영문법 판매 1위, 중학영문법 3800제의 초등시리즈

초등영문법 3800제

LEVEL 4

기초 2 단계

발행 초판 18쇄(2024년 8월 31일)
책임편집 서은숙 **편집** 성은혜 **원고집필** 정다혜, 권은정, 김주현, 정은주, 김유미, 홍주희 **연습문제집필** 조윤경, 권은정, 김송이, 김주희
워크북집필 윤정한, 정다혜, 김주희, 김송이 **원고검토** 유예슬, 최희찬, 박문정, 백경빈, 김미경, 김규은, 양원석, 고민정 **영문감수** Kathryn O'Handley
감수 오현진(강남구청 중등인강 강사) **교정** 황희진, 정다혜, 김주희, 이은영, 하은옥, 홍성경, 오정훈, 심가원, 이은혜, 신영은, 김송이, 하새롬
베타테스트 신재진, 이옥현, 유윤정, 정요한, 신소미, 장신혜, 변선영, 정은주
녹음 와이알 미디어 **녹음대본정리** 신소미, 김소정, 김건탁, 김윤아, 최안나 **녹음검수** 이상미, 신소미, 김소정, 김주희, 윤수경, 이옥현, 이유진, 최안나
사진검색 신의진, 김윤아, 이은혜, 손주연 **삽화** 박현주 **표지디자인** 김연실 **인디자인편집** 정은영, 박정민, 박경아, 김미라, 고연화
제작 이주영 **발행처** ㈜마더텅 **발행인** 문숙영 **주소** 서울시 금천구 가마산로 96, 708호

* 교재 및 기타 문의사항은 **이메일(mothert1004@toptutor.co.kr)**로 보내주시면 감사하겠습니다.
* 이 책에는 네이버에서 제공한 **나눔글꼴**이 적용되어 있습니다.
* 교재 구입 시 온/오프라인 서점에 교재가 없거나 파본으로 인한 교환, 반품을 원하는 경우에는 고객센터 전화 1661-1064(07:00~22:00)로 문의해 주시기 바랍니다.

마더텅 교재를 풀면서 궁금한 점이 생기셨나요?
교재 관련 내용 문의나 오류신고 사항이 있으면 아래 문의처로 보내주세요! 문의하신 내용에 대해 성심성의껏 답변해 드리겠습니다. 또한 교재의 내용 오류 또는 오·탈자, 그 외 수정이 필요한 사항에 대해 가장 먼저 신고해 주신 분께는 감사의 마음을 담아 CU 모바일 편의점 상품권 1천 원권을 보내드립니다!

*기한: 2024년 12월 31일 *오류신고 이벤트는 당사 사정에 따라 조기 종료될 수 있습니다. *홈페이지에 게시된 정오표 기준으로 최초 신고된 오류에 한하여 상품권을 보내드립니다.

카카오톡 mothertongue 이메일 mothert1004@toptutor.co.kr 문자 010-6640-1064(문자수신전용)
홈페이지 www.toptutor.co.kr 교재Q&A게시판 고객센터 전화 1661-1064(07:00~22:00)

초등영문법 3800제 **기초2단계**

이렇게 공부하세요.

LEVEL 4

STEP 1

문법 개념을 익힌 후 확인테스트를 풀어보면서 제대로 이해했는지 확인해요.

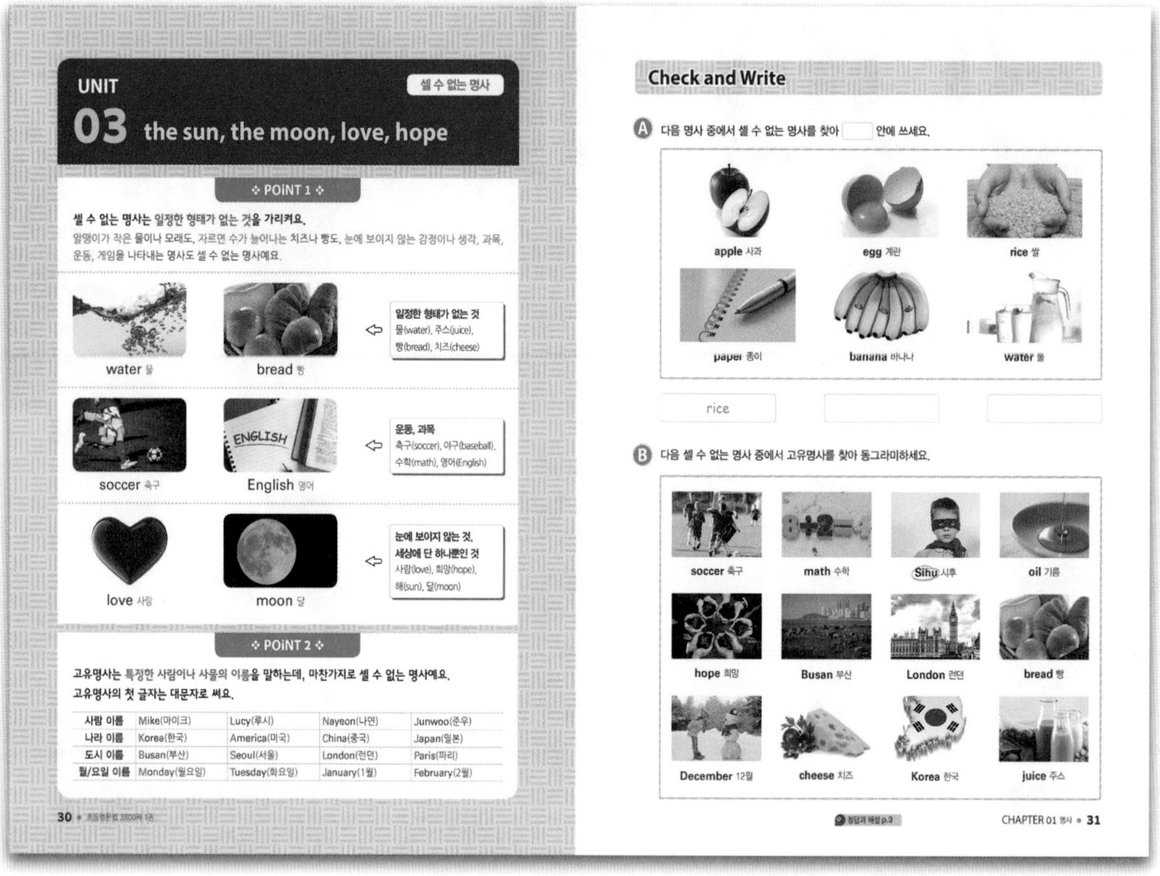
UNIT 셀 수 없는 명사
03 the sun, the moon, love, hope

POINT 1

셀 수 없는 명사는 일정한 형태가 없는 것을 가리켜요.
알갱이가 작은 물이나 모래도, 자르면 수가 늘어나는 치즈나 빵도, 눈에 보이지 않는 감정이나 생각, 과목, 운동, 게임을 나타내는 명사도 셀 수 없는 명사예요.

water 물 / bread 빵 — 일정한 형태가 없는 것: 물(water), 주스(juice), 빵(bread), 치즈(cheese)
soccer 축구 / English 영어 — 운동, 과목: 축구(soccer), 야구(baseball), 수학(math), 영어(English)
love 사랑 / moon 달 — 눈에 보이지 않는 것, 세상에 단 하나뿐인 것: 사랑(love), 희망(hope), 해(sun), 달(moon)

POINT 2

고유명사는 특정한 사람이나 사물의 이름을 말하는데, 마찬가지로 셀 수 없는 명사예요.
고유명사의 첫 글자는 대문자로 써요.

사람 이름	Mike(마이크)	Lucy(루시)	Nayeon(나연)	Junwoo(준우)
나라 이름	Korea(한국)	America(미국)	China(중국)	Japan(일본)
도시 이름	Busan(부산)	Seoul(서울)	London(런던)	Paris(파리)
월/요일 이름	Monday(월요일)	Tuesday(화요일)	January(1월)	February(2월)

30

Check and Write

A 다음 명사 중에서 셀 수 없는 명사를 찾아 안에 쓰세요.

apple 사과 / egg 계란 / rice 쌀 / paper 종이 / banana 바나나 / water 물

rice

B 다음 셀 수 없는 명사 중에서 고유명사를 찾아 동그라미하세요.

soccer 축구 / math 수학 / Sihu 시후 / oil 기름 / hope 희망 / Busan 부산 / London 런던 / bread 빵 / December 12월 / cheese 치즈 / Korea 한국 / juice 주스

CHAPTER 01 명사 31

STEP 2

Practice 1, 2, 3

Practice 1, 2, 3로 구성된 연습문제를 풀면서 앞에서 배운 문법이 적용된 풍부한 예문을 접할 수 있어요. 연습 문제들을 풀다보면, 서술형 문제도 더 이상 어렵지 않아요!

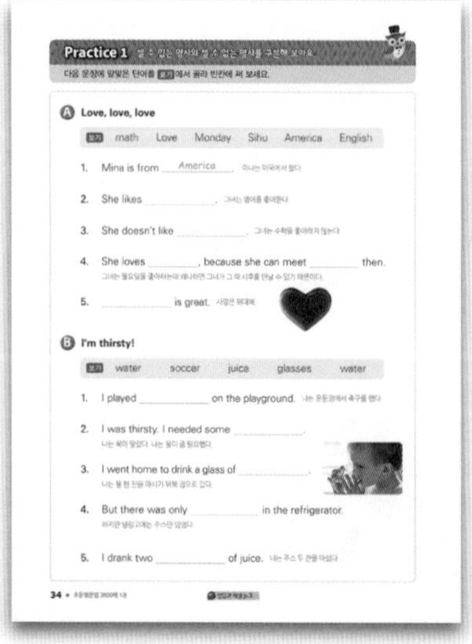

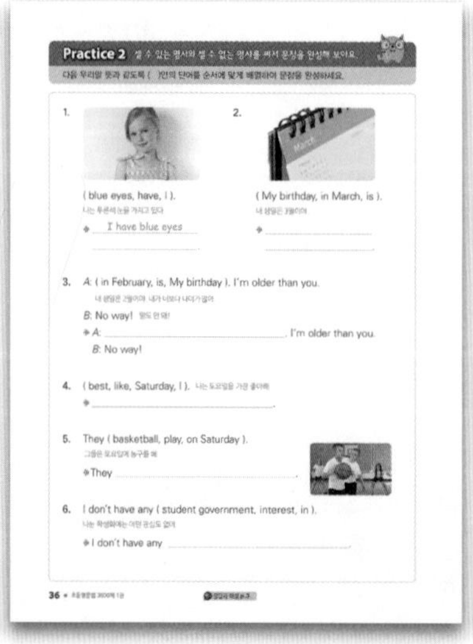

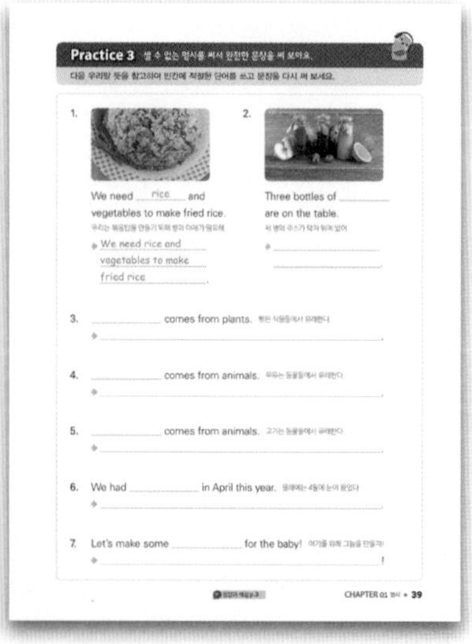

STEP 3

Let's Practice More!

문법 내용을 제대로 이해했는지 확인할 수 있도록 SET 01–08까지 다양한 유형의 연습문제를 실었어요.
문제를 하나하나 풀다보면 해당 UNIT의 핵심 개념을 제대로 익히게 될 거에요.

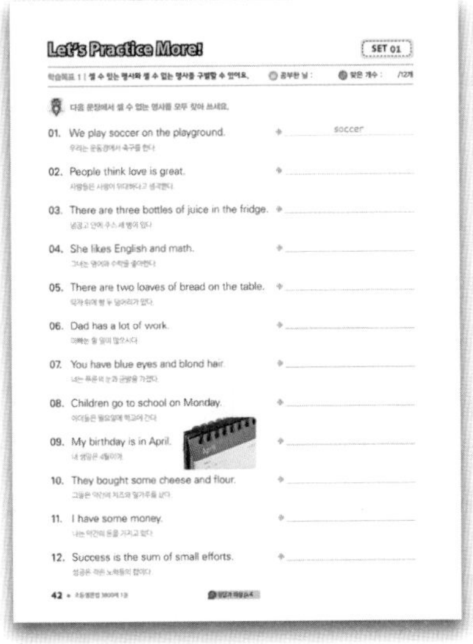

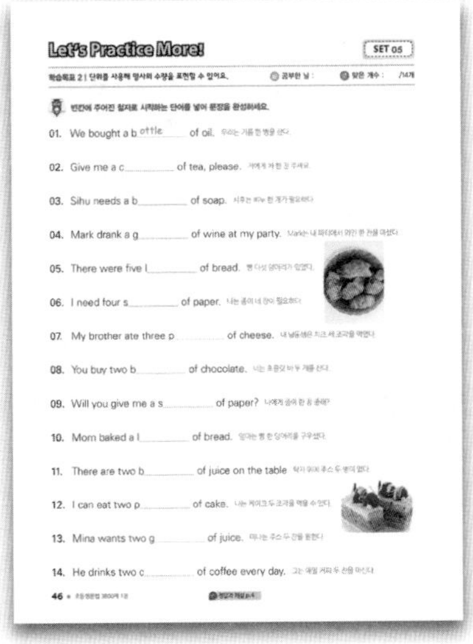

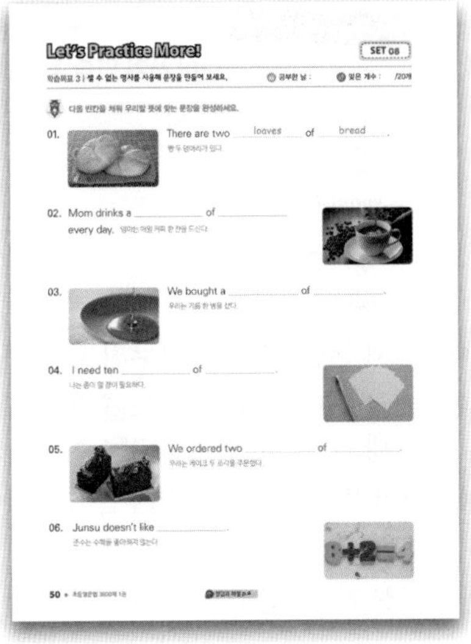

STEP 4

마무리 실전테스트

최종 마무리 테스트로서 권당 2회분의 실전테스트를 실었어요. 총 30문제의 진단평가 및
교내평가 유형의 실전문제로 앞에서 배운 내용을 복습하고 취약한 부분을 파악해 봐요.

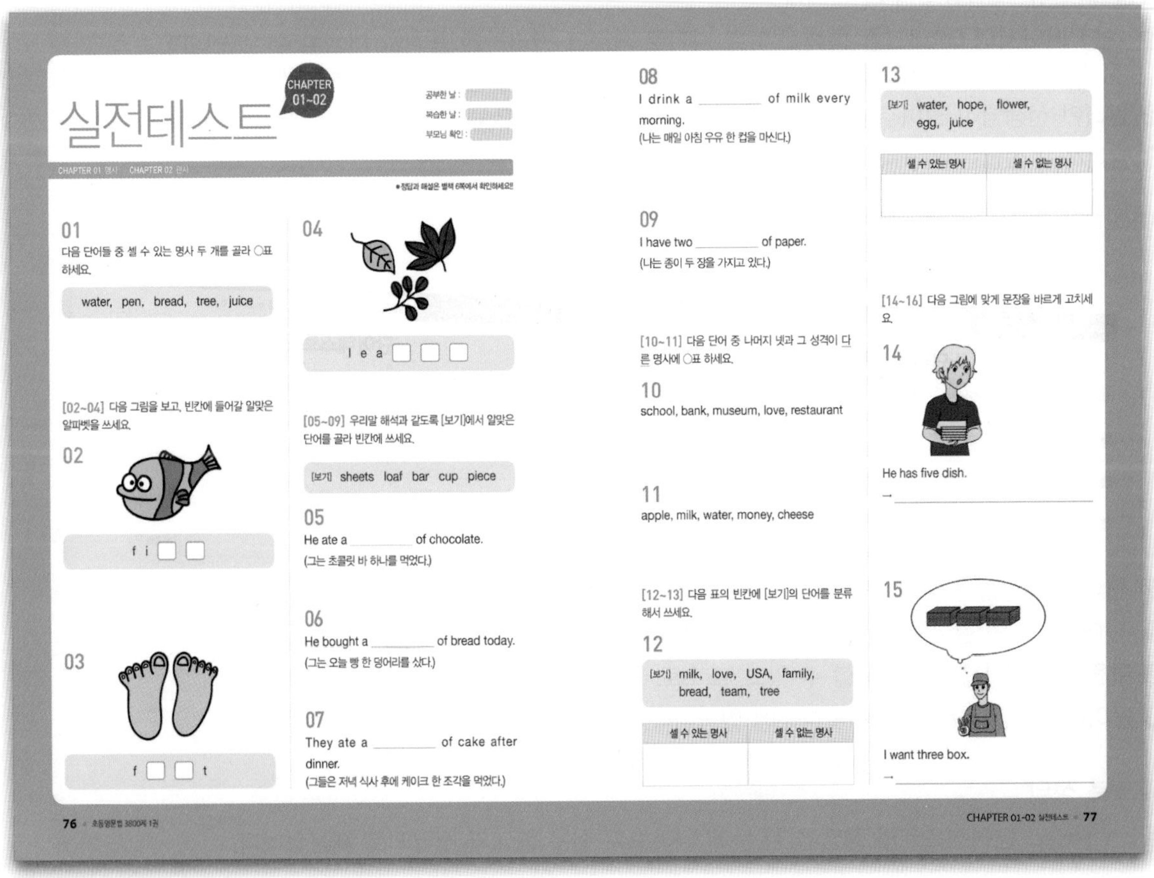

실전테스트 CHAPTER 01~02

공부한 날 :
복습한 날 :
부모님 확인 :

CHAPTER 01 명사 CHAPTER 02 관사

●정답과 해설은 별책 6쪽에서 확인하세요!

01
다음 단어들 중 셀 수 있는 명사 두 개를 골라 ○표 하세요.

water, pen, bread, tree, juice

[02~04] 다음 그림을 보고, 빈칸에 들어갈 알맞은 알파벳을 쓰세요.

02
fi□□

03
f□□t

04
lea□□□

[05~09] 우리말 해석과 같도록 [보기]에서 알맞은 단어를 골라 빈칸에 쓰세요.

[보기] sheets loaf bar cup piece

05
He ate a ________ of chocolate.
(그는 초콜릿 바 하나를 먹었다.)

06
He bought a ________ of bread today.
(그는 오늘 빵 한 덩어리를 샀다.)

07
They ate a ________ of cake after dinner.
(그들은 저녁 식사 후에 케이크 한 조각을 먹었다.)

08
I drink a ________ of milk every morning.
(나는 매일 아침 우유 한 컵을 마신다.)

09
I have two ________ of paper.
(나는 종이 두 장을 가지고 있다.)

[10~11] 다음 단어 중 나머지 넷과 그 성격이 다른 명사에 ○표 하세요.

10
school, bank, museum, love, restaurant

11
apple, milk, water, money, cheese

[12~13] 다음 표의 빈칸에 [보기]의 단어를 분류해서 쓰세요.

12
[보기] milk, love, USA, family, bread, team, tree

셀 수 있는 명사	셀 수 없는 명사

13
[보기] water, hope, flower, egg, juice

셀 수 있는 명사	셀 수 없는 명사

[14~16] 다음 그림에 맞게 문장을 바르게 고치세요.

14
He has five dish.
→

15
I want three box.
→

76 초등영문법 3800제 1권

CHAPTER 01-02 실전테스트 77

워크북 구성 및 활용법 워크북은 아래와 같은 방법으로 활용하세요.

1. 단어쓰기 연습

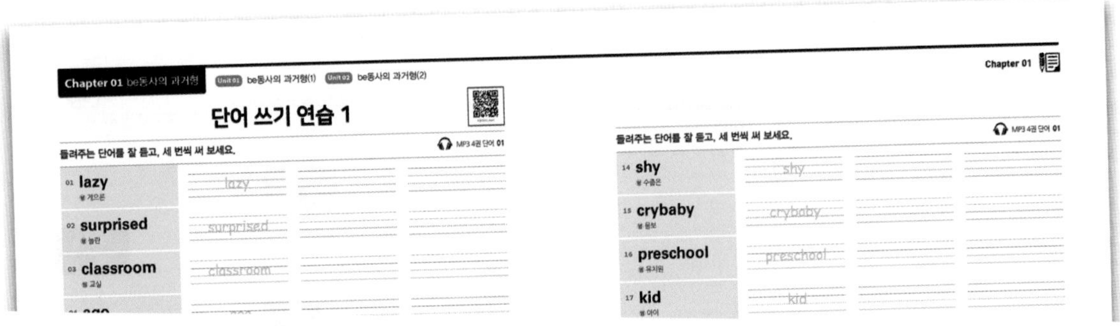
Chapter 01 be동사의 과거형 Unit 01 be동사의 과거형(1) Unit 02 be동사의 과거형(2)

단어 쓰기 연습 1

들려주는 단어를 잘 듣고, 세 번씩 써 보세요. MP3 4권 단어 01

01 lazy 게으른 lazy
02 surprised 놀란 surprised
03 classroom 교실 classroom

Chapter 01

들려주는 단어를 잘 듣고, 세 번씩 써 보세요. MP3 4권 단어 01

14 shy 수줍은 shy
15 crybaby 울보 crybaby
16 preschool 유치원 preschool
17 kid 아이 kid

❶ 먼저 본문 학습을 마무리 합니다.

❷ 해당 페이지의 QR코드를 통해 스마트 기기로 빠르고 편리하게 음원을 재생할 수 있습니다. 전체 음원 파일은 마더텅 홈페이지(www.toptutor.co.kr)에서 다운로드 가능합니다.

❸ 원어민 선생님이 읽어주는 영단어를 잘 듣고 안내선 안에 영어 단어 철자를 세 번씩 쓰세요.

2. 받아쓰기 시험 (Dictation Test)

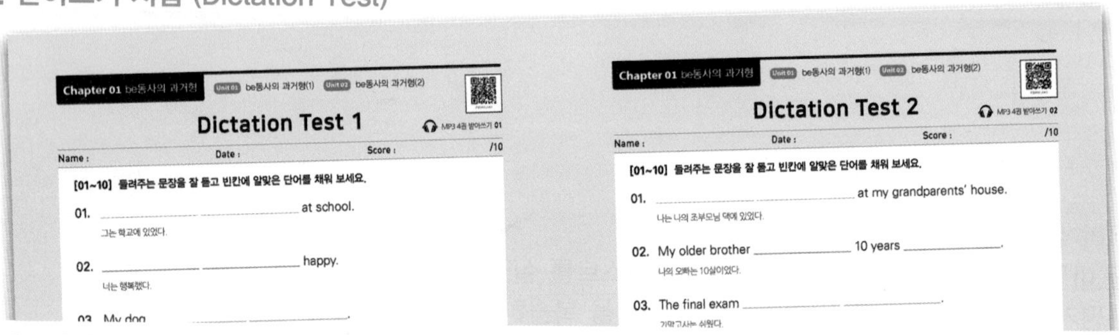
Chapter 01 be동사의 과거형 Unit 01 be동사의 과거형(1) Unit 02 be동사의 과거형(2)

Dictation Test 1

MP3 4권 받아쓰기 01

Name : Date : Score : /10

[01~10] 들려주는 문장을 잘 듣고 빈칸에 알맞은 단어를 채워 보세요.

01. ____________ at school.
그는 학교에 있었다.

02. ______ ______ happy.
너는 행복했다.

03. My dog ______ ______.

Chapter 01 be동사의 과거형 Unit 01 be동사의 과거형(1) Unit 02 be동사의 과거형(2)

Dictation Test 2

MP3 4권 받아쓰기 02

Name : Date : Score : /10

[01~10] 들려주는 문장을 잘 듣고 빈칸에 알맞은 단어를 채워 보세요.

01. ____________ at my grandparents' house.
나는 나의 조부모님 댁에 있었다.

02. My older brother ______ 10 years ______.
나의 오빠는 10살이었다.

03. The final exam ______ ______.

❶ 먼저 본문 학습을 마무리 합니다.

❷ 해당 페이지의 QR코드를 통해 스마트 기기로 빠르고 편리하게 음원을 재생할 수 있습니다. 전체 음원 파일은 마더텅 홈페이지(www.toptutor.co.kr)에서 다운로드 가능합니다.

❸ 원어민 선생님이 읽어주는 문장을 잘 듣고, 빈칸을 채우세요.

❹ 받아쓰기 정답은 워크북 뒷부분에 있습니다.

3. 단어테스트

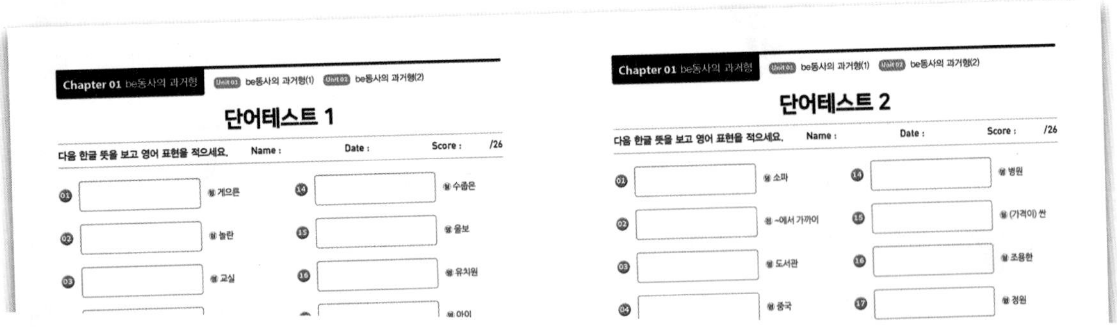
Chapter 01 be동사의 과거형 Unit 01 be동사의 과거형(1) Unit 02 be동사의 과거형(2)

단어테스트 1

다음 한글 뜻을 보고 영어 표현을 적으세요. Name : Date : Score : /26

01 게으른 14 수줍은
02 놀란 15 울보
03 교실 16 유치원
17 아이

Chapter 01 be동사의 과거형 Unit 01 be동사의 과거형(1) Unit 02 be동사의 과거형(2)

단어테스트 2

다음 한글 뜻을 보고 영어 표현을 적으세요. Name : Date : Score : /26

01 소파 14 병원
02 ~에서 가까이 15 (가격이) 싼
03 도서관 16 조용한
04 중국 17 정원

❶ 단어쓰기 연습을 하며, 단어들을 암기합니다.

❷ 단어테스트의 한글 뜻을 보고 암기한 영단어를 써 보세요.

❸ 학원에서 평가용으로 활용할 수 있고, 스스로 확인하는 용도로 활용할 수도 있습니다.

❹ 단어테스트 정답은 워크북 뒷부분에 있습니다.

4. 워크북 정답

Dictation Test와 단어테스트의 정답을 한 눈에 알아보기 쉬운 형태의 정답지로 제공합니다.

영문법 판매 1위, 중학영문법 3800제의 초등시리즈

초등영문법 3800제

LEVEL 4

기초2단계 CONTENTS

Chapter 01 be동사의 과거형

이 챕터에서는 동사의 형태로,
과거의 시제를 표현하는 'be동사의 과거형'에 대해 배워 보아요.

☆ 학습 방향 및 배울 내용 미리보기 ☆

☐ **Unit 01 : I was** at school.
be동사의 과거형 (1)
시제에 따라 달라지는 be동사의 형태, 그리고 주어에 따라 달라지는 be동사의 과거형에 대해 알아보아요.

▼

☐ **Unit 02 : I was** a student.
be동사의 과거형 (2)
be동사의 과거형의 의미와 과거동사와 함께 쓰이는 시간 표현들에 대해 알아보아요.

▼

☐ **Unit 03 :** They **were not** happy yesterday.
be동사 과거형의 부정문
be동사 과거형의 부정문을 만드는 방법과 줄여 쓰는 방법에 대해 배워 보아요.

▼

☐ **Unit 04 : Were you** in the library?
be동사 과거형의 의문문
be동사 과거형의 의문문을 만드는 방법과 be동사 과거형의 의문문에 대답하는 방법에 대해 배워 보아요.

단어 미리보기

이 챕터에 나올 단어들 중 이미 알고 있는 단어가 있나요?
맞는 뜻을 골라 체크해 봐요.

날짜 : 이름 : 알고 있는 단어의 수 : /24개

No.	아는 단어	단어	품사	알맞은 뜻에 체크 표시해 봐요.			
1	☑	lazy	형용사	게으른	☑	부지런한	☐
2	☐	surprised	형용사	놀란	☐	즐거운	☐
3	☐	ago	부사	~ 후에	☐	~ 전에	☐
4	☐	then	부사	그때	☐	~ 보다	☐
5	☐	now	부사	지금	☐	어제	☐
6	☐	shy	형용사	활발한	☐	수줍은	☐
7	☐	nurse	명사	의사	☐	간호사	☐
8	☐	America	명사	미국	☐	영국	☐
9	☐	bank	명사	서점	☐	은행	☐
10	☐	final	형용사	처음의	☐	마지막의	☐
11	☐	last	형용사	미래의	☐	지난	☐
12	☐	near	전치사	~에서 멀리	☐	~에서 가까이	☐
13	☐	a lot of	형용사	조금의	☐	많은	☐
14	☐	cheap	형용사	비싼	☐	싼	☐
15	☐	bored	형용사	지루한	☐	생기 있는	☐
16	☐	cook	명사	요리사	☐	박사	☐
17	☐	healthy	형용사	아픈	☐	건강한	☐
18	☐	old	형용사	낡은	☐	새로운	☐
19	☐	fresh	형용사	상한	☐	신선한	☐
20	☐	absent	형용사	결석한	☐	출석한	☐
21	☐	clear	형용사	어두운	☐	맑은	☐
22	☐	bike	명사	차	☐	자전거	☐
23	☐	problem	명사	문제	☐	질문	☐
24	☐	with	전치사	~와 따로	☐	~와 함께	☐

UNIT

01 I was at school.

be동사의 과거형 (1)

❖ POiNT 1 ❖

be동사의 과거형

동사의 형태로 과거, 현재, 미래의 '시제'를 표현할 수 있다는 거 알죠?
다른 동사들과 마찬가지로 be동사의 형태도 시제에 따라 달라져요.

be동사의 현재형	am/is/are	'~이다', '~(에) 있다', '~하다'
be동사의 과거형	was/were	'~이었다', '~(에) 있었다', '~했다'

❖ POiNT 2 ❖

주어에 따라 be동사의 과거형이 달라요!

	현재형	과거형
I	am	was
You/We/They	are	were
It/She/He	is	was

I/He/She was at school.
나는/그는/그녀는 학교에 있었다.

It was lazy.
그것은 게을렀다.

You were happy.
너는 행복했다.

We/They were friends.
우리는/그들은 친구였다.

Check and Write

다음 밑줄 친 be동사의 현재시제를 과거시제로 바꿔 보세요.

1. I am a superhero.

→ I [was] a superhero.

나는 슈퍼히어로였어.

2. We are in the park.

→ We ______ in the park last week.

우리는 지난주에 공원에 있었어.

3. My dog is sick.

→ My dog ______ sick.

나의 개는 아팠어.

4. She is surprised.

→ She ______ surprised.

그녀는 놀랐어.

5. You are in Jeju Island.

→ You ______ in Jeju Island.

너는 제주도에 있었어.

정답과 해설 p.2

UNIT

02 I was a student.

be동사의 과거형 (2)

❖ POiNT 1 ❖

be동사는 여러 의미를 가지고 있었죠?
과거형도 현재형과 마찬가지로 뒤에 오는 단어에 따라 여러 의미를 가져요!

I	am	a student.	나는 학생이다.
	was		나는 학생이었다.
They	are	in the classroom.	그들은 교실 안에 있다.
	were		그들은 교실 안에 있었다.
She	is	happy.	그녀는 행복하다.
	was		그녀는 행복했다.

❖ POiNT 2 ❖

과거동사와 함께 쓰이는 시간 표현들이 있어요!

yesterday 어제	yesterday morning 어제 아침	yesterday afternoon 어제 오후
yesterday evening 어제 저녁	last night 지난밤	the day before yesterday 그저께
last week 지난주	last month 지난달	last year 지난해
three hours ago 3시간 전에	a few minutes ago 몇 분 전에	then 그때

I was a preschool student last year.
나는 작년에 유치원생이었어. (O)

I am a preschool student last year.
나는 작년에 유치원생이야. (X)

I am an elementary school student now.
나는 지금 초등학생이야. (O)

※ 현재시제와 함께 쓰이는 표현에는 now(지금), right now(지금 당장)가 있어요!

Check and Write

다음 빈칸에 들어갈 단어로 적절한 것을 보기에서 골라 넣어보세요. (중복사용 가능)

보기 was am are

1. She [was] late yesterday.
그녀는 어제 늦었어.

2. They [ ] on the playground now.
그들은 지금 운동장에 있어.

3. It [ ] funny yesterday.
어제 재밌었어.

4. I [ ] angry now.
나 지금 화났어.

5. It [ ] rainy yesterday.
어제 비가 왔어.

정답과 해설 p.2

Practice 1 be동사의 과거형을 익혀 보아요.

우리말 뜻을 참고하여 be동사의 과거형을 빈칸에 써 보세요.

A The babies

1. I ___was___ big for my age.
   나는 나이에 비해 컸다.

2. My brother ________ small.
   나의 오빠는 작았다.

3. Nayeon ________ shy.
   나연이는 수줍음이 많았다.

4. You ________ a crybaby. (*crybaby: 울보)
   너는 울보였다.

5. We ________ at my grandparents' house.
   우리는 조부모님 댁에 있었다.

B Sihu's past

1. I ________ a preschool student.
   나는 유치원생이었다.

2. My older brother ________ 10 years old.
   나의 형은 10살이었다.

3. My parents ________ very busy.
   나의 부모님은 매우 바쁘셨다.

4. But, they ________ kind.
   하지만 그들은 다정했다.

5. My mom ________ a nurse, but she is a housewife now.
   우리 엄마는 간호사이셨지만 지금은 가정주부이시다.

정답과 해설 p.2

C In elementary school

1. Sihu and Junwoo __________ in the same class.
   시후와 준우는 같은 반이었다.

2. They __________ on the same soccer team.
   그들은 같은 축구팀에 있었다.

3. They __________ best friends.
   그들은 단짝이었다.

4. Mina __________ from America.
   미나는 미국 출신이었다.

5. She __________ a new kid in their class.
   그녀는 그들 반의 새로운(전학 온) 아이였다.

D Where were you yesterday?

1. My mother __________ at the bank.
   어머니는 은행에 계셨다.

2. My dog __________ on the couch.
   나의 개는 소파 위에 있었다.

3. My father __________ near my school.
   나의 아버지는 나의 학교 근처에 계셨다.

4. We __________ in a library.
   우리는 도서관에 있었다.

5. They __________ on the playground.
   그들은 운동장에 있었다.

정답과 해설 p.2

Practice 2 be동사의 과거형을 써서 문장을 완성해 보아요.

다음 우리말 뜻과 같도록 주어진 표현을 순서에 맞게 배열하여 문장을 완성하세요.

1. (in China, My family and I, were).
나의 가족과 나는 중국에 있었다.

➔ My family and I were in China.

2. (was, clean, My T-shirt).
내 티셔츠는 깨끗했어.

➔ ______________________ .

3. (My last vacation, fantastic, was)!
나의 지난 방학은 환상적이었어!

➔ ______________________ !

4. (It, rainy, was) yesterday. 어제 비가 왔어.

➔ ______________________ yesterday.

5. (was, It, sunny) in Busan.
부산은 (날씨가) 화창했어.

➔ ______________________ in Busan.

6. (was, I, so shy) yesterday.
나 어제 너무 부끄러웠어.

➔ ______________________ yesterday.

정답과 해설 p.2

7. (worried, I, was) about you.
난 너를 걱정했어.

➔ ______________________ about you.

8. (was, really strange, That).
그건 정말 이상했어.

➔ ______________________.

9. (was, in my backpack, My cat).
나의 고양이는 내 배낭 안에 있었어.

➔ ______________________
______________________.

10. (He, a crybaby, was).
그는 울보였다.

➔ ______________________
______________________.

11. (You, so cute, were) when you were a baby.
네가 아기였을 때 넌 너무 귀여웠단다.

➔ ______________________ when you were a baby.

12. (The final exam, easy, was).
기말시험은 쉬웠어요.

➔ ______________________.

13. (an interesting day, was, It).
그날은 재밌는 날이었어요.

➔ ______________________.

정답과 해설 p.2

14. My dad bought a lot of books yesterday.
(so unhappy, was, I)!
우리 아빠가 어제 많은 책을 사셨어. 난 정말 기분이 좋지 않았어!

➔ My dad bought a lot of books yesterday.
______________________________!

15. (in the hospital, My aunt, was) last month.
나의 이모는 지난달에 병원에 계셨어.

➔ ______________________________ last month.

16. (a nurse, was, She).
그녀는 간호사였어.

➔ ______________________________
______________________________.

17. (It, really cheap, was).
(값이) 정말 저렴했어.

➔ ______________________________
______________________________.

18. (a lovely baby, You, were).
너는 사랑스러운 아기였어.

➔ ______________________________.

19. (very quiet, He, was).
그는 매우 조용했어.

➔ ______________________________.

20. (was, The apple tree, in the garden).
그 사과나무는 정원에 있었어.

➔ ______________________________.

정답과 해설 p.2

Practice 3 be동사의 과거형을 써서 완전한 문장을 써 보아요.

[1 – 15] 우리말 뜻을 참고하여 주어진 표현을 사용해 문장을 완성해 보세요.

1. (in Jeju Island)

우리는 제주도에 있었어.

➔ We were in Jeju Island ______________________.

2. (really tired)

나는 정말 피곤했어.

➔ ______________________ ______________________.

3. (Yesterday, my 9th birthday)

어제는 나의 9번째 생일이었다.

➔ ______________________.

4. (Yesterday, a great day)

어제는 멋진 날이었어!

➔ ______________________!

5. (My birthday, last Friday)

내 생일은 지난 금요일이었어.

➔ ______________________.

6. (Sihu, my neighbor)

시후는 4년 전에 내 이웃이었어.

➔ ______________________ four years ago.

7. (my best friends)

그들은 나의 가장 친한 친구들이었어.

➔ ______________________.

정답과 해설 p.2

8. (Mina, the new girl, at school)

미나는 학교에 새로 온(전학 온) 여자애였다.

➔ ____.

9. (in the library)

우리는 도서관에 있었어.

➔ ______________________

______________________.

10. (The dishes, broken)

접시들이 깨져 있었어.

➔ ______________________

______________________.

11. (very shy) 그녀는 매우 수줍어했다.

➔ ____.

12. (in the E-mart)

나는 이마트에 있었어.

➔ ____.

13. (a police officer)

그는 경찰관이었어.

➔ ____.

14. (cute)

네가 아기였을 때 너는 귀여웠단다.

➔ ______________________________ when you were a baby.

정답과 해설 p.2

15. (a brave person)
그는 용감한 사람이었어.

➔ ______________________________.

[16–20] 우리말 뜻과 일치하도록 밑줄 친 부분을 바르게 고치고 전체 문장을 다시 써 보세요.

16. My uncle is a taxi driver.
나의 삼촌은 택시기사셨다.

➔ My uncle was a taxi driver.

17. My little brother were a preschool student last year.
나의 남동생은 작년에 유치원생이었다.

➔ ______________________________.

18. Today were a hard day.
오늘은 힘든 날이었다.

➔ ______________________________.

19. My cats was in my backpack.
나의 고양이들은 내 배낭 안에 있었다.

➔ ______________________________.

20. They are at the amusement park.
그들은 놀이공원에 있었다.

➔ ______________________________.

정답과 해설 p.2

Let's Practice More!

SET 01

학습목표 1 | 주어에 따라 달라지는 be동사의 과거형을 익혀 보아요.　공부한 날 :　맞은 개수 : /12개

다음 ( ) 안에서 알맞은 것을 고르세요.

01. I (was / were) big for my age. 나는 나이에 비해 컸다.

02. Nayeon (was / were) shy. 나연이는 수줍음이 많았다.

03. You (was / were) a crybaby. 너는 울보였다.

04. I (was / were) a preschool student. 나는 유치원생이었다.

05. My parents (was / were) very busy. 나의 부모님은 매우 바쁘셨다.

06. My mom (was / were) a nurse. 우리 엄마는 간호사이셨다.

07. Sihu and Junwoo (was / were) in the same class. 시후와 준우는 같은 반이었다.

08. They (was / were) on the same soccer team. 그들은 같은 축구팀에 있었다.

09. My mother (was / were) at the bank. 나의 어머니는 은행에 계셨다.

10. We (was / were) in a library. 우리는 도서관에 있었다.

11. My family and I (was / were) in China. 나의 가족과 나는 중국에 있었다.

12. Last vacation (was / were) fantastic! 지난 방학은 환상적이었어!

정답과 해설 p.2

Let's Practice More!

SET 02

학습목표 1 | 주어에 따라 달라지는 be동사의 과거형을 익혀 보아요. 공부한 날 : 맞은 개수 : /14개

다음 ( ) 안에서 알맞은 것을 고르세요.

01. It (was / were) rainy yesterday. 어제 비가 왔어.

02. It (was / were) sunny in Busan. 부산은 (날씨가) 화창했어.

03. I (was / were) so shy yesterday. 나는 어제 너무 부끄러웠어.

04. You (was / were) so cute when you were a baby.
네가 아기였을 때 넌 너무 귀여웠단다.

05. That (was / were) really strange. 그건 정말 이상했어.

06. You (was / were) a lovely baby. 너는 사랑스러운 아기였어.

07. My cat (was / were) in my backpack.
나의 고양이는 내 배낭 안에 있었어.

08. We (was / were) in Jeju Island. 우리는 제주도에 있었어.

09. I (was / were) really tired. 나는 정말 피곤했어.

10. Yesterday (was / were) my 11th birthday. 어제는 나의 11번째 생일이었다.

11. They (was / were) my best friends. 그들은 나의 가장 친한 친구들이었어.

12. The dishes (was / were) broken. 접시들이 깨져 있었어.

13. I (was / were) in the E-mart. 나는 이마트에 있었어.

14. You (was / were) tall. 너는 키가 컸어.

정답과 해설 p.2

Let's Practice More!

SET 03

학습목표 1 | 주어에 따라 달라지는 be동사의 과거형을 익혀 보아요. 공부한 날 : 맞은 개수 : /14개

다음 밑줄 친 부분이 맞으면 ○표, 틀리면 고쳐 써 보세요.

01. He was a police officer. → ○
그는 경찰관이었어.

02. My grandfather were a taxi driver. → ______
나의 할아버지는 택시기사이셨다.

03. Today was a hard day. → ______
오늘은 힘든 날이었다.

04. My cats was in my backpack. → ______
나의 고양이들은 내 가방 안에 있었다.

05. They was at the amusement park. → ______
그들은 놀이공원에 있었다.

06. My brother was small. → ______
나의 오빠는 작았다.

07. We was at my grandparents' house. → ______
우리는 조부모님 댁에 있었다.

08. They was kind. → ______
그들은 친절했다.

09. Mina were from America. → ______
미나는 미국 출신이었다.

10. She was a new kid in their class. → ______
그녀는 그들 반의 새로운(전학 온) 아이였다.

11. My dog were on the couch. → ______
나의 개는 소파 위에 있었다.

12. They were on the playground. → ______
그들은 운동장에 있었다.

13. My T-shirt were clean. → ______
내 티셔츠는 깨끗했어.

14. I was worried about you. → ______
난 너를 걱정했어.

정답과 해설 p.2

Let's Practice More!

SET 04

학습목표 2 | be동사의 여러 의미를 익혀 보아요.　　공부한 날 :　　맞은 개수 : /14개

다음 문장에서 밑줄 친 be동사(was, were)의 알맞은 의미를 골라 보세요.

01. He was a crybaby. (~이었다 / ~에 있었다)

02. We were friends. (~이었다 / ~에 있었다)

03. My aunt was in the hospital last month. (~이었다 / ~에 있었다)

04. You were a lovely baby. (~이었다 / ~에 있었다)

05. The apple tree was in the garden. (~이었다 / ~에 있었다)

06. They were my best friends. (~이었다 / ~에 있었다)

07. He was my neighbor four years ago. (~이었다 / ~에 있었다)

08. Yesterday was a great day! (~이었다 / ~에 있었다)

09. We were in the library. (~이었다 / ~에 있었다)

10. I was a superhero. (~이었다 / ~에 있었다)

11. He was a brave person. (~이었다 / ~에 있었다)

12. My father was near my school. (~이었다 / ~에 있었다)

13. It was an interesting day. (~이었다 / ~에 있었다)

14. She was a student. (~이었다 / ~에 있었다)

정답과 해설 p.3

Let's Practice More!

SET 05

학습목표 2 | be동사의 여러 의미를 익혀 보아요. 공부한 날 : 맞은 개수 : /12개

다음 우리말 뜻과 같아지도록 빈칸에 알맞은 be동사를 쓰세요.

01. He ___was___ a brave person.
그는 용감한 사람이었어.

02. My uncle __________ a taxi driver.
나의 삼촌은 택시기사이셨다.

03. My little brother __________ a preschool student last year.
나의 남동생은 작년에 유치원생이었다.

04. I __________ big for my age.
나는 나이에 비해 크다.

05. Nayeon __________ shy.
나연이는 수줍음이 많았다.

06. You __________ a crybaby.
너는 울보였다.

07. My older brother __________ 10 years old.
나의 형은 10살이었다.

08. They __________ best friends.
그들은 단짝이었다.

09. I __________ worried about you.
난 너를 걱정했어.

10. That __________ strange.
그건 이상했어.

11. My cat __________ in my backpack.
나의 고양이는 내 배낭 안에 있었어.

12. We __________ in the library.
우리는 도서관에 있었어.

정답과 해설 p.3

Let's Practice More!

SET 06

학습목표 3 | 시간 표현에 따라 달라지는 be동사를 익혀 보아요. 공부한 날 : 맞은 개수 : /14개

주어진 우리말 뜻을 보고 밑줄 친 부분이 맞으면 ○표, 틀리면 고쳐 써 보세요.

01. You <u>are</u> so cute when you were a baby. ➔ were
네가 아기였을 때 넌 너무 귀여웠단다.

02. The final exam <u>was</u> easy yesterday. ➔ ________
어제 기말시험은 쉬웠어요.

03. He <u>is</u> a firefighter now. ➔ ________
그는 지금 소방관이다.

04. He <u>is</u> very quiet yesterday. ➔ ________
그는 어제 매우 조용했어.

05. My birthday <u>is</u> last Friday. ➔ ________
내 생일은 지난 금요일이었어.

06. My aunt <u>was</u> in the hospital last month. ➔ ________
나의 이모는 지난달에 병원에 계셨어.

07. She <u>was</u> very hungry now. ➔ ________
그녀는 지금 매우 배가 고프다.

08. My brother <u>is</u> small at that time. ➔ ________
나의 오빠는 그때 작았다.

09. I <u>am</u> a preschool student two years ago. ➔ ________
나는 2년 전에 유치원생이었다.

10. My parents <u>are</u> very busy yesterday. ➔ ________
나의 부모님은 어제 매우 바쁘셨다.

11. My family and I <u>were</u> in China last year. ➔ ________
나의 가족과 나는 작년에 중국에 있었다.

12. Sihu and Junwoo <u>are</u> in the same class this year. ➔ ________
시후와 준우는 올해 같은 반이다.

13. My mother <u>is</u> at the bank this morning. ➔ ________
어머니는 오늘 아침 은행에 계셨다.

14. My dog <u>is</u> on the couch a moment ago. ➔ ________
나의 개는 방금 전에 소파 위에 있었다.

정답과 해설 p.3

Let's Practice More!

SET 07

학습목표 4 | **현재시제 문장을 과거시제 문장으로 바꿔 보아요.** 공부한 날 : 맞은 개수 : /20개

다음 ( ) 안의 표현을 문장 끝에 덧붙여 과거시제 문장으로 쓰세요.

01. They are on the same soccer team. (last year)

➔ They were on the same soccer team last year.

그들은 작년에 같은 축구팀에 있었다.

02. They are best friends. (two years ago)

➔ ______________________________.

그들은 2년 전에 단짝이었다.

03. My father is near my school. (two hours ago)

➔ ______________________________.

나의 아버지는 2시간 전에 나의 학교 근처에 계셨다.

04. We are in an airport. (yesterday)

➔ ______________________________.

우리는 어제 공항에 있었다.

05. My family and I are in China. (last year)

➔ ______________________________.

나의 가족과 나는 작년에 중국에 있었다.

06. It is rainy. (yesterday evening)

➔ ______________________________.

어제 저녁에 비가 왔어.

07. I am so shy. (yesterday)

➔ ______________________________.

나 어제 너무 부끄러웠어.

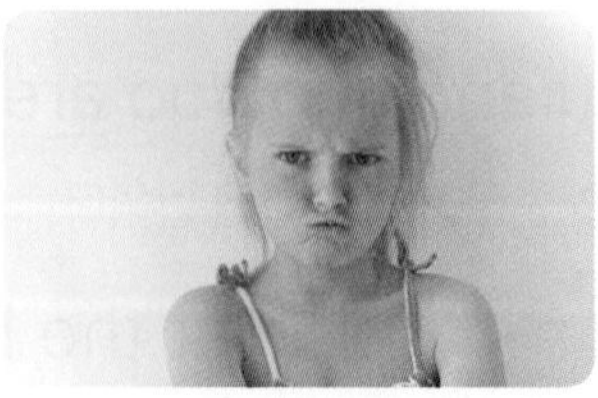

08. I am so angry! (then)

➔ ______________________________!

나는 그때 너무 화가 났었어!

09. My aunt is in the hospital. (last month)

➔ ______________________________.

나의 이모는 지난달에 병원에 계셨어.

정답과 해설 p.3

10. He is very quiet. (yesterday)

➜ ____.

그는 어제 매우 조용했어.

11. The apple tree is in the garden. (last year)

➜ ____.

그 사과나무는 작년에 정원에 있었어.

12. I am really tired. (yesterday)

➜ ____.

나는 어제 정말 피곤했어.

13. Jane is my neighbor. (four years ago)

➜ ____.

Jane은 4년 전에 나의 이웃이었어.

14. The dishes are broken. (two days ago)

➜ ____.

접시들이 이틀 전에 깨졌어.

15. They are at the amusement park. (an hour ago)

➜ ____.

그들은 한 시간 전에 놀이공원에 있었다.

16. He is a police officer. (three years ago)

➜ ____.

그는 3년 전에 경찰관이었어.

17. My little brother is a preschool student. (last year)

➜ ____.

나의 남동생은 작년에 유치원생이었다.

18. My cats are in my backpack. (yesterday morning)

➜ ____.

어제 아침 나의 고양이들은 내 배낭 안에 있었다.

19. She is very hungry. (two hours ago)

➜ ____.

그녀는 2시간 전에 매우 배가 고팠다.

20. We are at my grandparents' house. (the day before yesterday)

➜ ____.

우리는 그저께 조부모님 댁에 있었다.

정답과 해설 p.3

Let's Practice More!

SET 08

학습목표 4 | 현재시제 문장을 과거시제 문장으로 바꿔 보아요. 공부한 날 : 맞은 개수 : /20개

다음 현재시제 문장을 주어진 주어로 시작하는 과거시제 문장으로 바꿔 보세요.

01. 

They are on the playground.

➔ I was on the playground.

나는 운동장에 있었다.

02. 

The kitchen is clean.

➔ My room ______________.

내 방은 깨끗했어.

03. My older brother is 10 years old.

➔ They ______________.

그들은 10살이었다.

04. They are kind.

➔ She ______________.

그녀는 다정했다.

05. Mina is from America.

➔ I ______________.

나는 미국 출신이었다.

06. She is a new kid in their class.

➔ Sihu ______________.

시후는 그들 반의 새로운(전학 온) 아이였다.

07. I am in the E-mart.

➔ They ______________.

그들은 이마트에 있었어.

08. She is a nurse.

➔ They ______________.

그들은 간호사들이었다.

09. It is really cheap.

➔ These pencils ______________.

이 연필들은 (값이) 정말 저렴했어.

정답과 해설 p.3

10. We are in Jeju Island.

➜ My friends ______________________________.

내 친구들은 제주도에 있었어.

11. We are in the library.

➜ She ______________________________.

그녀는 도서관에 있었어.

12. My cats are in my backpack.

➜ My dog ______________________________.

나의 개는 내 배낭 안에 있었다.

13. They are at the amusement park.

➜ I ______________________________.

나는 놀이공원에 있었다.

14. I am big for my age.

➜ He ______________________________.

그는 나이에 비해 컸다.

15. Nayeon is shy.

➜ I ______________________________.

나는 수줍음이 많았다.

16. You are a crybaby.

➜ Nayeon ______________________________.

나연이는 울보였다.

17. My parents are very busy.

➜ My father ______________________________.

나의 아빠는 매우 바쁘셨다.

18. They are on the same soccer team.

➜ We ______________________________.

우리는 같은 축구팀에 있었다.

19. They are best friends.

➜ Sihu and Junwoo ______________________________.

시후와 준우는 단짝이었다.

20. My mother is at the market.

➜ They ______________________________.

그들은 시장에 있었다.

정답과 해설 p.3

UNIT 03 They were not happy yesterday.

be동사 과거형의 부정문

❖ POiNT 1 ❖

be동사 과거형의 부정문

'~이/가 아니었다, ~에 없었다'라고 말하려면 어떻게 해야 할까요?

be동사 과거형 뒤에 not을 붙여주면 돼요.

I/He/She/It/단수 명사	was + not
You/We/They/복수 명사	were + not

❖ POiNT 2 ❖

was not은 wasn't로, were not은 weren't로 줄여 쓸 수 있어요!

be동사의 과거형	I/He/She was happy yesterday. 나/그/그녀는 어제 행복했어. You/We/They were happy yesterday. 너/우리/그들은(는) 어제 행복했어. I/He/She was a preschool student last year. 나/그/그녀는 작년에 유치원생이었어. You were preschool students last year. 너희들은 작년에 유치원생이었어. We/They were preschool students last year. 우리/그들은(는) 작년에 유치원생이었어.
be동사 과거형의 부정문	I/He/She was not[wasn't] happy yesterday. 나/그/그녀는 어제 행복하지 않았어. You/We/They were not[weren't] happy yesterday. 너/우리/그들은(는) 어제 행복하지 않았어. I/He/She was not[wasn't] a preschool student last year. 나/그/그녀는 작년에 유치원생이 아니었어. You were not[weren't] preschool students last year. 너희들은 작년에 유치원생이 아니었어. We/They were not[weren't] preschool students last year. 우리/그들은(는) 작년에 유치원생이 아니었어.

Check and Write

다음 밑줄 친 be동사의 형태를 부정형으로 바꿔 보세요.

1. She <u>was</u> bored.
그녀는 지루해했어.
→ She [was not[wasn't]] bored.
그녀는 지루해하지 않았어.

2. They <u>were</u> in the classroom.
그들은 교실에 있었어.
→ They [ ] in the classroom.
그들은 교실에 있지 않았어.

3. He <u>was</u> big.
그는 (덩치가) 컸어.
→ He [ ] big.
그는 (덩치가) 크지 않았어.

4. We <u>were</u> players.
우리는 선수들이었어.
→ We [ ] players.
우리는 선수들이 아니었어.

정답과 해설 p.3

UNIT 04 Were you in the library?

be동사 과거형의 의문문

❖ POiNT 1 ❖

be동사 과거형의 의문문
'~이었니(였니)?/~에 있었니?'라고 말하려면 어떻게 해야 할까요?
be동사와 주어의 순서를 바꾸어주면 돼요.
[Was/Were + 주어 + (보어)~?]

주어가 단수일때

	be동사의 현재형	be동사의 과거형
평서문	He is in the classroom. 그는 교실에 있어.	He was in the classroom ten minutes ago. 그는 10분 전에 교실에 있었어.
의문문	Is he in the classroom? 그는 교실에 있니?	Was he in the classroom ten minutes ago? 그는 10분 전에 교실에 있었니?

주어가 복수일때

	be동사의 현재형	be동사의 과거형
평서문	We are friends. 우리는 친구입니다.	We were friends. 우리는 친구였습니다.
의문문	Are we friends? 우리는 친구입니까?	Were we friends? 우리는 친구였습니까?

❖ POiNT 2 ❖

be동사 과거형의 의문문에 대한 대답
긍정이면, [Yes, 주어 + was/were.]
부정이면, [No, 주어 + wasn't/weren't.]

Were you in the library? 너 도서관에 있었니?

-Yes, I was. 응, 도서관에 있었어.
-No, I wasn't. 아니, 도서관에 있지 않았어.

Check and Write

다음 주어진 문장을 의문문으로 바꿔 보세요.

1. It was rainy yesterday.

➔ Was it rainy yesterday?

어제 비가 왔니?

2. They were friends.

➔

그들은 친구였니?

3. She was glad.

➔

그녀는 기뻐했니?

4. You were bored.

➔

너는 지루했니?

정답과 해설 p.3

Practice 1 be동사 과거형의 부정문과 의문문을 익혀 보아요.

주어진 우리말 뜻을 참고하여 빈칸에 알맞은 말을 써 보세요.

A My mom was tired!

1. My mom ___was___ ___not___ a housewife.
   우리 엄마는 전업주부가 아니셨어.

2. __________ she busy? 그녀는 바쁘셨니?

3. Yes, she __________. 응, 그녀는 바쁘셨어.
   She __________ so tired. 그녀는 매우 피곤하셨어.

4. She __________ __________ healthy.
   그녀는 건강하지 않으셨어.

5. __________ she healthy now?
   그녀가 지금은 건강하시니?

B The baby needed his mom!

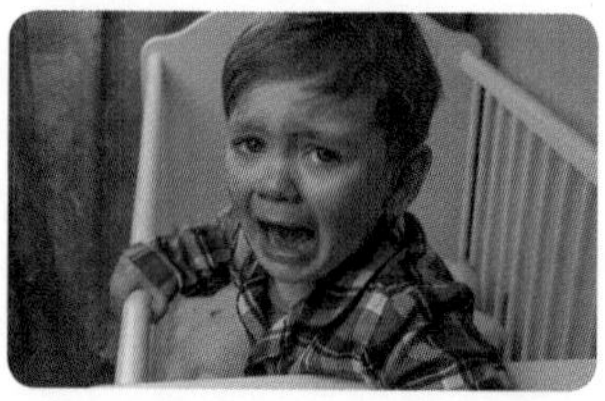

1. *A*: The baby cried all last night.
   어제 아기가 밤새 울었어.
   B: __________ the baby sick? 아기가 아팠니?

2. *A*: No, he __________ __________.
   아니, 그는 아프지 않았어.

3. *A*: He __________ __________ hungry.
   그는 배고프지 않았어.

4. *B*: Then, what __________ the problem?
   그럼 문제가 뭐였어?

5. *A*: Mom __________ __________ at home.
   엄마가 집에 없었어.

정답과 해설 p.3

C Twins!

1. *Nari* : __________ Nayeon and I alike long ago?

   나연이와 저는 옛날에 닮았었어요?

2. *Nayeon*: I __________ tall, but you were not tall.

   나는 키가 컸지만 너는 크지 않았어.

3. *Mom* : You __________ __________ different.

   너희들은 다르지 않았어.

   You had the same dream, too.

   너희들은 같은 꿈도 가지고 있었단다.

4. *Nari* : What __________ that? 그게 뭐였어요?

5. *Mom* : It __________ to be a cook.

   그것은 요리사가 되는 것이었단다.

6. *Nari* : But, Nayeon's food __________ __________ tasty!

   하지만 나연이의 음식은 맛이 없었어요!

D Mom knows everything!

1. *Mom* : Where __________ you at 5:00?

   너 다섯 시에 어디에 있었니?

2. *Mom* : You __________ __________ at home.

   너는 집에 없었어.

3. *Mom* : __________ you in an Internet cafe?

   너는 피시방에 있었니?

   Jinwoo : How did you know that?

   어떻게 그걸 아셨어요?

Practice 2 be동사 과거형의 부정문과 의문문을 완성해 보아요.

다음 우리말 뜻과 같도록 주어진 표현을 순서에 맞게 배열하여 문장을 완성하세요.

1. (you, late, Were)?
너 늦었었니?

➔ Were you late ______ ?

2. (in the classroom, Was, Junwoo)? 준우는 교실에 있었니?

➔ ______ ?

3. (were, Where, you)? 너 어디에 있었어?

➔ ______ ?

4. (not, was, late, I) for school today.
나는 오늘 학교에 지각하지 않았어.

➔ ______ for school today.

5. (in the teachers' room, Mr. Lee, Was)?
이 선생님이 교무실에 계셨니?

➔ ______ ?

6. (not, He, was, in the teachers' room).
그는 교무실에 계시지 않았어.

➔ ______ .

7. (not, It, was, my fault)! (*fault: 잘못, 책임)
그건 내 잘못이 아니었어!

➔ ______ !

정답과 해설 p.3

8. (your day, How, was)?
오늘 하루 어땠어?

➔ ______________________________?

9. (it, delicious, Was)?
그것은 맛있었니?

➔ ______________________________
______________________________?

10. (interesting, was, not, The book). 그 책은 재미있지 않았어.

➔ ______________________________
______________________________.

11. (cute, Was, I) when I was young?
내가 어렸을 때 나는 귀여웠어요?

➔ ______________________________ when I was young?

12. (they, Were, twins)?
그들이 쌍둥이였니?

➔ ______________________________?

13. (not, It, boring, was).
그건 지루하지 않았어.

➔ ______________________________.

14. (he, Was, smaller) last year? 그는 작년에 (덩치가) 더 작았어? (*smaller: 더 작은)

➔ ______________________________ last year?

정답과 해설 p.3

15. (big, He, not, was) last year.
그는 작년에는 (덩치가) 크지 않았다.

➔ ______________________________ last year.

16. I am sorry. (with you, wasn't, I).
미안해. 나는 너와 함께 있지 않았어.

➔ I am sorry. ______________________________.

17. (clear, was, The sky) last night.
어젯밤에 하늘은 맑았어.

➔ ______________________________ last night.

18. (not, was, snowy, It) yesterday.
어제는 눈이 오지 않았어.

➔ ______________________________ yesterday.

19. (were, in the same class, not, We) last year.
우리는 작년에 같은 반이 아니었어.

➔ ______________________________ last year.

20. So, (were, close, we, not) at first.
그래서 우리는 처음에 친하지 않았어.

➔ So, ______________________________ at first.

정답과 해설 p.4

Practice 3 be동사 과거형의 평서문과 부정문, 의문문을 써 보아요.

우리말 뜻을 참고하여 주어진 표현을 사용해 문장을 완성하세요.

1. (Mina, sick)
미나는 아팠어?

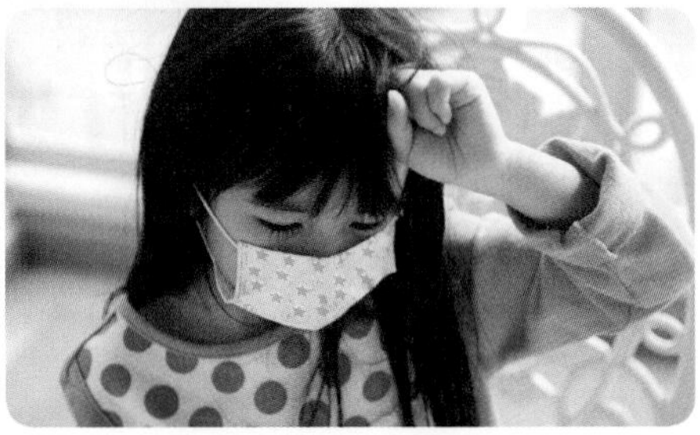

➔ Was Mina sick ______________________?

2. (close, at first)
그들은 처음엔 친하지 않았어.

➔ ______________________ ______________________.

3. (your cat, in your house) 너의 고양이는 너의 집에 있었니?
➔ ______________________?

4. (My cat, in my house) 내 고양이는 우리 집에 없었어.
➔ ______________________.

5. (with your dog) 그것은 너의 개와 함께 있었어.
➔ ______________________.

6. (My dog, at home) 나의 개는 집에 없었어.
➔ ______________________.

7. (in the same class) 너는 작년에 시후와 같은 반이었어?
➔ ______________________ with Sihu last year?

8. (in the same class) 나는 그와 같은 반이 아니었어.
➔ ______________________ with him.

9. (good at math) 나는 수학을 잘하지 못했어.
➔ ______________________.

정답과 해설 p.4

10. (the English test, difficult) 영어 시험이 어려웠니?

➔ ______________________________?

11. (best friends) 너희는 작년에 단짝이었니?

➔ ______________________________ last year?

12. (best friends) 우리는 그땐 단짝이 아니었지만, 지금은 단짝이야.

➔ ______________________________ then,

but ______________________________ now.

13. (absent from school) 너 어제 학교 결석했어?

➔ ______________________________ yesterday?

14. (The salad, fresh)

나는 배탈이 났었어. 샐러드가 신선하지 않았어. **(*stomachache: 배탈)**

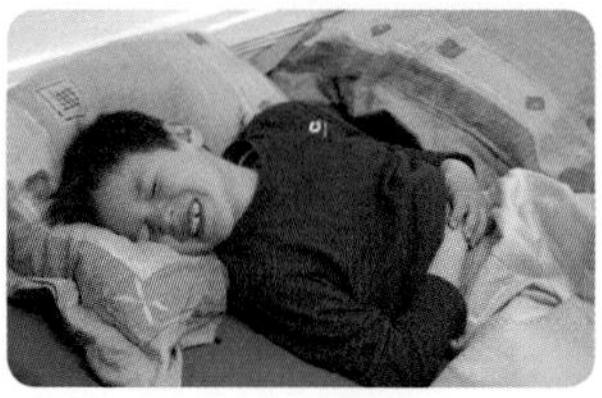

➔ I had a stomachache. ____________________.

15. (it, my fault) 그게 내 잘못이었니?

➔ ______________________________?

16. (The math test, easy) 수학 시험은 쉽지 않았어.

➔ ______________________________.

17. (good at English) 그들은 영어를 잘했니?

➔ ______________________________?

18. (a crybaby) 그는 울보였어?

➔ ______________________________?

19. (your bike, old) 너의 자전거는 낡았었니?

➔ ______________________________?

20. (My bike, too small) 내 자전거는 나에게 너무 작지는 않았지만, 나는 새 자전거를 원했어.

➔ ____________________ for me, but I wanted a new bike.

정답과 해설 p.4

Let's Practice More!

SET 01

학습목표 1 | be동사 과거형의 부정문 형태를 연습해 보아요.　공부한 날 :　맞은 개수 : /12개

다음 문장을 읽고 밑줄 친 부분이 맞으면 ○표, 틀리면 ×표를 하세요.

01. My mom was not a housewife. → ○
나의 엄마는 전업주부가 아니셨어.

02. She were not tired. → ______
그녀는 피곤하지 않았어.

03. Mom were not at home. → ______
엄마는 집에 계시지 않았어.

04. I was tall, but you was not tall. → ______
나는 키가 컸지만 너는 크지 않았어.

05. You were not different. → ______
너는 다르지 않았어.

06. The book were not interesting. → ______
그 책은 재미있지 않았어.

07. Your food were not tasty! → ______
너의 음식은 맛이 있지 않았어!

08. You were not at home. → ______
너는 집에 있지 않았어.

09. He was not sick. → ______
그는 아프지 않았어.

10. I was not late for school yesterday. → ______
나는 어제 학교에 늦지 않았어.

11. It were not boring. → ______
그것은 지루하지 않았어.

12. That were not my fault! → ______
그것은 내 잘못이 아니었어!

정답과 해설 p.4

Let's Practice More!

SET 02

학습목표 1 | be동사 과거형의 부정문 형태를 연습해 보아요. 공부한 날 : 맞은 개수 : /14개

다음 ( ) 안에서 알맞은 것을 골라 보세요.

01. He (was not / were not) healthy.
그는 건강하지 않았어.

02. He (was not / were not) hungry.
그는 배고프지 않았어.

03. I (was not / were not) late for school yesterday.
나는 어제 학교에 늦지 않았어.

04. He (was not / were not) in the teachers' room.
그는 교무실에 있지 않았어.

05. We (was not / were not) in the same class last year.
우리는 작년에 같은 반이 아니었어.

06. It (was not / were not) my fault!
그것은 내 잘못이 아니었어!

07. We (was not / were not) close at first.
우리는 처음에 친하지 않았어.

08. The book (was not / were not) interesting.
그 책은 재미있지 않았어.

09. He (was not / were not) a fool.
그는 바보가 아니었어.

10. They (was not / were not) good at English.
그들은 영어를 잘 하지 못했어.

11. You (was not / were not) absent from school yesterday.
너는 어제 학교에 결석하지 않았어.

12. The math test (was not / were not) easy.
그 수학 시험은 쉽지 않았어.

13. You (was not / were not) late.
너는 늦지 않았어.

14. It (was not / were not) yours.
그것은 너의 것이 아니었어.

정답과 해설 p.4

Let's Practice More!

SET 03

학습목표 2 | be동사 과거형의 부정문을 줄여 쓸 수 있어요. 공부한 날 : 맞은 개수 : /14개

밑줄 친 부정형의 줄임말이 맞으면 ○표, 틀리면 고쳐 써 보세요.

01. He weren't lazy. → wasn't
그는 게으르지 않았어.

02. My cat wasn't in my house. → ________
나의 고양이는 내 집에 있지 않았어.

03. My dog weren't at home. → ________
나의 개는 집에 있지 않았어.

04. I weren't good at math. → ________
나는 수학을 잘 하지 못했어.

05. It weren't yours. → ________
그것은 너의 것이 아니었어.

06. You wasn't different. → ________
너는 다르지 않았어.

07. The math test weren't easy. → ________
그 수학 시험은 쉽지 않았어.

08. My bike weren't small. → ________
나의 자전거는 작지 않았어.

09. The salad wasn't fresh. → ________
그 샐러드는 신선하지 않았어.

10. She wasn't healthy. → ________
그녀는 건강하지 않았어.

11. You weren't at home. → ________
너는 집에 있지 않았어.

12. He wasn't a fool. → ________
그는 바보가 아니었어

13. They wasn't twins. → ________
그들은 쌍둥이가 아니었어.

14. He wasn't big last year. → ________
그는 작년에 (덩치가) 크지 않았어.

정답과 해설 p.4

Let's Practice More!

SET 04

학습목표 2 | be동사 과거형의 부정문을 줄여 쓸 수 있어요. 공부한 날 : 맞은 개수 : /12개

밑줄 친 부정형을 줄여 쓰세요.

01. Junwoo was not in the classroom. → wasn't
준우는 교실에 있지 않았어.

02. Our teachers were not in the teachers' room. → ______
우리의 선생님들은 교무실에 계시지 않았어.

03. It was not delicious. → ______
그것은 맛이 없었어.

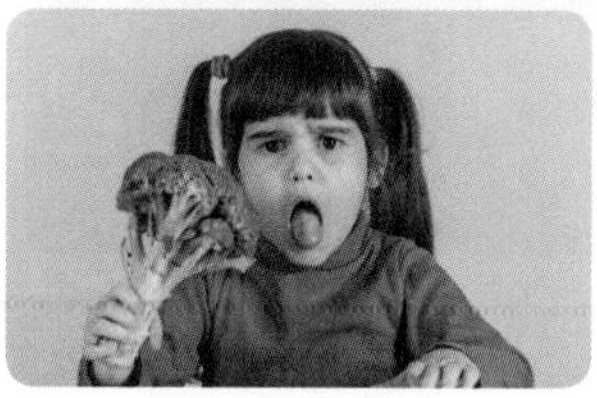

04. They were not twins. → ______
그들은 쌍둥이가 아니었어.

05. It was not boring. → ______
그것은 지루하지 않았어.

06. The babies were not small last year. → ______
그 아기들은 작년에 작지 않았어.

07. I was not with you. → ______
나는 너와 함께 있지 않았어.

08. It was not snowy yesterday. → ______
어제 눈이 오지 않았어.

09. We were not in the same class last year. → ______
우리는 작년에 같은 반이 아니었어.

10. We were not close at first. → ______
우리는 처음에 친하지 않았어.

11. Mina was not sick. → ______
미나는 아프지 않았어.

12. It was not with your dog. → ______
그것은 너의 개와 함께 있지 않았어.

정답과 해설 p.4

Let's Practice More!

SET 05

학습목표 3 | be동사 과거형의 의문문 형태를 연습해 보아요. 공부한 날 : 맞은 개수 : /14개

다음 빈칸에 Was와 Were 중 알맞은 것을 쓰세요.

01. ___Was___ your cat at your home?
너의 고양이는 너의 집에 있었니?

02. __________ she healthy then?
그때 그녀는 건강했니?

03. __________ the English test difficult?
그 영어 시험은 어려웠니?

04. __________ you best friends last year?
너희들은 작년에 단짝이었니?

05. __________ you absent from school yesterday?
너는 어제 학교에 결석했니?

06. __________ it my fault?
그것은 내 잘못이었니?

07. __________ they good at English?
그들은 영어를 잘 했니?

08. __________ he a crybaby?
그는 울보였니?

09. __________ your bike old?
너의 자전거는 낡았었니?

10. __________ she busy?
그녀는 바빴니?

11. __________ you in the same class with Sihu last year?
너는 작년에 시후와 같은 반이었니?

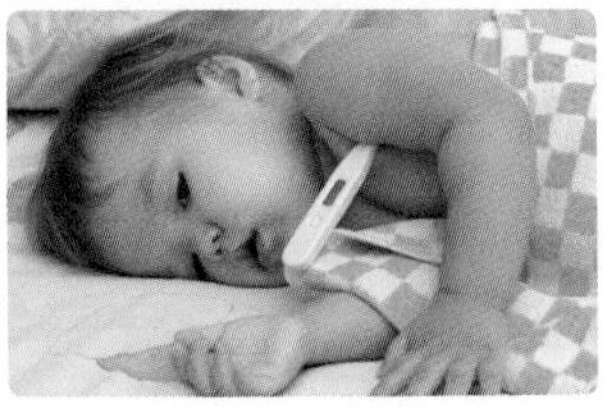

12. __________ the baby sick?
그 아기는 아팠니?

13. __________ the problem easy?
그 문제는 쉬웠니?

14. __________ Nayeon and I alike long ago?
나연이와 나는 오래 전에 닮았었니?

정답과 해설 p.4

Let's Practice More!

SET 06

학습목표 4 | be동사 과거형의 의문문에 대한 대답을 연습해 보아요. 공부한 날 : 맞은 개수 : /14개

다음 문장을 읽고 빈칸에 적절한 대답을 써 보세요.

01. 

Were Nayeon and I alike long ago? 나연이와 저는 옛날에 닮았었어요?

A: Yes, ___you were___.

B: No, ___you weren't___.

02. 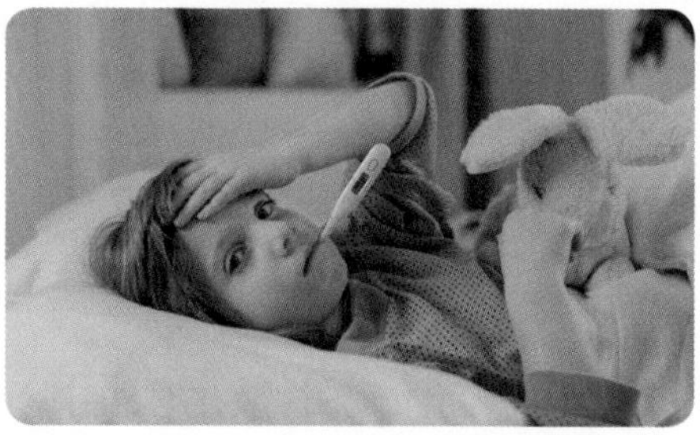

Was Mina sick? 미나는 아팠어?

A: Yes, ________________.

B: No, ________________.

03. Were they in an Internet cafe? 그들은 피시방에 있었니?

A: Yes, ________________.

B: No, ________________.

04. Were you late? 너 늦었니?

A: Yes, ________________.

B: No, ________________.

05. Was I cute when I was young? 내가 어렸을 때 나는 귀여웠어요?

A: Yes, ________________.

B: No, ________________.

06. Was he small last year? 그는 작년에 (덩치가) 작았어?

A: Yes, ________________.

B: No, ________________.

정답과 해설 p.4

07. Was your sister at your home? 너의 여동생은 너의 집에 있었니?

A: Yes, ______________________________.

B: No, ______________________________.

08. Was the English test difficult? 영어 시험이 어려웠니?

A: Yes, ______________________________.

B: No, ______________________________.

09. Was it my fault? 그게 내 잘못이었니?

A: Yes, ______________________________.

B: No, ______________________________.

10. Was he a crybaby? 그는 울보였어?

A: Yes, ______________________________.

B: No, ______________________________.

11. Was your bike old? 너의 자전거는 낡았었니?

A: Yes, ______________________________.

B: No, ______________________________.

12. Was she busy? 그녀는 바빴니?

A: Yes, ______________________________.

B: No, ______________________________.

13. Was your daughter sick? 네 딸이 아팠니?

A: Yes, ______________________________.

B: No, ______________________________.

14. Were you best friends last year? 너희는 작년에 단짝이었니?

A: Yes, ______________________________.

B: No, ______________________________.

정답과 해설 p.4

Let's Practice More!

SET 07

학습목표 5 | be동사 과거형의 부정문과 의문문 만드는 방법을 확실히 다져보아요.

공부한 날 : 　　　맞은 개수 : /20개

괄호 안의 지시에 따라 문장을 바꿔 보세요.

01.

She was so tired. (의문문)

➔ Was she so tired ?

그녀는 매우 피곤했니?

02.

He was hungry. (부정문)

➔ ______________________.

그는 배고프지 않았어.

03. My mom was a housewife. (부정문)

➔ ______________________.

우리 엄마는 전업주부가 아니셨어.

04. They were healthy. (의문문)

➔ ______________________?

그들은 건강했니?

05. He was sick. (부정문)

➔ ______________________.

그는 아프지 않았어.

06. Mom was at home. (부정문)

➔ ______________________.

엄마가 집에 안 계셨어.

07. Your dreams were the same, too. (의문문)

➔ ______________________?

너희들의 꿈도 똑같았니?

08. She was a cook. (의문문)

➔ ______________________?

그녀는 요리사였니?

09. You were in an Internet cafe. (부정문)

➔ ______________________.

너는 피시방에 없었어.

정답과 해설 p.4

10.
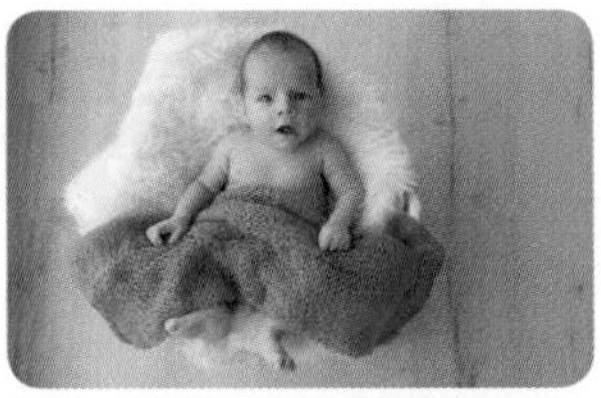

I was cute when
I was young. (의문문)

→ ______________________

______________________?

내가 어렸을 때 나는 귀여웠어요?

11.

The sky was clear
last year. (의문문)

→ ______________________

______________________?

작년에 하늘은 맑았니?

12. Junwoo was in the classroom. (의문문)

→ ____?

준우는 교실에 있었니?

13. Mr. Lee was in the teachers' room. (의문문)

→ ____?

이 선생님이 교무실에 계셨니?

14. It was delicious. (의문문)

→ ____?

그것은 맛있었니?

15. He was big last year. (부정문)

→ ____.

그는 작년에는 (덩치가) 크지 않았다.

16. I was with you. (부정문)

→ ____.

나는 너와 함께 있지 않았어.

17. It was snowy yesterday. (부정문)

→ ____.

어제는 눈이 오지 않았어.

18. He was lazy. (부정문)

→ ____.

그는 게으르지 않았어.

19. My cats were in my house. (의문문)

→ ____?

내 고양이들은 우리 집에 있었니?

20. You were with your dog. (의문문)

→ ________________________________?

너는 너의 강아지와 함께 있었니?

Let's Practice More!

SET 08

학습목표 5 | be동사 과거형의 부정문과 의문문 만드는 방법을 확실히 다져보아요.

공부한 날 : 맞은 개수 : /20개

다음 우리말 해석에 맞도록 빈칸을 채워 문장을 완성해 보세요.

01. I was tall, but you ___were___ ___not___ tall.
나는 키가 컸지만 너는 크지 않았어.

02. __________ __________ that?
그게 뭐였어요?

03. __________ they fire fighters?
그들은 소방관들이었니?

04. Nayeon's food __________ __________ tasty!
나연이의 음식은 맛이 없었어요!

05. __________ __________ you at 5:00?
너 다섯 시에 어디에 있었니?

06. __________ the problem easy?
그 문제는 쉬웠어?

07. __________ she busy?
그녀는 바빴니?

08. __________ __________ your day?
오늘 하루 어땠어?

09. The sky __________ __________ clear yesterday.
어제 하늘은 맑지 않았어.

정답과 해설 p.5

10. ___________ your dogs at home?
너의 개들은 집에 있었니?

11. I ___________ ___________ good at math.
나는 수학을 잘하지 못했어.

12. ___________ the salad fresh?
그 샐러드는 신선했니?

13. My bike ___________ ___________ small.
내 자전거는 작지 않았어.

14. He ___________ ___________ in the teachers' room.
그는 교무실에 계시지 않았어.

15. He ___________ ___________ a fool.
그는 바보가 아니었어.

16. The math test ___________ ___________ easy.
수학 시험은 쉽지 않았어.

17. ___________ the English test difficult?
영어 시험은 어려웠니?

18. Mina ___________ ___________ sick.
미나는 아프지 않았어.

19. ___________ it snowy yesterday?
어제 눈이 왔었니?

20. We ___________ ___________ close at first.
우리는 처음에 친하지 않았어.

정답과 해설 p.5

Chapter 02 일반동사의 과거형

이 챕터에서는 동사의 형태로,
과거에 일어난 일을 표현하는 '일반동사의 과거형'에 대해 배워 보아요.

☆ 학습 방향 및 배울 내용 미리보기 ☆

☐ **Unit 01 : I wanted** a skateboard last year.
일반동사의 과거형(규칙변화)
일반동사를 과거형으로 만드는 규칙에 대해 알아보아요.

▼

☐ **Unit 02 :** They **read** many books last month.
일반동사의 과거형(불규칙변화)
일반동사를 과거형으로 만들 때 불규칙적으로 변화하는 동사들에 대해 알아보아요.

▼

☐ **Unit 03 : I didn't** sleep well yesterday.
일반동사 과거형의 부정문
일반동사 과거형의 부정문을 만드는 방법에 대해 배워 보아요.

▼

☐ **Unit 04 : Did** she like EXO?
일반동사 과거형의 의문문
일반동사 과거형의 의문문을 만드는 방법과 일반동사 과거형의 의문문에 대답하는 방법에 대해 배워 보아요.

단어 미리보기

이 챕터에 나올 단어들 중 이미 알고 있는 단어가 있나요?
맞는 뜻을 골라 체크해 봐요.

날짜 : 이름 : 알고 있는 단어의 수 : /24개

No.	아는 단어	단어	품사	알맞은 뜻에 체크 표시해 봐요.			
1	☑	skateboard	명사	스케이트보드	☑	칠판	☐
2	☐	study	동사	즐기다	☐	공부하다	☐
3	☐	hard	부사	열심히	☐	즐겁게	☐
4	☐	drink	동사	먹다	☐	마시다	☐
5	☐	hear	동사	듣다	☐	보다	☐
6	☐	hurt	동사	자르다	☐	아프다	☐
7	☐	many	형용사	적은	☐	많은	☐
8	☐	laugh	동사	웃다	☐	울다	☐
9	☐	letter	명사	편지	☐	일기	☐
10	☐	arm	명사	손	☐	팔	☐
11	☐	later	부사	나중에	☐	일찍	☐
12	☐	worry	동사	걱정하다	☐	즐거워하다	☐
13	☐	well	부사	힘들게	☐	잘	☐
14	☐	melt	동사	녹다	☐	줍다	☐
15	☐	get	동사	주다	☐	얻다	☐
16	☐	ill	형용사	아픈	☐	좋은	☐
17	☐	shine	동사	빛나다	☐	비가 오다	☐
18	☐	dry	동사	마르다	☐	습기가 차다	☐
19	☐	clean	동사	더럽히다	☐	청소하다	☐
20	☐	exercise	동사	운동하다	☐	경험하다	☐
21	☐	window	명사	유리	☐	창문	☐
22	☐	fruit	명사	과일	☐	채소	☐
23	☐	happen	동사	끝나다	☐	일어나다	☐
24	☐	sell	동사	사다	☐	팔다	☐

UNIT 일반동사의 과거형(규칙변화)

01 I wanted a skateboard last year.

❖ POiNT 1 ❖

일반동사의 과거형으로 과거에 일어난 일을 표현할 수 있어요!

'~했다'라고 해석하고, yesterday(어제), last week(지난주), last month(지난달), two days ago(이틀 전)와 같이 과거를 나타내는 시간 표현과 함께 쓰일 수 있어요.

현재

I want a skateboard now.

나는 지금 스케이트보드를 원해요.

과거

I wanted a skateboard last year.

나는 작년에 스케이트보드를 원했어요.

❖ POiNT 2 ❖

일반동사 과거형의 규칙변화

일반동사를 과거형으로 만드는 규칙이 있어요!

	동사원형	과거형	동사원형	과거형
대부분의 동사+-ed	help 돕다	**helped**	want 원하다	**wanted**
-e로 끝나는 동사 +-d	like 좋아하다	**liked**	die 죽다	**died**
〈자음+-y〉로 끝나는 동사 : y를 i로 바꾸고 +-ed	cry 울다	**cried**	study 공부하다	**studied**
〈모음+-y〉로 끝나는 동사+-ed	enjoy 즐기다	**enjoyed**	stay 머무르다	**stayed**

Check and Write

다음 밑줄 친 일반동사의 현재시제를 과거시제로 바꿔 보세요.

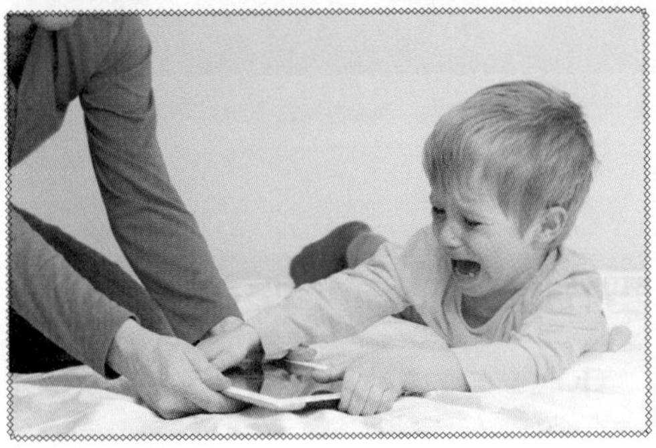

1. He always <u>cries</u>.
   ➔ He always [cried].
   그는 항상 울었어.

2. They <u>look</u> at me.
   ➔ They [ ] at me.
   그들은 나를 보았어.

3. You <u>study</u> very hard.
   ➔ You [ ] very hard.
   너는 아주 열심히 공부했어.

4. I <u>like</u> my father.
   ➔ I [ ] my father.
   나는 나의 아빠를 좋아했어.

정답과 해설 p.5

UNIT 02 일반동사의 과거형(불규칙변화)

They read many books last month.

❖ POiNT ❖

	동사원형	과거형	동사원형	과거형
불규칙변화 동사	take 데리고 가다	**took**	go 가다	**went**
	have 가지다	**had**	make 만들다	**made**
	eat 먹다	**ate**	see 보다	**saw**
	meet 만나다	**met**	run 달리다	**ran**
	tell 말하다	**told**	drink 마시다	**drank**
	write 쓰다	**wrote**	get 얻다	**got**
	know 알다	**knew**	give 주다	**gave**
	win 이기다	**won**	hear 듣다	**heard**
	fall 떨어지다	**fell**	do 하다	**did**
	feel 느끼다	**felt**	buy 사다	**bought**
변하지 않는 동사	read 읽다	**read**	cut 자르다	**cut**
	put 놓다	**put**	hit 치다	**hit**
	hurt 상처 입히다/아프다	**hurt**	let ~하게 하다	**let**

＊동사 read의 현재형 발음은 [ri:d], 과거형의 발음은 [red]예요!

I always read many books. 나는 항상 많은 책을 읽어요.
They read many books last month. 그들은 지난달에 많은 책을 읽었어요.

Check and Write

다음 밑줄 친 일반동사의 현재시제를 과거시제로 바꿔 보세요.

1. We <u>see</u> something.

   → We [saw] something.

   우리는 무언가를 봤어.

2. She <u>writes</u> in a diary.

   → She [ ] in a diary.

   그녀는 일기를 썼어.

3. You <u>put</u> a mouse on a bike.

   → You [ ] a mouse on a bike.

   너는 쥐를 자전거 위에 올려놨어.

4. They <u>make</u> a cake.

   → They [ ] a cake.

   그들은 케이크를 만들었어.

정답과 해설 p.5

Practice 1 일반동사의 과거형을 익혀 보아요.

다음 문장에 알맞은 동사를 보기에서 골라 빈칸에 과거형으로 바꿔 써 보세요.

A Junwoo's day

보기 win give get play

1. We __played__ soccer yesterday.
우리는 어제 축구를 했다.

2. Sihu ________ a goal. 시후가 골을 넣었다.

3. We ________ the game. 우리는 그 경기를 이겼다.

4. I ________ him a thumbs-up. 나는 그에게 엄지를 척 세워주었다.

B No comic books in class!

보기 call hurt scold write read laugh

1. I ________ a comic book in English class yesterday.
나는 어제 영어 시간에 만화책을 읽었다.

2. I ________ loudly because it was so funny.
그게 너무 웃겼기 때문에 나는 크게 웃었다.

3. The teacher ________ my name. 선생님은 내 이름을 부르셨다.

4. He ________ me. 그는 나를 혼내셨다.

5. I ________ a very long letter of apology.
나는 아주 긴 반성문을 썼다. (*a letter of apology: 반성문)

6. My arm ________ so much last night. 어젯밤에 팔이 너무 아팠다.

정답과 해설 p.5

C We are friends!

보기 hear have feel go know

1. Nayeon __________ Mina's secret.
나연이는 미나의 비밀을 알았다.

2. Junwoo __________ it and teased Mina.
준우가 그것을 듣고 미나를 놀렸다.

3. She was absent from school the next day. 그녀는 다음 날 학교에 결석했다.

Junwoo __________ sorry. 준우는 미안함을 느꼈다.

4. He __________ to Mina's house. 그는 미나의 집으로 갔다.

5. Mina was at home because she __________ a cold.
미나는 감기에 걸려서 집에 있었다.

D Daddy worries!

보기 run tell get play want

1. Last night my dad __________ me, "You can go to Sihu's house on Saturday." 나의 아빠는 어젯밤에 말씀하셨다, "토요일에 시후네 집에 가도 된다."

2. I __________ to Sihu's house. 나는 시후의 집으로 달려갔다.

3. We __________ all day long. 우리는 하루 종일 놀았다.

4. But, I __________ a phone call later that night. It was my daddy. 하지만, 나는 그날 밤 늦게 전화를 받았다. 아빠였다.

5. He __________ me to come home.
아빠는 내가 집으로 오기를 원하셨다.

My dad always worries! 우리 아빠는 항상 걱정하신다!

정답과 해설 p.5

Practice 2 일반동사의 과거형을 써서 문장을 완성해 보아요.

다음 우리말 뜻과 같도록 주어진 표현을 순서에 맞게 배열하여 문장을 완성하세요.

1. (did, I, my homework) last night. 어젯밤에 나는 숙제를 했다.
   ➔ I did my homework last night.

2. (got up, late, I). 난 늦게 일어났어.
   ➔ ______________________________.

3. (arrived home, early, I) today. 나는 오늘 집에 일찍 도착했다.
   ➔ ______________________________ today.

4. (cut, the paper, I) with scissors. 나는 가위로 종이를 잘랐다.
   ➔ ______________________________ with scissors.

5. (My mom, my test paper, saw).
   우리 엄마는 내 시험지를 보셨다.
   ➔ ______________________________.

6. (saw, I, her angry face). 나는 그녀의 화난 얼굴을 보았다.
   ➔ ______________________________.

7. After dinner, (went, we, to a movie). 저녁을 먹은 후, 우리는 영화를 보러 갔다.
   ➔ After dinner, ______________________________.

8. (watched, We, a comedy film). 우리는 코미디 영화를 보았다.
   ➔ ______________________________.

9. (had, a lot of dreams, I) when I was a kid. 내가 어렸을 때 나는 많은 꿈들이 있었다.
   ➔ ______________________________ when I was a kid.

정답과 해설 p.5

10. (a time capsule, made, I) with a shoe box.
나는 신발 상자로 타임캡슐 하나를 만들었다.

➔ ______________________________ with a shoe box.

11. (played, chess, We).
우린 체스를 했어.

➔ ______________________________
______________________________.

12. (a glass of water, drank, She). 그녀는 물 한 잔을 마셨다.

➔ ______________________________
______________________________.

13. (a book, I, read) last weekend. 지난 주말에 나는 책을 읽었다.

➔ ______________________________ last weekend.

14. (I, them, believed). 나는 그들을 믿었어.

➔ ______________________________.

15. (Charlie, at home, stayed) because he was sick.
Charlie는 아팠기 때문에 집에 있었다.

➔ ______________________________
because he was sick.

16. (my favorite toy, put, I) in it.
나는 내가 가장 좋아하는 장난감을 그 안에 넣었다.

➔ ______________________________ in it.

정답과 해설 p.5

Practice 3 일반동사의 과거형을 써서 완전한 문장을 써 보아요.

우리말 뜻을 참고하여 다음 주어진 표현을 활용해 문장을 완성해 보세요.
(주어진 동사를 과거형으로 바꿔 쓰세요.)

1. (go to school)
나는 학교에 갔다.

➔ I went to school.

2. (feel good)
나는 기분이 좋았다.

➔ ________________.

3. (visit, my uncle) 나는 일요일에 삼촌을 방문했다.
➔ ________________ on Sunday.

4. (get up, at 9 o'clock) 나는 9시에 일어났어.
➔ ________________.

5. (The class, start, early) 수업은 일찍 시작했다.
➔ ________________.

6. (meet, on Friday) 나는 금요일에 그를 만났다.
➔ ________________.

7. (eat fruit) 그녀는 과일을 먹었다.
➔ ________________.

8. (take care of, little brother) 그녀는 그녀의 남동생을 돌봤다.
➔ ________________.

9. (go to city hall) 우리는 어제 시청에 갔어.
➔ ________________ yesterday.

10. (see, "Pororo") 그는 아침에 '뽀로로'를 봤다.
➔ ________________ in the morning.

정답과 해설 p.5

11. (take a picture)

그들은 사진을 찍었다.

➔ ____________________
____________________.

12. (Leaves, fall from the tree)

나뭇잎들이 나무에서 떨어졌다.

➔ ____________________
____________________.

13. (fall asleep) (*fall asleep : 잠이 들다) 그는 잠이 들었다.

➔ ____.

14. (tell a lie) 그녀는 거짓말을 했다.

➔ ____.

15. (meet, friends) 그녀는 그녀의 친구들을 만났다.

➔ ____.

16. (father, write a letter) 그녀의 아버지는 편지를 썼다.

➔ ____.

17. (hit a home run) 그는 홈런을 쳤다.

➔ ____.

18. (answer my question) 그녀는 나의 질문에 대답했다.

➔ ____.

19. (buy a car) 그는 작년에 차를 샀어.

➔ ______________________________ last year.

20. (cry, all day long) 그는 하루 종일 울었다.

➔ ____.

정답과 해설 p.5

Let's Practice More!

SET 01

학습목표 1 | 일반동사 과거형의 규칙변화를 연습해 보아요.　　공부한 날 :　　맞은 개수 :　　/12개

다음 문장을 읽고 밑줄 친 부분이 맞으면 ○표, 틀리면 ×표를 하세요.

01. We plaied basketball yesterday. → ×
우리는 어제 농구를 했다.

02. He wanted me to come back home. → ______
그는 내가 집으로 돌아오기를 원했다.

03. I arriveed home early today. 나는 오늘 집에 일찍 도착했다. → ______

04. We watched a comedy film. 우리는 코미디 영화를 보았다. → ______

05. I believeed them. 나는 그들을 믿었다. → ______

06. The teacher called my name. 선생님은 내 이름을 부르셨다. → ______

07. He scolded me. 그는 나를 혼내셨다. → ______

08. The class started early. 수업은 일찍 시작했다. → ______

09. She answered my question. 그녀는 나의 질문에 대답했다. → ______

10. He cryed all day long. 그는 하루 종일 울었다. → ______

11. You baked some cookies. 너는 쿠키를 좀 구웠다. → ______

12. I liveed with my family. → ______
나는 가족과 함께 살았어.

정답과 해설 p.5

Let's Practice More!

SET 02

학습목표 1 | 일반동사 과거형의 규칙변화를 연습해 보아요. 공부한 날 : 맞은 개수 : /14개

다음 ( ) 안에서 알맞은 것을 골라 보세요.

01. They (laughed / laughd) loudly. 그들은 크게 웃었다.

02. We (plaied / played) all day long. 우리는 하루 종일 놀았다.

03. My brother (helpped / helped) many people. 나의 형은 많은 사람들을 도왔다.

04. Charlie (stayed / staied) at home. Charlie는 집에 있었다.

05. I (visited / visitted) my uncle on Sunday. 나는 일요일에 삼촌을 방문했다.

06. I (liveed / lived) alone. 나는 혼자 살았다.

07. The teacher (called / calld) my name. 선생님은 내 이름을 부르셨다.

08. He (scolded / scoldeed) me. 그는 나를 혼내셨다.

09. He (wantd / wanted) me to come back home. 그는 내가 집으로 돌아오기를 원했다.

10. I (arriveed / arrived) home early today. 나는 오늘 집에 일찍 도착했다.

11. We (watched / watcheed) a comedy film. 우리는 코미디 영화를 보았다.

12. I (believd / believed) them. 나는 그들을 믿었어.

13. The class (started / startted) early. 수업은 일찍 시작했다.

14. He (cryed / cried) all day long. 그는 하루 종일 울었다.

정답과 해설 p.6

Let's Practice More!

SET 03

학습목표 1 | 일반동사 과거형의 규칙변화를 연습해 보아요. 공부한 날 : 맞은 개수 : /14개

다음 문장을 읽고 밑줄 친 부분을 올바르게 고쳐 보세요.

01. She answerred my question. 그녀는 나의 질문에 대답했다. → answered

02. He cryed all day long. 그는 하루 종일 울었다. → ________

03. You bakeed some cookies. 너는 쿠키를 좀 구웠다. → ________

04. I liveed with my family. 나는 가족과 함께 살았어. → ________

05. I laugheed loudly. 나는 크게 웃었다. → ________

06. We plaied all day long. 우리는 하루 종일 놀았다. → ________

07. My brother helpped sick people. 나의 형은 아픈 사람들을 도왔다. → ________

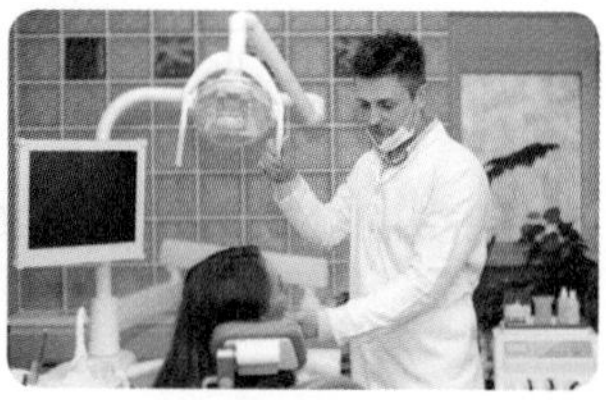

08. Charlie staied at home. Charlie는 집에 있었다. → ________

09. I visitted my grandparents on Sunday. 나는 일요일에 조부모님을 방문했다. → ________

10. He watcheed a soccer game yesterday. 그는 어제 축구 경기를 봤다. → ________

11. The teacher calld my name. 선생님은 내 이름을 부르셨다. → ________

12. My mom scoldded me. 엄마는 나를 혼내셨다. → ________

13. My sister wantted me to come back home. 나의 언니는 내가 집으로 돌아오기를 원했다. → ________

14. She arriveed home early today. 그녀는 오늘 집에 일찍 도착했다. → ________

정답과 해설 p.6

Let's Practice More!

SET 04

학습목표 2 | 일반동사 과거형의 불규칙 변화를 연습해 보아요. 공부한 날 : 맞은 개수 : /12개

다음 문장을 읽고 밑줄 친 부분이 맞으면 ○표, 틀리면 고쳐 써 보세요.

01. Sihu getted a goal. 시후가 골을 넣었다. → got

02. We won the game. 우리는 그 경기를 이겼다. → ______

03. I gived him a thumbs-up. 나는 그에게 엄지를 척 세워주었다. → ______

04. I read a comic book in English class yesterday. 나는 어제 영어 시간에 만화책을 읽었다. → ______

05. I writed a letter of apology. 나는 반성문을 썼다. → ______

06. My arm hurted last night. 어젯밤에 팔이 아팠다. → ______

07. Nayeon knew Mina's secret. 나연이는 미나의 비밀을 알았다. → ______

08. Junwoo heard it and teased Mina. 준우가 그것을 듣고 미나를 놀렸다. → ______

09. She meeted her friends. 그녀는 그녀의 친구들을 만났다. → ______

10. Dad drinked beer. 아빠는 맥주를 드셨어. → ______

11. She taked care of her little brother. 그녀는 그녀의 남동생을 돌봤다. → ______

12. Leaves fell from a tree. 나뭇잎들이 나무에서 떨어졌다. → ______

정답과 해설 p.6

Let's Practice More!

SET 05

학습목표 2 | 일반동사 과거형의 불규칙 변화를 연습해 보아요.　　공부한 날 :　　맞은 개수 :　　/14개

다음 우리말 해석을 보고 ( ) 안의 단어를 이용해 문장을 완성해 보세요.

01. She (ate) fruit. (eat) 그녀는 과일을 먹었다.

02. I ( ) a phone call. (get) 나는 전화를 받았다.

03. We ( ) the game. (win) 우리는 그 경기를 이겼다.

04. Junwoo ( ) sorry. (feel) 준우는 미안함을 느꼈다.

05. He ( ) to Mina's house. (go) 그는 미나의 집으로 갔다.

06. My dad ( ) me about it. (tell) 나의 아빠는 그것에 대해 나에게 말씀하셨다.

07. I ( ) to Sihu's house. (run) 나는 시후의 집으로 달려갔다.

08. I ( ) my homework last night. (do) 어젯밤에 나는 숙제를 했다.

09. I ( ) the paper with scissors. (cut) 나는 가위로 종이를 잘랐다.

10. My mom ( ) my test paper. (see) 우리 엄마는 내 시험지를 보셨다.

11. He ( ) a glass of water. (drink)
그는 물 한 잔을 마셨다.

12. I ( ) a lot of dreams. (have) 나는 많은 꿈들이 있었다.

13. I ( ) a time capsule with a shoe box. (make)
나는 신발 상자로 타임캡슐 하나를 만들었다.

14. I ( ) a book last weekend. (read)
지난 주말에 나는 책 한 권을 읽었다.

정답과 해설 p.6

Let's Practice More!

SET 06

학습목표 3 | 일반동사 과거형을 확실히 다져 보아요. 공부한 날 : 맞은 개수 : /14개

다음 ( ) 안에서 알맞은 것을 고르세요.

01. She (studies / studied) in the library yesterday.
그녀는 어제 도서관에서 공부했다.

02. We (go / went) to city hall last weekend.
우리는 지난 주말에 시청에 갔어.

03. He (watched / watches) "Pororo" in the morning.
그는 아침에 '뽀로로'를 봤다.

04. He (falls / fell) asleep early last night.
그는 어젯밤에 일찍 잠이 들었다.

05. He (bought / buys) a car last year.
그는 작년에 차를 샀어.

06. We (play / played) soccer yesterday.
우리는 어제 축구를 했다.

07. My arm (hurts / hurt) last night.
어젯밤에 팔이 아팠다.

08. My dad (told / tells) me about it.
나의 아빠는 그것에 대해 나에게 말씀하셨다.

09. I (get / got) up late this morning.
난 오늘 아침에 늦게 일어났어.

10. Sihu (got / gets) a goal in the last round.
시후가 마지막 라운드에서 골을 넣었다.

11. I (wrote / write) a letter of apology last night.
나는 어젯밤에 반성문을 썼다.

12. Junwoo (hears / heard) Mina's secret yesterday.
준우는 어제 미나의 비밀을 들었다.

13. He (goes / went) to Mina's house last Friday.
그는 지난 금요일에 미나의 집으로 갔다.

14. I (do / did) my homework an hour ago.
나는 한 시간 전에 숙제를 했다.

정답과 해설 p.6

Let's Practice More!

SET 07

학습목표 4 | 일반동사의 현재시제와 과거시제를 비교해 보아요. 공부한 날 : 맞은 개수 : /20개

다음 문장을 ( ) 안의 지시대로 바꿔 보세요.

01. I give him a thumbs-up.
(과거시제로)

➔ I gave him a thumbs-up.

나는 그에게 엄지를 척 세워주었다.

02. We play chess.
(과거시제로)

➔ ______________________.

우린 체스를 했어.

03. We won the game. (현재시제로)

➔ ______________________.

우리는 그 경기를 이긴다.

04. Nayeon knows Mina's secret. (과거시제로)

➔ ______________________.

나연이는 미나의 비밀을 알았다.

05. Junwoo feels sorry. (과거시제로)

➔ ______________________.

준우는 미안함을 느꼈다.

06. I ran to Sihu's house. (현재시제로)

➔ ______________________.

나는 시후의 집으로 달려간다.

07. She got a phone call. (현재시제로)

➔ ______________________.

그녀는 전화를 받는다.

08. I get up late. (과거시제로)

➔ ______________________.

난 늦게 일어났어.

09. I cut the paper with scissors. (과거시제로)

➔ ______________________.

나는 가위로 종이를 잘랐다.

정답과 해설 p.6

10. My mom sees my test paper. (과거시제로)

➔ ______________________________.

우리 엄마는 내 시험지를 보셨다.

11. He watched a comedy film. (현재시제로)

➔ ______________________________.

그는 코미디 영화를 본다.

12. They put their favorite toys in the box. (현재시제로)

➔ ______________________________.

그들은 그들이 가장 좋아하는 장난감들을 그 상자에 넣는다.

13. Jane goes to school. (과거시제로)

➔ ______________________________.

Jane은 학교에 갔다.

14. My younger brother feels good. (과거시제로)

➔ ______________________________.

내 남동생은 기분이 좋았다.

15. Janet and I got up at 9 o'clock. (현재시제로)

➔ ______________________________.

Janet과 나는 9시에 일어나.

16. They take a picture. (과거시제로)

➔ ______________________________.

그들은 사진을 찍었다.

17. She tells a lie. (과거시제로)

➔ ______________________________.

그녀는 거짓말을 했다.

18. Her father writes a letter. (과거시제로)

➔ ______________________________.

그녀의 아버지는 편지를 썼다.

19. He hit a home run. (현재시제로)

➔ ______________________________.

그는 홈런을 친다.

20. She drinks a glass of water. (과거시제로)

➔ ______________________________.

그녀는 물 한 잔을 마셨다.

정답과 해설 p.6

Let's Practice More!

SET 08

학습목표 5 | 일반동사의 과거형을 이용해서 다양한 문장을 만들어 보아요. 공부한 날 : 맞은 개수 : /20개

다음 우리말 해석을 보고 ( ) 안의 단어를 이용해 문장을 완성해 보세요.

01. Mina was at home because she (had) a cold. (have)
미나는 감기에 걸려서 집에 있었다.

02. I ( ) her angry face. (see)
나는 그녀의 화난 얼굴을 보았다.

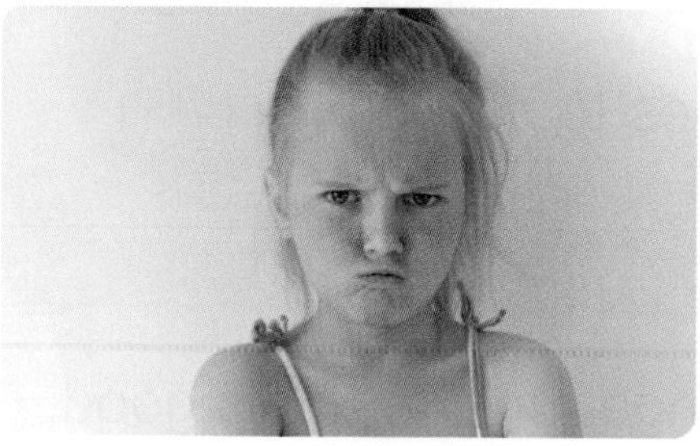

03. After dinner, we ( ) to a movie. (go) 저녁을 먹은 후, 우리는 영화를 보러 갔다.

04. We ( ) chess. (play) 우린 체스를 했어.

05. I ( ) a lot of dreams. (have) 나는 많은 꿈들이 있었다.

06. I ( ) a time capsule with a shoe box. (make)
나는 신발 상자로 타임캡슐 하나를 만들었다.

07. I ( ) a book last weekend. (read) 지난 주말에 나는 책 한 권을 읽었다.

08. I ( ) my favorite toy in the box. (put)
나는 내가 가장 좋아하는 장난감을 그 상자 안에 넣었다.

09. I ( ) good. (feel) 나는 기분이 좋았다.

정답과 해설 p.6

10. I ( ) up at 9 o'clock. (get) 나는 9시에 일어났어.

11. I ( ) him on Friday. (meet) 나는 금요일에 그를 만났다.

12. She ( ) fruit. (eat) 그녀는 과일을 먹었다.

13. I ( ) with my family. (live) 나는 가족과 함께 살았어.

14. Leaves ( ) from a tree. (fall) 나뭇잎들이 나무에서 떨어졌다.

15. She ( ) a lie. (tell) 그녀는 거짓말을 했다.

16. Her father ( ) a letter. (write) 그녀의 아버지는 편지를 썼다.

17. He ( ) a home run. (hit) 그는 홈런을 쳤다.

18. He ( ) a car last year. (buy) 그는 작년에 차를 샀어.

19. Dad ( ) a cup of coffee. (drink)
아빠는 커피 한 잔을 드셨어.

20. She ( ) care of her little brother. (take)
그녀는 그녀의 남동생을 돌봤다.

정답과 해설 p.6

일반동사 과거형의 부정문

UNIT 03 I didn't sleep well yesterday.

❖ POiNT 1 ❖

일반동사 현재형의 부정문

'~하지 않는다'라는 일반동사 현재형의 부정문 만드는 법을 기억하나요?

3인칭 단수 주어	주어+does not[doesn't]+동사원형
그 외의 주어	주어+do not[don't]+동사원형

I don't sleep well these days.

나는 요즘 잠을 잘 못 자.

He doesn't sleep well these days.

그는 요즘 잠을 잘 못 자.

❖ POiNT 2 ❖

일반동사 과거형의 부정문

그렇다면 '~하지 않았다'라고 말하려면 어떻게 해야 할까요?

주어에 상관없이 동사원형 앞에 do의 과거형인 did를 쓰고, not을 붙여주면 돼요!

주어에 상관없이	주어+did not[didn't]+동사원형

I did not[didn't] sleep well yesterday.

나는 어제 잠을 잘 자지 못했어.

She did not[didn't] sleep well yesterday.

그녀는 어제 잠을 잘 자지 못했어.

You did not[didn't] do your homework.

너는 숙제를 하지 않았어.

They did not[didn't] do their homework.

그들은 숙제를 하지 않았어.

*** did not 뒤에는 반드시 동사원형이 온다는 것을 기억해요!**

동사원형이란? want, give, sing과 같이 주어나 시제에 따라 바뀌지 않는 동사의 원래 형태를 말해요.

Check and Write

다음 밑줄 친 일반동사를 부정형으로 바꿔 보세요. (단, 부정형을 줄여 쓰세요.)

1. They turned on the light.
   → They [didn't turn] on the light.
   그들은 불을 켜지 않았어.

2. He bought popcorn.
   → He [ ] popcorn.
   그는 팝콘을 사지 않았어.

3. It melted away.
   → It [ ] away.
   그것은 녹아 없어지지 않았어.

4. We talked loudly.
   → We [ ] loudly.
   우리는 크게 말하지 않았어요.

정답과 해설 p.6

UNIT

04 Did she like EXO?

일반동사 과거형의 의문문

❖ POiNT 1 ❖

일반동사 현재형의 의문문

'~하니?'라고 묻는 일반동사 현재형의 의문문 만드는 법을 기억하나요?

3인칭 단수 주어	Does+주어+동사원형 ~?
그 외의 주어	Do+주어+동사원형 ~?

❖ POiNT 2 ❖

일반동사 과거형의 의문문

'~했니?'라고 말하려면 'Does'와 'Do' 대신, 주어에 상관없이 조동사 do의 과거형 Did를 쓰면 돼요.

주어에 상관없이	Did+주어+동사원형 ~?

현재형의 의문문	과거형의 의문문
Do you study hard? 너는 공부를 열심히 하니?	Did you study hard? 너는 공부를 열심히 했니?
Does she like EXO? 그녀는 엑소를 좋아하니?	Did she like EXO? 그녀는 엑소를 좋아했니?

❖ POiNT 3 ❖

일반동사 과거형의 의문문에 대한 대답

긍정이면, [Yes, 주어 + did.]
부정이면, [No, 주어 + didn't.]

Did you understand? 너 이해했니?

– Yes, I did. 응, 이해했어.

– No, I didn't. 아니, 이해 못했어.

Check and Write

다음 주어진 평서문을 의문문으로 바꿔 보세요.

1. You won at chess.

→ Did you win at chess ?

너 체스에서 이겼니?

2. They remembered you.

→ ____________________ ?

그들은 너를 기억했니?

3. She had lunch.

→ ____________________ ?

그녀는 점심을 먹었니?

4. You got the call.

→ ____________________ ?

너는 전화를 받았니?

정답과 해설 p.6

Practice 1 일반동사 과거형의 부정문과 의문문을 익혀 보아요.

다음 문장에 알맞은 단어를 보기에서 골라 빈칸에 써 보세요. (단, 한 단어를 여러 번 쓸 수 있어요.)

A He's crying again!

보기 Did[did] didn't sleep have stop get

1. I ___didn't___ ___sleep___ well yesterday. 나는 어제 잠을 잘 못 잤어.

2. Hayul __________ __________.
하율이가 잠을 자지 않았어.

3. He __________ __________ crying.
그는 울음을 멈추지 않았어.

4. __________ he __________ a nightmare? 그는 악몽을 꾸었니?

5. He __________ __________ a nightmare.
그는 악몽을 꾸지 않았어.

6. Dad __________ __________ up.
아빠는 깨지 않으셨어.

B We have to do our homework!

보기 Did[did] played got win play didn't

1. __________ you __________ basketball yesterday?
너희 어제 농구를 했니?

2. No, we __________. 아니요, 하지 않았어요.

3. We __________ soccer. 우린 축구를 했어요.

정답과 해설 p.6

4. __________ you __________ the game? 너희 그 경기를 이겼니?

5. Yes, we __________. 네, 이겼어요.

6. Sihu __________ a goal. 시후가 골을 넣었어요.

7. __________ you do your homework?
너희 숙제는 했니?

8. Phew... No, we __________ yet.
휴… 아니요, 아직 안 했어요.

C Mina is ill.

보기 answer come go Did[did] didn't

1. __________ you __________ Mina's call yesterday?
어제 미나의 전화 받았니?

2. No, I __________. 아니, 못 받았어.

3. __________ Mina __________ to school today?
오늘 미나가 학교에 왔니?

4. No, she __________. She is ill.
아니, 그녀는 오지 않았어. 그녀는 아파.

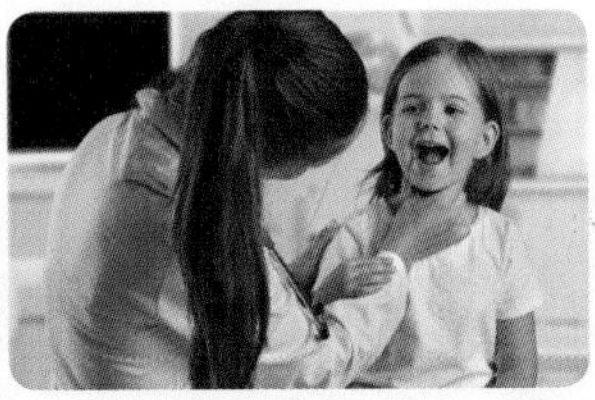

5. __________ Mina __________ to see a doctor? 미나는 병원에 갔니?

6. Yes, she __________. 응, 갔어.

정답과 해설 p.6

Practice 2 일반동사 과거형의 부정문과 의문문을 완성해 보아요.

다음 우리말 뜻과 같도록 주어진 표현을 순서에 맞게 배열하여 문장을 완성하세요.

1. (did not, shine, The sun).

햇빛이 비치지 않았어.

➔ The sun did not shine.

2. (The playground, dry, didn't).

운동장이 마르지 않았어.

➔ ______________________.

3. So, (play soccer, we, didn't) in the playground.

그래서 우리는 운동장에서 축구를 하지 않았어.

➔ So, ______________________ in the playground.

4. (you, the window, Did, break)? 네가 창문을 깼니?

➔ ______________________?

5. Junwoo (didn't, the classroom, clean). 준우는 교실 청소를 하지 않았어요.

➔ Junwoo ______________________.

6. (talk to him, didn't, I). 나는 그에게 말을 건네지 않았어.

➔ ______________________.

7. (exercise, We, didn't). 우리는 운동을 하지 않았어.

➔ ______________________.

8. (Did, make that pizza, you)?

네가 그 피자를 만들었니?

➔ ______________________?

9. (Did, push the button, you)?

네가 버튼을 눌렀니?

➔ ______________________?

정답과 해설 p.6

10. (see Sihu, you, Did) on the street? 너 길에서 시후를 봤니?

➔ ______________________ on the street?

11. No, (didn't, see, I, him). 아니, 나는 그를 보지 않았어.

➔ No, ______________________.

12. (watch that movie, Did, you)? 너 그 영화 봤니?

➔ ______________________?

13. (watch, that movie, didn't, I). 나는 그 영화를 보지 않았어.

➔ ______________________.

14. (have lunch, Did, you)? 너 점심 먹었니?

➔ ______________________?

15. (bring his umbrella, didn't, He). 그는 그의 우산을 갖고 오지 않았어.

➔ ______________________.

16. (taste good, didn't, The soup). 그 수프는 맛이 좋지 않았어.

➔ ______________________.

17. (raise his hand, Did, he)? 그는 손을 들었니?

➔ ______________________?

18. (know her name, didn't, We). 우리는 그녀의 이름을 몰랐어.

➔ ______________________.

19. (She, have a family, didn't). 그녀는 가족이 없었어.

➔ ______________________.

20. (see my pencil case, you, Did)? 너 내 필통 봤니?

➔ ______________________?

정답과 해설 p.7

Practice 3 일반동사 과거형의 부정문과 의문문을 완성해 보아요.

우리말 뜻을 참고하여 주어진 표현을 활용해 문장을 완성해 보세요.

1. (The alarm, ring)

알람이 울리지 않았어.

➔ The alarm did not[didn't] ring.

2. (wake you up)

내가 너희들을 깨웠니?

➔ ____________________?

3. (go to bed, late, last night) 너 어젯밤에 늦게 잤니?

➔ ____________________?

4. (Mom, wake me up) 엄마는 나를 깨우지 않으셨어.

➔ ____________________.

5. (The school bus, come, in time) 학교 버스는 제 시간에 오지 않았어.

➔ ____________________.

6. (bring, textbook) 나는 내 교과서를 가져오지 않았어.

➔ ____________________.

정답과 해설 p.7

7. (do your homework) 너 숙제 했어?

➔ ____?

8. (want to study)

나는 공부하고 싶지 않았어.

➔ ____________________

____________________.

9. (The store, sell fruit)

그 가게는 과일을 팔지 않았어.

➔ ____________________

____________________.

10. (bring, notebook) 나는 내 노트를 가져오지 않았어.

➔ ____.

11. (arrive, early) 그는 일찍 도착했니?

➔ ____?

12. (write, a letter of apology) 너 반성문 썼니?

➔ ____?

13. (study hard) 그들은 공부를 열심히 했니?

➔ ____?

정답과 해설 p.7

14. (Mom, see, report card) 엄마는 내 성적표를 보지 않으셨어.

➔ ______________________________.

15. (it, happen, at night) 그것은 밤에 일어났니?

➔ ______________________________?

16. (keep the secret)

그는 비밀을 지켰니?

➔ ______________________________

______________________________?

17. (fight)

그들은 싸우지 않았어.

➔ ______________________________

______________________________.

18. (respect) (*respect : 존경하다, 존중하다) 너는 그를 존경했니?

➔ ______________________________?

19. (get, your report card)

너 네 성적표 받았니?

➔ ______________________________

______________________________?

20. (drink milk)

그는 우유를 마시지 않았어.

➔ ______________________________

______________________________.

정답과 해설 p.7

Let's Practice More!

SET 01

학습목표 1 | 일반동사 과거형의 부정문 형태를 연습해 보아요. 공부한 날 : 맞은 개수 : /12개

다음 문장을 읽고 밑줄 친 부분이 맞으면 ○표, 틀리면 고쳐 써 보세요.

01. I did not sleeping yesterday. → sleep
나는 어제 잠을 못 잤어.

02. I did not see him. → ________
나는 그를 보지 않았어.

03. He did not having a nightmare. → ________
그는 악몽을 꾸지 않았어.

04. Dad did not get up. → ________
아빠는 일어나지 않으셨어.

05. We did not won the game. → ________
우리는 경기에서 이기지 못했어요.

06. We did not do our homework yet. → ________
우리는 아직 숙제를 안 했어요.

07. I did not getting the call. → ________
나는 전화를 못 받았어.

08. She did not coming to school. → ________
그녀는 학교에 오지 않았어.

09. The sun did not shined. → ________
햇빛이 비치지 않았어.

10. The playground did not dry. → ________
운동장이 마르지 않았어.

11. Junwoo did not cleaned the classroom. → ________
준우는 교실 청소를 하지 않았어요.

12. We did not exercise. → ________
우리는 운동을 하지 않았어.

정답과 해설 p.7

Let's Practice More!

SET 02

학습목표 1 | 일반동사 과거형의 부정문 형태를 연습해 보아요. 공부한 날 : 맞은 개수 : /14개

다음 ( ) 안에서 알맞은 것을 골라 보세요.

01. I did not (see / saw) him.
나는 그를 보지 않았어.

02. I did not (watched / watch) that movie.
나는 그 영화를 보지 않았어.

03. The soup did not (tasting / taste) good.
그 수프는 맛이 좋지 않았어.

04. We did not (knew / know) her name.
우리는 그녀의 이름을 몰랐어

05. She did not (have / having) a family.
그녀는 가족이 없었어.

06. The alarm did not (ring / rang).
알람이 울리지 않았어.

07. Mom did not (waked / wake) me up.
엄마는 나를 깨우지 않으셨어.

08. The school bus did not (came / come) in time.
학교 버스는 제 시간에 오지 않았어.

09. The store did not (sell / selling) fruit.
그 가게는 과일을 팔지 않았어.

10. I did not (bringing / bring) my cell phone.
나는 내 휴대폰을 가져오지 않았어.

11. Mom did not (see / saw) my report card.
엄마는 내 성적표를 보지 않으셨어.

12. They did not (fight / fought).
그들은 싸우지 않았어.

13. He did not (drank / drink) milk.
그는 우유를 마시지 않았어.

14. He did not (stopping / stop) crying.
그는 울음을 멈추지 않았어.

정답과 해설 p.7

Let's Practice More!

SET 03

학습목표 2 | 일반동사 과거형의 부정문을 줄여 쓸 수 있어요. 공부한 날 : 맞은 개수 : /14개

밑줄 친 부정형의 줄임말이 맞으면 ○표, 틀리면 고쳐 써 보세요.

01. We did'nt play basketball. → didn't
우리는 농구를 하지 않았어요.

02. I did'nt talk to him. → ________
나는 그에게 말을 건네지 않았어.

03. He didn't bring his umbrella. → ________
그는 그의 우산을 갖고 오지 않았어.

04. I didnt bring my textbook. → ________
나는 내 교과서를 가져오지 않았어.

05. I didn't want to study. → ________
나는 공부하고 싶지 않았어.

06. I did'nt sleep well yesterday. → ________
나는 어제 잠을 잘 못 잤어.

07. The baby didn't sleep. → ________
아기가 잠을 자지 않았어.

08. He didn't' stop crying. → ________
그는 울음을 멈추지 않았어.

09. Dad did'nt get up. → ________
아빠는 일어나지 않으셨어.

10. We didn't win the game. → ________
우리는 경기에서 이기지 못했어요.

11. We didn't do our homework yet. → ________
우리는 아직 숙제를 안 했어요.

12. The sun didn't shine. → ________
햇빛이 비치지 않았어.

13. The playground didn't dry. → ________
운동장이 마르지 않았어.

14. I did'nt see him. → ________
나는 그를 보지 않았어.

정답과 해설 p.7

Let's Practice More!

SET 04

학습목표 3 | 일반동사 과거형의 의문문을 연습해 보아요. 공부한 날 : 맞은 개수 : /14개

다음 우리말 해석을 보고 ( ) 안에서 올바른 것을 고르세요.

01. (Did / Do) you pass the exam? 너는 시험에 통과했니?

02. Did she (like / liked) me? 그녀는 나를 좋아했어?

03. (Do / Did) you win the game? 너는 그 경기를 이겼니?

04. Did you (doing / do) your homework? 너는 숙제를 했니?

05. (Did / Do) you answer Mina's call yesterday?
너는 어제 미나의 전화를 받았니?

06. (Does / Did) Mina come to school today? 오늘 미나가 학교에 왔니?

07. Did Mina (goes / go) to see a doctor? 미나는 병원에 갔니?

08. Did you (break / broke) the window? 네가 창문을 깼니?

09. Did you (make / made) that pizza?
네가 저 피자를 만들었니?

10. (Do / Did) you push the button? 네가 버튼을 눌렀니?

11. Did you (see / saw) Sihu on the street? 너 길에서 시후를 봤니?

12. Did you (watch / watched) the movie? 너 그 영화 봤니?

13. (Do / Did) they have lunch? 그들은 점심 먹었니?

14. (Did / Does) he raise his hand? 그는 손을 들었니?

정답과 해설 p.7

Let's Practice More!

SET 05

학습목표 3 | 일반동사 과거형의 의문문을 연습해 보아요. 공부한 날 : 맞은 개수 : /14개

다음 우리말 해석을 보고 빈칸에 알맞은 말을 써 보세요.

01. (Did) I wake you up? 내가 너희들을 깨웠니?

02. ( ) you go to bed late last night? 너 어젯밤에 늦게 잤니?

03. Did you ( ) your homework? 너 숙제 했어?

04. ( ) he arrive early? 그는 일찍 도착했니?

05. Did you ( ) a letter of apology? 너 반성문 썼니?

06. ( ) they study hard? 그들은 공부를 열심히 했니?

07. ( ) you get the report card? 너 성적표 받았니?

08. ( ) you play basketball yesterday?
너희 어제 농구를 했니?

09. Did you ( ) my pencil case? 너희들 내 필통 봤니?

10. ( ) it happen at night? 그것은 밤에 일어났니?

11. Did he ( ) a nightmare? 그는 악몽을 꾸었니?

12. Did you ( ) that movie? 너희들 그 영화 봤니?

13. ( ) you win the game? 너희 그 경기를 이겼니?

14. Did you ( ) the dishes? 너 설거지 했니?

정답과 해설 p.7

Let's Practice More!

SET 06

학습목표 4 | 일반동사 과거형의 의문문에 대한 대답을 연습해 보아요. 공부한 날 : 맞은 개수 : /12개

다음 문장을 읽고 빈칸에 적절한 대답을 써 보세요.

01. Did you answer Mina's call yesterday? 어제 미나의 전화 받았니?

A: Yes, ___I did___. 응, 받았어.

B: No, ___I didn't___. 아니, 못 받았어.

02. Did Mike come to school today? 오늘 Mike가 학교에 왔니?

A: Yes, ______________. 응, 왔어.

B: No, ______________. 아니, 안 왔어.

03. Did your sister go to see a doctor? 너의 여동생은 병원에 갔니?

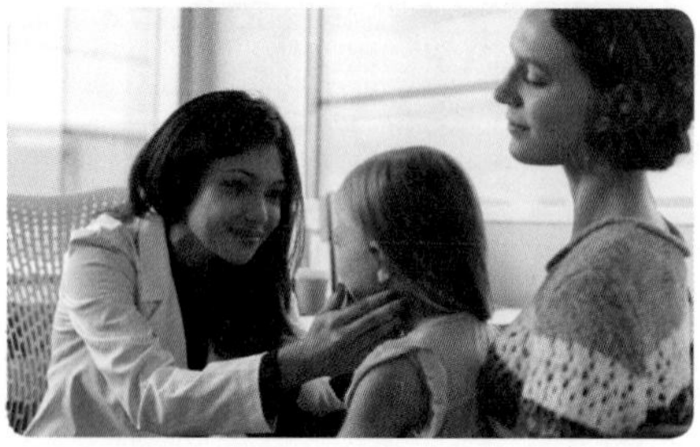

A: Yes, ______________.

응, 갔어.

B: No, ______________.

아니, 안 갔어.

04. Did you break the window?

네가 창문을 깼니?

A: Yes, ______________.

응, 깼어.

B: No, ______________.

아니, 깨지 않았어.

05. Did they make the pizza? 그들이 그 피자를 만들었니?

A: Yes, ______________. 응, 만들었어.

B: No, ______________. 아니, 만들지 않았어.

정답과 해설 p.7

06. Did you push the button? 네가 버튼을 눌렀니?

A: Yes, ______________________. 응, 눌렀어.

B: No, ______________________. 아니, 누르지 않았어.

07. Did you watch that movie? 너희들 그 영화 봤니?

A: Yes, ______________________. 응, 봤어.

B: No, ______________________. 아니, 안 봤어.

08. Did your friends have lunch? 너의 친구들은 점심 먹었니?

A: Yes, ______________________. 응, 먹었어.

B: No, ______________________. 아니, 안 먹었어.

09. Did he raise his hand? 그는 손을 들었니?

A: Yes, ______________________. 응, 들었어.

B: No, ______________________. 아니, 안 들었어.

10. Did you see my pencil case? 너희들 내 필통 봤니?

A: Yes, ______________________. 응, 봤어.

B: No, ______________________. 아니, 못 봤어.

11. Did I wake you up? 내가 너희들을 깨웠니?

A: Yes, ______________________. 응, 깨웠어

B: No, ______________________. 아니, 깨우지 않았어.

12. Did you go to bed late last night? 너 어젯밤에 늦게 잤니?

A: Yes, ______________________. 응, 늦게 잤어.

B: No, ______________________. 아니, 늦게 자지 않았어.

정답과 해설 p.7

Let's Practice More!

SET 07

학습목표 5 | 일반동사 과거형의 부정문과 의문문 만드는 방법을 확실히 다져 보아요. 공부한 날 : 맞은 개수 : /20개

( ) 안의 지시에 따라 문장을 바꿔 보세요.

01. She had a family. (의문문)

➜ Did she have a family ?

그녀는 가족이 있었니?

02. The store sold fruit. (의문문)

➜ ________________?

그 가게는 과일을 팔았니?

03. He had a nightmare. (부정문)

➜ ________________.

그는 악몽을 꾸지 않았어.

04. We played basketball. (부정문)

➜ ________________.

우리는 농구를 하지 않았어요.

05. We played soccer. (부정문)

➜ ________________.

우린 축구를 하지 않았어요.

06. Sihu got a goal. (의문문)

➜ ________________?

시후가 골을 넣었니?

07. I got the call. (부정문)

➜ ________________.

나는 전화를 못 받았어.

08. She came to school. (의문문)

➜ ________________?

그녀가 학교에 왔니?

09. Junwoo cleaned the classroom. (의문문)

➜ ________________?

준우는 교실 청소를 했니?

정답과 해설 p.7

10. I talked to him. (부정문)

➔ ______________________________________.

나는 그에게 말을 건네지 않았어.

11. We exercised. (부정문)

➔ ______________________________.

우리는 운동을 하지 않았어.

12. They saw him. (의문문)

➔ ______________________________________?

그들은 그를 봤니?

13. He brought his umbrella. (의문문)

➔ ______________________________________?

그는 그의 우산을 갖고 왔니?

14. I watched that movie. (부정문)

➔ ______________________________.

나는 그 영화를 보지 않았어.

15. The soup tasted good. (의문문)

➔ ______________________________________?

그 수프는 맛이 좋았니?

16. We knew her name. (부정문)

➔ ______________________________________.

우리는 그녀의 이름을 몰랐어.

17. The alarm rang. (의문문)

➔ ______________________________?

알람이 울렸니?

18. Mom woke me up. (부정문)

➔ ______________________________________.

엄마는 나를 깨우지 않으셨어.

19. I brought my textbook. (부정문)

➔ ______________________________________.

나는 내 교과서를 가져오지 않았어.

20. I wanted to study. (부정문)

➔ ______________________________________.

나는 공부하고 싶지 않았어.

정답과 해설 p.8

Let's Practice More!

SET 08

학습목표 5 | 일반동사 과거형의 부정문과 의문문 만드는 방법을 확실히 다져보아요. 공부한 날 : 맞은 개수 : /20개

다음 우리말 해석에 맞도록 빈칸을 채워 문장을 완성해 보세요.

01. He ___did___ ___not___ wear socks.
그는 양말을 신지 않았어.

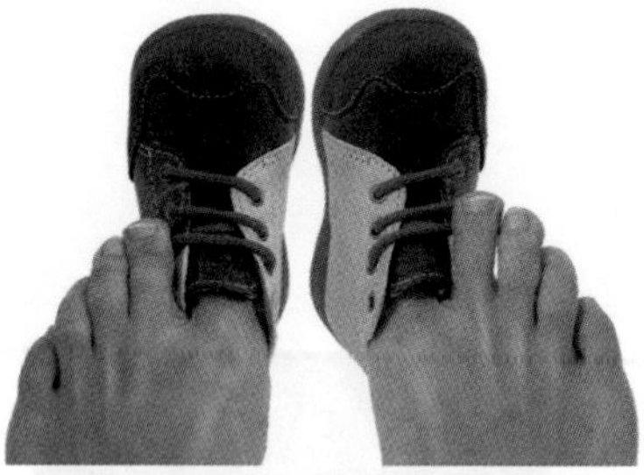

02. ________ ________ walk your dog?
넌 너의 개를 산책시켰니?

03. ________ you ________ your homework? 너 숙제 했어?

04. I ________ ________ bring my cell phone. 나는 내 휴대폰을 가져오지 않았어.

05. ________ you ________ a letter of apology? 너 반성문 썼니?

06. ________ they ________ hard? 그들은 공부를 열심히 했니?

07. Mom ________ see my report card. 엄마는 내 성적표를 보지 않으셨어.

08. ________ ________ get the report card? 너 성적표 받았니?

09. They ________ ________ fight. 그들은 싸우지 않았어.

정답과 해설 p.8

10. __________ he __________ the secret? 그는 비밀을 지켰니?

11. I __________ sleep well yesterday. 나는 어제 잠을 잘 못 잤어.

12. We __________ play soccer. 우린 축구를 하지 않았어요.

13. __________ Sihu __________ a goal? 시후가 골을 넣었나요?

14. We __________ play baseball in the playground.
우리는 운동장에서 야구를 하지 않았어.

15. __________ you respect __________?
너는 그를 존경했니?

16. __________ he __________ milk?
그는 우유를 마셨니?

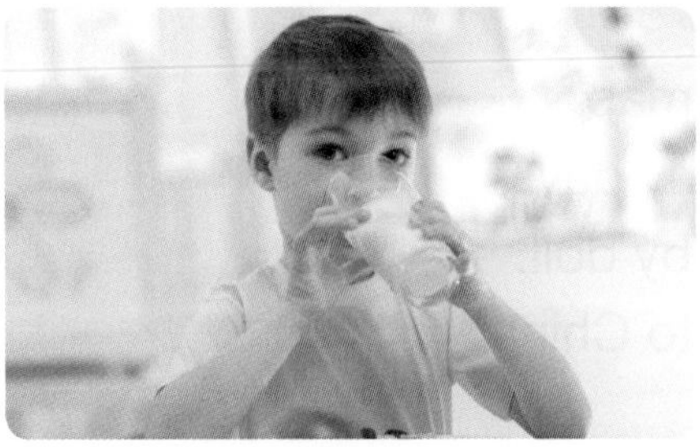

17. Hayul __________ sleep. 하율이가 잠을 자지 않았어.

18. We __________ do our homework yet. 우리는 아직 숙제를 안 했어요.

19. __________ you answer Mina's call yesterday? 어제 미나의 전화 받았니?

20. I __________ get the call. 나는 전화를 못 받았어.

정답과 해설 p.8

실전테스트

CHAPTER 01~02

공부한 날 :

복습한 날 :

부모님 확인 :

CHAPTER 01 be동사의 과거형　CHAPTER 02 일반동사의 과거형

●정답과 해설은 별책 8쪽에서 확인하세요!!

01

다음 빈칸에 알맞은 be동사 과거형을 쓰세요.

(1) am – ____________

(2) aren't – ____________

(3) isn't – ____________

02

다음 중 과거형을 나타내는 문장이 아닌 것을 고르세요.

① She saw a map.
② It was a rainy day.
③ I want a baby doll.
④ They went to China.

03

다음 문장을 의문문으로 알맞게 바꾼 것을 고르세요.

He got a chance.

① Did he get a chance?
② Did he got a chance?
③ Did he gets a chance?
④ Does he got a chance?

04

다음 중 밑줄 친 부분이 어색한 것을 고르세요.

① Were you in your room?
② He watched TV last night.
③ She was a singer.
④ He look happy.

05

다음 빈칸에 들어갈 수 없는 말을 고르세요.

Did you go to the bookstore ____________?

① last week
② this morning
③ yesterday
④ tomorrow

06

다음 문장을 부정문으로 바꿀 때 didn't가 들어갈 위치로 알맞은 곳을 고르세요.

① You ② read ③ the ④ book.

[07~10] 다음 중 동사의 현재형과 과거형이 잘못 짝지어진 것을 고르세요.

07

① read – read ② come – come
③ walk – walked ④ get – got

08

① write – writed ② move – moved
③ jump – jumped ④ learn – learned

09

① sing – sang ② start – started
③ use – used ④ go – goed

10

① wake – woked ② say – said
③ save – saved ④ help – helped

11

다음 중 짝지어진 대화가 어색한 것을 고르세요.

① A: Did you finish your homework?
B: Yes, I did.
② A: Are you a student?
B: Yes, I was.
③ A: Did you have lunch?
B: No, I didn't.
④ A: Is she your aunt?
B: Yes, she is.

12

다음 문장을 의문문으로 바꿀 때 빈칸에 들어갈 알맞은 말을 고르세요.

He saw the movie.
→ ________ he see the movie?

① Was ② Did
③ Does ④ Do

13

다음 대화의 빈칸에 들어갈 알맞은 말을 고르세요.

A: Were you a nurse?
B: ____________________

① I am a nurse.
② No, you are.
③ Yes, I was.
④ Yes, I were.

[14~16] 다음 문장을 부정문으로 고쳐 보세요.

14

We ate pizza.

⇨ ____________________

15

She woke up early this morning.

⇨ ____________________

16

I did my homework.

⇨ ____________________

[17~20] 다음 밑줄 친 부분을 줄여서 문장을 다시 쓰세요.

17
They <u>are not</u> kind to my kids.

⇨ ______________________________

18
I <u>did not</u> wash the dishes.

⇨ ______________________________

19
He <u>was not</u> a scientist.

⇨ ______________________________

20
You <u>were not</u> his friend.

⇨ ______________________________

[21~24] [보기]에서 가장 적절한 be동사 형태를 골라 다음 문장의 빈칸을 완성하세요.

[보기] am, are, is, was, were

21
I __________ at home yesterday.
(나는 어제 집에 있었다.)

22
They __________ in the 4th grade this year.
(그들은 올해 4학년이다.)

23
We __________ in the bathroom an hour ago.
(우리는 한 시간 전에 욕실에 있었다.)

24
It __________ dark outside now.
(밖은 지금 어둡다.)

[25~28] 다음 그림을 보고, 질문에 맞는 답을 빈 칸에 쓰세요.

25

A: Was she a teacher?

B: No, __________ __________.

26

A: Did the dog like some chocolate?

B: No, __________ __________.

27

A: __________ he play baseball yesterday?

B: Yes, __________ __________.

28

A: Were they sad?

B: No, __________ __________.

[29~30] 다음 해석에 맞게 단어들을 바르게 배열하여 문장을 쓰세요. (단, 동사를 시제에 맞게 바꾸세요.)

29

우리는 어제 영화를 보았다.

(movie / a / watch / We / yesterday).

⇨ ______________________________

30

그녀는 지난 주에 일본에 갔다.

(Japan / go to / last week / She).

⇨ ______________________________

Chapter 03 현재시제 / 과거시제

이 챕터에서는 동사의 '현재시제'와 '과거시제'의 용법에 대해 배워 보아요.

☆ 학습 방향 및 배울 내용 미리보기 ☆

☐ **Unit 01 : I have** a fever.

현재시제

동사의 현재시제는 어떤 경우에 쓰는지 알아보아요.

▼

☐ **Unit 02 :** He **had** many friends at school.

과거시제

동사의 과거시제는 어떤 경우에 쓰는지 알아보아요.

단어 미리보기

이 챕터에 나올 단어들 중 이미 알고 있는 단어가 있나요?
맞는 뜻을 골라 체크해 봐요.

날짜 : 이름 : 알고 있는 단어의 수 : /24개

No.	아는 단어	단어	품사	알맞은 뜻에 체크 표시해 봐요.			
1	✔	fever	명사	축제	☐	열	✔
2	☐	east	명사	서쪽	☐	동쪽	☐
3	☐	autumn	명사	가을	☐	겨울	☐
4	☐	save	동사	아끼다	☐	열다	☐
5	☐	take	동사	버리다	☐	(사진) 찍다	☐
6	☐	October	명사	12월	☐	10월	☐
7	☐	upset	형용사	화난	☐	즐거운	☐
8	☐	sleepy	형용사	졸린	☐	활기찬	☐
9	☐	catch	동사	떨어지다	☐	잡다	☐
10	☐	close	형용사	가까운	☐	먼	☐
11	☐	truth	명사	진실	☐	거짓	☐
12	☐	finger	명사	젓가락	☐	손가락	☐
13	☐	ghost	명사	유령	☐	신부	☐
14	☐	lonely	형용사	외로운	☐	행복한	☐
15	☐	joy	명사	화남	☐	기쁨	☐
16	☐	knock	동사	두드리다	☐	닫다	☐
17	☐	arrive	동사	출발하다	☐	도착하다	☐
18	☐	use	동사	사용하다	☐	허락하다	☐
19	☐	share	동사	공유하다	☐	빛나다	☐
20	☐	for	전치사	~동안	☐	~까지	☐
21	☐	about	전치사	~에서 부터	☐	~에 대해	☐
22	☐	mind	동사	신경쓰다	☐	혼내다	☐
23	☐	church	명사	공장	☐	교회	☐
24	☐	shape	명사	장난감	☐	모양	☐

UNIT 01 I have a fever.

❖ POiNT ❖

현재시제는 이럴 때 써요.

현재의 상태	I **have** a fever. 나 열이 있어. She **is** a teacher. 그녀는 선생님이다.	
현재의 습관, 성격	Junsu usually **sleeps** until 2:00 p.m. on weekends. 준수는 보통 주말에 오후 2시까지 잠을 자. I always **have** lunch with my friends. 난 항상 친구들과 함께 점심을 먹어. He **has** a bad temper. 그는 나쁜 성질을 가지고 있어.	
불변의 진리, 과학적 사실	The sun **rises** in the east. 해는 동쪽에서 뜬다. Leaves **fall** from the trees in autumn. 가을에 나뭇잎들은 나무에서 떨어진다.	
속담, 격언	A stitch in time **saves** nine. 제때의 한 땀이 아홉 바느질을 아낀다. Time **is** gold. 시간은 금이다.	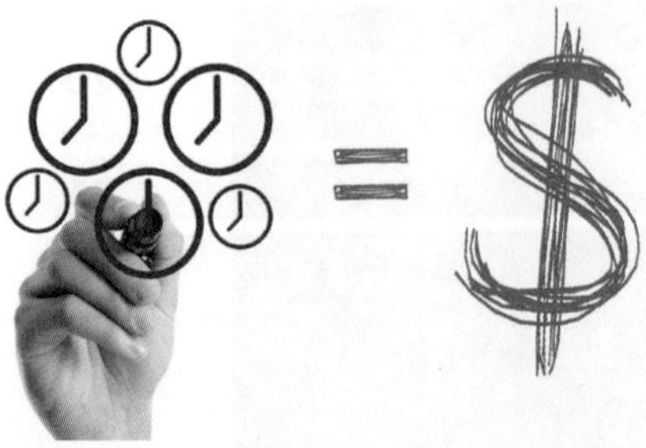

Check and Write

주어진 동사원형을 현재시제로 써서 문장을 완성해 보세요.

1. yawn

→ The dog yawns.
그 개는 하품을 해.

2. form

→ The swans ______ a heart shape.
백조들이 하트모양을 만들어.

3. take

→ They ______ a funny picture.
그들은 웃긴 사진을 찍어.

4. be

→ She ______ sleepy.
그녀는 졸려.

정답과 해설 p.8

UNIT 02 He **had** many friends at school.

과거시제

❖ POiNT ❖

과거시제는 이럴 때 써요.

과거의 습관, 사실	I **went** to church every Sunday. 나는 일요일마다 교회에 갔었어. She **got up** early in those days. 그녀는 그 당시에 일찍 일어났어.

역사적 사실	The Korean War **broke out** in 1950. (*break out: 발생하다) 한국전쟁은 1950년에 발생했다. Columbus **discovered** America on October 12, 1492. 콜럼버스는 1492년 10월 12일에 아메리카 대륙을 발견했다.

과거에 끝난 일시적 동작, 상태	I **had** a long wait at the McDonald's, but I **didn't** mind. 난 맥도날드에서 오래 기다렸지만, 신경 쓰진 않았어.  I **wanted** a bicycle for my birthday. 나는 내 생일 선물로 자전거를 원했어. He **had** many friends at school. 그는 학교에 친구가 많았어. 

Check and Write

주어진 동사원형을 과거시제로 써서 문장을 완성해 보세요.

1. paint

➔ He painted his face yesterday.
그는 어제 그의 얼굴을 색칠했어.

2. play

➔ They ______ together.
그들은 함께 놀았어.

3. be

➔ He ______ upset last night.
그는 어젯밤에 화났었어.

4. have

➔ They ______ a birthday party.
그들은 생일 파티를 했어.

정답과 해설 p.8

Practice 1 동사의 현재시제와 과거시제를 익혀 보아요.

다음 문장에 알맞은 단어를 보기에서 골라 빈칸에 알맞게 변형하여 써 보세요.
(단, 한 단어는 여러 번 쓸 수 있어요.)

A Pokémon GO!

보기 do　be　play　go　have

1. What ___did___ you do yesterday?
어제 너는 뭐 했어?

2. I ___________ to Sokcho.
나는 속초에 갔어.

3. What ___________ you do there?
거기서 뭘 했는데?

4. I ___________ "Pokémon GO."
나는 '포켓몬 고'를 했어.

5. Wow, ___________ it fun?
와, 그거 재밌었어?

6. Yes. I ___________ a great time.
응. 나는 좋은 시간을 보냈어.

B On Sunday!

보기 talk　be　get　do　want　go

1. ___________ up right now!
당장 일어나!

2. Oh, no... I ___________ sleepy now...
싫어요... 저 지금 졸려요...

정답과 해설 p.8

3. And it __________ Sunday, today!
그리고 오늘은 일요일이에요!

4. I __________ to sleep late on Sunday.
나는 일요일에 늦게까지 자고 싶어요.

5. When __________ you go to bed last night?
어젯밤에 몇 시에 잤니?

6. I __________ to bed at 1:00 a.m.
저 어제 한 시에 잤어요.

7. Why __________ you stay up so late?
너 왜 그렇게 늦게까지 깨어있었니?

8. I __________ to Mina on the phone.
나는 미나랑 전화로 이야기했어요.

C We can play it!

보기	do	be	play

1. I __________ a search on the Internet about "Pokémon GO."
나는 '포켓몬 고'에 대해 인터넷으로 검색해 봤어.

2. What __________ that?
그게 뭔데?

3. It __________ a game where you catch "Pokémon."
그것은 '포켓몬'을 잡는 게임이야.

4. We can __________ it in Seoul.
우리는 서울에서 그 게임을 할 수 있어.

5. It __________ also possible in Sokcho.
그것은 또한 속초에서도 가능해.

정답과 해설 p.8

Practice 2 동사의 현재시제와 과거시제가 쓰인 문장을 완성해 보아요.

다음 우리말 뜻과 같도록 주어진 표현을 순서에 맞게 배열하여 문장을 완성하세요.

1. (aren't, friends, We) now.
우리는 이제 친구가 아니야.

➔ We aren't friends
__________ now.

2. (The sun, in the east, rises).
태양은 동쪽에서 떠오른다.

➔ __________
__________.

3. (laughed at, me, He). (*laugh at: ~를 비웃다)
그가 나를 비웃었어.

➔ __________.

4. (were, They, close).
그들은 친했었잖아.

➔ __________.

5. (is, My mother, inside the house, not) right now.
나의 엄마는 지금 집 안에 없어요.

➔ __________ right now.

6. (went to bed, early, He) last night.
그는 어젯밤 일찍 잠자리에 들었어.

➔ __________ last night.

정답과 해설 p.8

7. (quiet, It, is) now.
지금은 조용해.

➔ ______________________ now.

8. (his finger, cut, Sihu).
시후는 그의 손가락을 베였어.

➔ ______________________
______________________.

9. (the news, heard, He), too.
그도 그 소식을 들었어.

➔ ______________________
______________________, too.

10. (her foot, She, broke).
그녀는 발이 부러졌어.

➔ ______________________.

11. (didn't, They, know the truth).
그들은 진실을 몰랐어.

➔ ______________________.

12. (a good idea, not, It, is).
그건 좋은 생각이 아니야.

➔ ______________________.

13. (it, I, regret, may).
나는 그것을 후회할지도 몰라.

➔ ______________________.

정답과 해설 p.8

14. (understand, I, can, you) now.
난 이제 너를 이해할 수 있어.

➔ ________________________________ now.

15. (always, I, share joy) with my friends.
난 항상 친구들과 기쁨을 나눠.

➔ ________________________________ with my friends.

16. (on the playground, I, fell down). 난 운동장에서 넘어졌어.

➔ ________________________________
________________________________.

17. (It, not, was, your fault).
그건 너의 잘못이 아니었어.

➔ ________________________________
________________________________.

18. (was, I, not, with you).
난 너와 함께 있지 않았어.

➔ ________________________________.

19. (some subjects, failed, I).
난 몇몇 과목에서 낙제했어.

➔ ________________________________.

20. (lonely, He, felt) yesterday.
그는 어제 외로움을 느꼈어.

➔ ________________________________ yesterday.

정답과 해설 p.9

Practice 3 동사의 현재시제와 과거시제를 구분해서 문장을 써 보아요.

우리말 뜻을 참고하여 다음 주어진 표현을 활용해 문장을 완성해 보세요.
(단, 필요한 경우 주어와 시제에 따라 동사를 알맞게 변형하세요.)

1. (see a ghost)
그는 귀신을 봤어.

➔ He saw a ghost
______________.

2. (It, a big doll)
그것은 커다란 인형이었어.

➔ ______________
______________.

3. (go to school)
우리는 학교에 가.

➔ ______________________________.

4. (have a nightmare)
하율이는 어제 악몽을 꿨어.

➔ Hayul ______________________ yesterday.

5. (sleep, in his parents' room)
이제 그는 그의 부모님 방에서 자.

➔ Now, ______________________________.

6. (It, a ghost)
그건 귀신이 아니었어.

➔ ______________________________.

정답과 해설 p.9

7. (collect, many acorns) (*acorn: 도토리)

나 도토리 많이 모았어!

➔ ____!

8. (Today, Dana's birthday)

오늘은 다나의 생일이야.

➔ ____________________

____________________.

9. (Yesterday, New Year's Day)

어제는 새해 첫날이었어.

➔ ____________________

____________________.

10. (feel lonely)

나는 어제 외로웠다.

➔ ______________________________ yesterday.

11. (best friends once)

우리는 한때는 제일 친한 친구였는데 지금은 아니야.

➔ ______________________________, but now we're not.

12. (soulmates)

지금 우리는 소울메이트야.

➔ ______________________________ now.

13. (use, my smartphone)

나는 어제 스마트폰을 사용했어.

➔ ______________________________________ yesterday.

정답과 해설 p.9

14. (Mom, upset)
엄마는 그것 때문에 속상해 하셨어.

➔ ________________________________ about it.

15. (play video games)
나는 비디오게임을 하루에 30분만 해.

➔ ________________________________ for only 30 minutes a day.

16. (live on the farm)
어렸을 때 그는 농장에 살았어.

➔ ____________________
when he was young.

17. (knock on the door)
그는 문을 두드렸어.

➔ ____________________
____________________.

18. (eat some pizza)
그들은 어제 피자를 좀 먹었어.

➔ ________________________________ yesterday.

19. (arrive, early)
우리는 아침 일찍 도착했어.

➔ ________________________________ in the morning.

20. (usually, take the bus)
그녀는 보통 버스를 타.

➔ ____.

정답과 해설 p.9

Let's Practice More!

SET 01

학습목표 1 | 동사의 현재시제와 과거시제를 복습해 보아요.   공부한 날 :   맞은 개수 :   /12개

다음 밑줄 친 부분을 우리말 해석에 알맞게 고쳐 써 보세요.

01. She tells the secret. → told
그녀는 비밀을 말했다.

02. I meeted her in the market yesterday. → ______
나는 어제 그녀를 시장에서 만났어.

03. I goed to bed at 1:00 a.m. → ______
저 새벽 한 시에 잤어요.

04. We isn't friends now. → ______
우리는 이제 친구가 아니야.

05. They eated some pizza yesterday. → ______
그들은 어제 피자를 좀 먹었어.

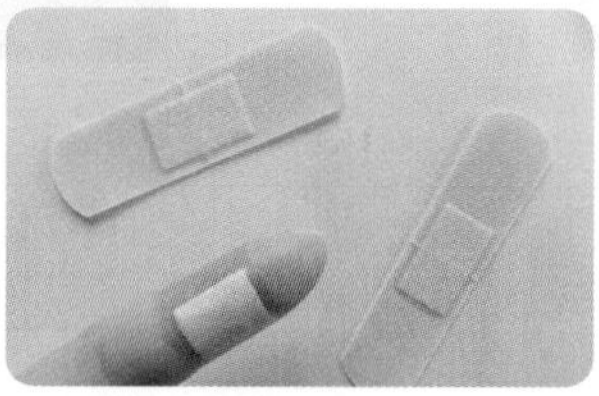

06. Sihu cuted his finger. → ______
시후는 그의 손가락을 베였어.

07. She playes video games. → ______
그녀는 비디오 게임을 해.

08. He heared the news. → ______
그는 그 소식을 들었어.

09. She breaked her arm. → ______
그녀는 팔이 부러졌어.

10. I falled down in the park. → ______
난 공원에서 넘어졌어.

11. He sleepes in his parents' room. → ______
그는 그의 부모님 방에서 자.

12. What doed you do yesterday? → ______
어제 너는 뭐했어?

정답과 해설 p.9

Let's Practice More!

SET 02

학습목표 2 | 현재시제와 과거시제는 어느 때 쓰이는지 익혀 보아요. 공부한 날 : 맞은 개수 : /14개

다음 문장에서 밑줄 친 동사의 시제가 나타내는 것을 고르세요.

01. I have a fever. (현재의 상태 / 과거의 습관)
나 열이 있어.

02. It is Sunday, today! (현재의 상태 / 현재의 습관)
오늘은 일요일이에요!

03. The sun rises in the east. (과거의 사실 / 불변의 진리)
태양은 동쪽에서 떠오른다.

04. She usually takes the bus. (현재의 습관 / 과거의 습관)
그녀는 보통 버스를 타.

05. We aren't friends now. (현재의 상태 / 현재의 습관)
우리는 이제 친구가 아니야.

06. Time is gold. (현재의 습관 / 격언)
시간은 금이다.

07. My mother is not inside the house. (현재의 상태 / 현재의 습관)
우리 엄마는 집 안에 없어요.

08. I always share joy with my friends. (불변의 진리 / 현재의 습관)
난 항상 친구들과 기쁨을 나눠.

09. The earth moves around the sun. (과거의 사실 / 불변의 진리)
지구는 태양 주위를 돈다.

10. Today is Dana's birthday. (현재의 상태 / 현재의 습관)
오늘은 다나의 생일이야.

11. I always have lunch with my friends. (과거의 습관 / 현재의 습관)
난 항상 친구들과 함께 점심을 먹어.

12. I am full. (현재의 상태 / 현재의 습관)
나 배불러.

13. A stitch in time saves nine. (과거의 사실 / 속담)
제때의 한 땀이 아홉 비느질을 이낀다.

14. It is quiet now. (현재의 상태 / 현재의 습관)
지금은 조용해.

정답과 해설 p.9

Let's Practice More!

SET 03

학습목표 2 | 현재시제와 과거시제는 어느 때 쓰이는지 익혀 보아요. 공부한 날 : 맞은 개수 : /14개

다음 문장에서 밑줄 친 동사의 시제가 나타내는 것을 고르세요.

01. The Korean War broke out in 1950. (과거의 습관 / 역사적 사실)
한국전쟁은 1950년에 일어났다.

02. I fell down on the playground. (과거의 사실 / 역사적 사실)
난 운동장에서 넘어졌어.

03. My grandmother went to church. (과거의 사실 / 현재의 상태)
할머니는 교회에 가셨어.

04. She broke her arm. (과거의 사실 / 현재의 상태)
그녀는 팔이 부러졌어.

05. I go to church every Sunday. (현재의 습관 / 역사적 사실)
나는 일요일마다 교회에 간다.

06. Columbus discovered America on October 12, 1492. (불변의 진리 / 역사적 사실)
콜럼버스는 1492년 10월 12일에 아메리카 대륙을 발견했다.

07. He laughed at me. (과거의 사실 / 역사적 사실)
그가 나를 비웃었어.

08. He went to bed early last night. (과거의 사실 / 역사적 사실)
그는 어젯밤 일찍 잠자리에 들었어.

09. Sihu cut his finger. (과거의 사실 / 역사적 사실)
시후는 그의 손가락을 베였어.

10. My brother uses his smartphone every night. (현재의 습관 / 과거의 사실)
나의 남동생은 매일 밤 스마트폰을 사용한다.

11. World War II broke out in 1939. (불변의 진리 / 역사적 사실)
세계 2차 대전은 1939년에 일어났다.

12. I was not with you. (과거의 사실 / 현재의 상태)
난 너와 함께 있지 않았어.

13. I failed some subjects. (과거의 사실 / 역사적 사실)
난 몇몇 과목에서 낙제했어.

14. Hangul was created by King Sejong in 1443. (불변의 진리 / 역사적 사실)
한글은 1443년에 세종대왕에 의해 창제되었다.

정답과 해설 p.9

Let's Practice More!

SET 04

학습목표 3 | 현재시제와 과거시제를 비교해 보아요.　　공부한 날 :　　맞은 개수 :　　/12개

다음 우리말 해석을 보고 밑줄 친 부분이 맞으면 ○표, 틀리면 고쳐 써 보세요.

01. I learn fast. → learned
나는 빨리 배웠어.

02. They were close. → ______
그들은 친했었잖아.

03. My grandmother goes to church. → ______
할머니는 교회에 가셨어.

04. She cut her finger. → ______
그녀는 그녀의 손가락을 베였어.

05. Hayul has a nightmare yesterday. → ______
하율이는 어제 악몽을 꿨어.

06. It is not your fault. → ______
그건 너의 잘못이 아니었어.

07. She breaks her arm. → ______
그녀는 팔이 부러졌어.

08. He saw a ghost. → ______
그는 귀신을 봤어.

09. It was quiet now. → ______
지금은 조용해.

10. They didn't know the truth. → ______
그들은 진실을 몰랐어.

11. We arrives early in the morning. → ______
우리는 아침 일찍 도착했어.

12. We were not friends now. → ______
우리는 이제 친구가 아니야.

정답과 해설 p.9

Let's Practice More!

SET 05

학습목표 3 | 현재시제와 과거시제를 비교해 보아요. 공부한 날 : 맞은 개수 : /14개

다음 우리말 해석을 보고 ( ) 안의 단어를 이용해 문장을 완성해 보세요.

01. He ___sends___ a letter to her. (send) 그는 그녀에게 편지를 보내.

02. He __________ at me. (laugh) 그가 나를 비웃었어.

03. Today __________ my birthday. (be) 오늘은 내 생일이야.

04. I __________ my smartphone. (use)
나는 스마트폰을 사용했어.

05. My mother __________ her finger. (cut) 나의 엄마는 손가락을 베이셨어.

06. She usually __________ the bus. (take) 그녀는 보통 버스를 타.

07. He __________ the news. (hear) 그는 그 소식을 들었어.

08. I __________ many acorns! (collect) 나 도토리 많이 모았어!

09. I __________ sleepy now. (be) 저 지금 졸려요.

10. They __________ some pizza yesterday. (eat) 그들은 어제 피자를 좀 먹었어.

11. I __________ some subjects. (fail) 난 몇몇 과목에서 낙제했어.

12. The sun __________ in the east. (rise) 태양은 동쪽에서 떠오른다.

13. Mom __________ upset about it. (be)
엄마는 그것 때문에 속상해 하셨어.

14. He __________ on the door. (knock) 그는 문을 두드렸어.

정답과 해설 p.9

Let's Practice More!

SET 06

학습목표 3 | 현재시제와 과거시제를 비교해 보아요. 공부한 날 : 맞은 개수 : /14개

다음 우리말 해석을 보고 밑줄 친 동사의 시제가 맞으면 ○표, 틀리면 고쳐 써 보세요.

01. She <u>cleans</u> her room yesterday. → cleaned
그녀는 어제 그녀의 방을 청소했어.

02. Today <u>was</u> my dad's birthday. → ________
오늘은 나의 아빠의 생신이야.

03. Yesterday <u>was</u> New Year's Day. → ________
어제는 새해 첫날이었어.

04. They <u>eat</u> some pizza yesterday. → ________
그들은 어제 피자를 좀 먹었어.

05. I <u>feel</u> sad last night. → ________
나는 어젯밤에 슬펐다.

06. She usually <u>took</u> the bus. → ________
그녀는 보통 버스를 타.

07. He <u>felt</u> lonely yesterday. → ________
그는 어제 외로움을 느꼈어.

08. I always <u>shared</u> joy with my friends. → ________
난 항상 친구들과 기쁨을 나눠.

09. He <u>went</u> to bed early last night. → ________
그는 어젯밤 일찍 잠자리에 들었어.

10. I <u>was</u> sleepy now. → ________
저 지금 졸려요.

11. They <u>are</u> close 2 years ago. → ________
2년 전에 그들은 친했었잖아.

12. We <u>go</u> to school every day. → ________
우리는 매일 학교에 가.

13. He <u>lives</u> on the farm when he was young. → ________
어렸을 때 그는 농장에 살았어.

14. It <u>was</u> Sunday, today! → ________
오늘은 일요일이에요!

정답과 해설 p.9

Let's Practice More!

SET 07

학습목표 4 | 현재시제와 과거시제로 다양한 표현을 완성해 보아요.　　공부한 날 :　　맞은 개수 :　　/20개

다음 문장을 ( ) 안의 지시대로 고쳐 보세요.

01.

They fought. (현재시제로)

➔ They fight.

그들은 싸운다.

02.

She breaks her arm. (과거시제로)

➔ ______________________.

그녀는 팔이 부러졌어.

03. She wanted a bicycle for her birthday. (현재시제로)

➔ ______________________.

그녀는 그녀의 생일 선물로 자전거를 원해.

04. He sees a ghost. (과거시제로)

➔ ______________________.

그는 귀신을 봤어.

05. It was a big doll. (현재시제로)

➔ ______________________.

그것은 커다란 인형이야.

06. I collect many coins! (과거시제로)

➔ ______________________!

나는 동전을 많이 모았어!

07. It was not a ghost. (현재시제로)

➔ ______________________.

그건 귀신이 아니야.

08. He sleeps in his parents' room. (과거시제로)

➔ ______________________.

그는 그의 부모님 방에서 잤어.

09. He lives on the farm. (과거시제로)

➔ ______________________.

그는 농장에 살았어.

정답과 해설 p.9

10. We were best friends. (현재시제로)

➔ ____.

우리는 가장 친한 친구야.

11. I use your headphones. (과거시제로)

➔ ______________________________________.

나는 너의 헤드폰을 사용했어.

12. Mom is upset about it. (과거시제로)

➔ ____.

엄마는 그것 때문에 속상해 하셨어.

13. They ate some pizza. (현재시제로)

➔ ____.

그들은 피자를 먹어.

14. I feel sad. (과거시제로)

➔ ______________________________________.

나는 슬펐다.

15. What do you do there? (과거시제로)

➔ ____?

거기서 뭘 했는데?

16. I went to bed at 1:00 a.m. (현재시제로)

➔ ____.

저는 새벽 한 시에 자요.

17. Why do you stay up late? (과거시제로)

➔ ____?

너 왜 늦게까지 깨어있었니?

18. He knocks on the door. (과거시제로)

➔ ____.

그는 문을 두드렸어.

19. My mother was not inside the house. (현재시제로)

➔ ____.

나의 엄마는 집 안에 없어요.

20. They didn't know the truth. (현재시제로)

➔ ____.

그들은 진실을 몰라.

정답과 해설 p.9

Let's Practice More!

SET 08

학습목표 4 | 현재시제와 과거시제로 다양한 표현을 완성해 보아요. 공부한 날 : 맞은 개수 : /20개

다음 우리말 해석을 보고 ( ) 안의 단어를 이용해 문장을 완성해 보세요.

01. 

I ___ate___ chicken yesterday. (eat) 나는 어제 치킨을 먹었어.

02. 

He ________ in his parents' room. (sleep) 그는 그의 부모님 방에서 자.

03. What ________ you do yesterday? (do) 어제 너는 뭐 했어?

04. I ________ to Sokcho. (go) 나는 속초에 갔어.

05. I ________ "Pokémon GO." (play) 나는 '포켓몬 고'를 했어.

06. ________ it fun? (be) 재밌었어?

07. I ________ a great time. (have) 나는 좋은 시간을 보냈어.

08. The Korean War ________ out in 1950. (break) 한국전쟁은 1950년에 발발했다.

09. It ________ not your fault. (be) 그건 너의 잘못이 아니었어.

정답과 해설 p.10

10. He __________ lonely yesterday. (feel) 그는 어제 외로움을 느꼈어.

11. We __________ soulmates now. (be) 지금 우리는 소울메이트야.

12. He __________ his face yesterday. (paint) 그는 어제 그의 얼굴을 칠했어.

13. I __________ down on the playground. (fall) 난 운동장에서 넘어졌어.

14. I __________ video games. (play) 나는 비디오게임을 해.

15. She __________ a search on the Internet about it. (do)
그녀는 그것에 대해 인터넷을 검색했어.

16. We __________ early in the morning. (arrive) 우리는 아침 일찍 도착했어.

17. A stitch in time __________ nine. (save) 제때의 한 땀이 아홉 바느질을 아낀다.

18. We __________ best friends once. (be) 우리는 한때는 제일 친한 친구였어.

19. He __________ up early in those days. (get) 그는 그 당시에 일찍 일어났어.

20. She __________ to sleep late on Saturday. (want)
그녀는 토요일에 늦게까지 자고 싶어 해.

정답과 해설 p.10

Chapter 04 미래시제

이 챕터에서는 미래의 예측이나 계획을 나타내는
동사의 '미래시제'의 용법에 대해 배워 보아요.

☆ 학습 방향 및 배울 내용 미리보기 ☆

☐ **Unit 01 : I will** be back in a moment.

미래시제 will

미래시제 will을 사용하여 긍정문, 부정문, 의문문을 만드는 방법에 대해 알아보아요.

▼

☐ **Unit 02 : I am going to** fail my math test!

미래시제 be going to

미래시제 be going to를 사용하여 긍정문, 부정문, 의문문을 만드는 방법, 그리고 주어와 be going to를 줄여 쓰는 방법을 배워 보아요.

단어 미리보기

이 챕터에 나올 단어들 중 이미 알고 있는 단어가 있나요?
맞는 뜻을 골라 체크해 봐요.

날짜 : 이름 : 알고 있는 단어의 수 : /24개

No.	아는 단어	단어	품사	알맞은 뜻에 체크 표시해 봐요.			
1	✔	bite	명사	한 입	✔	자전거	☐
2	☐	back	부사	잠깐	☐	다시	☐
3	☐	step	동사	밟다	☐	찌르다	☐
4	☐	happen	동사	완료하다	☐	일어나다	☐
5	☐	again	부사	다시	☐	이미	☐
6	☐	hard	부사	서투르게	☐	열심히	☐
7	☐	fail	동사	실패하다	☐	서두르다	☐
8	☐	worry	동사	걱정하다	☐	괴롭히다	☐
9	☐	tonight	부사	오늘 낮에	☐	오늘 밤에	☐
10	☐	move	동사	옮기다	☐	건너다	☐
11	☐	deliver	동사	뛰어넘다	☐	배달하다	☐
12	☐	mail	명사	우편	☐	매일	☐
13	☐	next	형용사	예전의	☐	다음의	☐
14	☐	Thursday	명사	화요일	☐	목요일	☐
15	☐	magic	명사	마술	☐	미술	☐
16	☐	music	명사	기술	☐	음악	☐
17	☐	triangle	명사	실로폰	☐	트라이앵글	☐
18	☐	soon	부사	벌써	☐	곧	☐
19	☐	picnic	명사	소풍	☐	연습	☐
20	☐	careful	형용사	겁 없는	☐	조심하는	☐
21	☐	sure	형용사	확신하는	☐	경계하는	☐
22	☐	ready	형용사	게으른	☐	준비된	☐
23	☐	forgive	동사	용서하다	☐	사과하다	☐
24	☐	dish	명사	접시	☐	세제	☐

UNIT 미래시제 will

01 I will be back in a moment.

❖ POiNT 1 ❖

미래시제 '~할 것이다'라는 의미로 조동사 will이나 be going to라는 표현을 써서 미래의 예측이나 계획을 나타내요.
미래시제는 tomorrow(내일), this afternoon(오늘 오후), next week(다음 주), later(나중에)와 같은 표현과 함께 자주 쓰여요.

❖ POiNT 2 ❖

긍정문	주어 + **will** + 동사원형 ~할 것이다	One bite and all your dreams **will** come true. 한 입이면 모든 너의 꿈들은 이루어질 거야. [백설공주] I left my cell phone at home. I **will** be back in a moment. 나 내 핸드폰을 집에 두고 왔어. 나 금방 돌아올게. 
부정문	주어 + **will not(=won't)** + 동사원형 ~하지 않을 것이다	*Nayeon*: Ouch! You stepped on my foot. 아야! 너 내 발을 밟았어. *Sihu*: I'm sorry. It **won't** happen again. 미안해. 그건 다신 일어나지 않을 거야. It **won't** cost much... just your voice. 대가는 크지 않을 거야... 그냥 너의 목소리(면 돼). [인어공주]
의문문	**Will** + 주어 + 동사원형 ~? ~할 거야?	**Will** it snow tomorrow? 내일 눈이 올까? **Will** you finish the homework by tomorrow? 넌 숙제를 내일까지 끝낼 거야?

Check and Write

다음 밑줄 친 동사를 조동사 will을 써서 미래시제로 바꿔보세요.

1. He <u>goes</u> to the pool.

   ➔ He [will go] to the pool.

   그는 수영장에 갈 거야.

2. It <u>snows</u>.

   ➔ It [ ].

   눈이 올 거야.

3. I <u>go</u> to bed.

   ➔ I [ ] to bed.

   나는 자러 갈 거야.

4. She <u>studies</u> hard.

   ➔ She [ ] hard.

   그녀는 열심히 공부할 거야.

정답과 해설 p.10

UNIT 미래시제 be going to

02 I am going to fail my math test!

❖ POiNT 1 ❖

be going to는 조동사 will 대신 쓸 수 있어요. 'go(가다)'와는 다른 뜻이에요!

긍정문	주어 + **be going to** + 동사원형 ~할 것이다	I can't sleep. I **am going to** fail my math test! 난 잘 수 없어. 난 내 수학 시험을 망칠 거야! Don't worry. 걱정하지 마. Everything **is going to** be fine. 모든 것은 괜찮을 거야. 
부정문	주어 + **be동사** + **not** + **going to** + 동사원형 ~하지 않을 것이다	I **am[I'm] not going to** lie to you. 난 당신에게 거짓말 하지 않을 거야. We **are not[aren't] going to** eat out tonight. 우리는 오늘 밤에 외식 하지 않을 거야.
의문문	**be동사** + 주어 + **going to** + 동사원형 ~? ~할 거야?	**Are** you **going to** eat that? 너 저거 먹을 거야? **Is** she **going to** move to another school? 그녀는 다른 학교로 옮길 거래?

❖ POiNT 2 ❖

'주어 + be going to'는 줄여 쓸 수 있어요.

I am going to ⇨ I'**m** going to

You/We/They are going to ⇨ You'**re**/We'**re**/They'**re** going to

He/She/It is going to ⇨ He'**s**/She'**s**/It'**s** going to

Check and Write

다음 밑줄 친 동사를 be going to를 이용하여 미래시제로 바꿔보세요.

1. It is rainy.
   → It [is going to be] rainy.
   비가 올 거야.

2. He sleeps.
   → He [ ].
   그는 잠을 잘 거야.

3. They watch "Frozen."
   → They [ ] "Frozen."
   그들은 '겨울왕국'을 볼 거야.

4. I study hard.
   → I [ ] hard.
   나는 열심히 공부할 거야.

정답과 해설 p.10

Practice 1 will과 be going to를 익혀 보아요.

다음 문장에 알맞은 말을 보기 에서 골라 빈칸에 써 보세요. (단, 한 번 쓴 말을 여러 번 쓸 수 있어요.)

A Let's go to see a movie!

보기 going are to

1. *Dad* : Let's go to see a movie tonight!
오늘 밤에 영화 보러 가자!
Suho : What __are__ we __going__ __to__ see?
우리 뭐 볼 거예요?

2. *Dad* : We ________ ________ ________ see "Zootopia."
우리는 '주토피아'를 볼 거야.

B Mail delivery

보기 will[Will] am going to arrive deliver be

1. *Mail carrier* : I ________ ________ ________ ________ a piece of registered mail soon.
우편 배달원 : 제가 곧 등기우편 한 통을 배달할 건데요.
(*deliver: 배달하다, registered mail: 등기우편)

2. *Sihu* : When ________ you ________?
언제 도착하세요?

3. *Mail carrier* : I think I ________ ________ around four.
우편 배달원 : 4시쯤 도착할 거 같아요.

4. *Sihu* : Nobody ________ ________ at home.
집에 아무도 없을 거예요.

정답과 해설 p.10

5. *Mail carrier* : __________ anyone __________ there tomorrow?
우편 배달원 : 내일은 거기 누군가 계신가요?

Sihu : I will be studying at home tomorrow.
내일은 제가 집에서 공부하고 있을 거예요.

6. *Mail carrier* : Then I __________ __________ it tomorrow.
우편 배달원 : 그럼 제가 그것을 내일 배달할게요.

C School talent show

보기 will is going to are going to do play dance hold

1. We __________ __________ a school talent show next Thursday.
우리는 다음 주 목요일에 학예회를 개최할 것이다. (*school talent show: 학예회)

2. Some students __________ __________ __________ __________.
몇몇 학생들은 춤을 출 것이다.

3. Jinwoo __________ __________ __________ __________ a magic show.
진우는 마술쇼를 할 것이다.

4. Suho and his friends __________ __________ music.
수호와 그의 친구들은 음악을 연주할 것이다.

5. Mina and Sihu __________ __________ the recorder.
미나와 시후는 리코더를 연주할 것이다.

6. Dana and Jihye __________ __________ the xylophone.
다나와 지혜는 실로폰을 연주할 것이다.

7. Suho __________ __________ __________ __________ the triangle.
수호는 트라이앵글을 연주할 것이다.

정답과 해설 p.10

D Farewell party

보기	will	not	hold	move	go

1. Taeyeon __________ __________ to another school soon.
   태연이는 곧 다른 학교로 전학을 갈 것이다.

2. Some of the students __________ __________ a farewell party.
   몇몇 학생들이 송별회를 할 것이다. (*farewell party: **송별회**)

3. But, I __________ __________ __________ to the party.
   하지만 나는 파티에 가지 않을 것이다.

Cultural Tips
재미로 익히는 문화상식

한국과 미국의 동물울음소리는 어떻게 다를까요?

정답과 해설 p.10

Practice 2 will과 be going to를 써서 문장을 완성해 보아요.

다음 우리말 뜻과 같도록 주어진 표현을 순서에 맞게 배열하여 문장을 완성하세요.

1. *Sihu* : Let's go to see a movie today.
오늘 영화 보러 가자.
Jinwoo : Good! (are, What, going to see, we)?
좋아! 우리 뭐 볼까?
➔ Good! What are we going to see?

2. (we, will, meet, When)? 우리 언제 만날 거야?
➔ ____________________?

3. (watch a movie, We, will) tonight. 우리 오늘 밤에 영화 볼 거야.
➔ ____________________ tonight.

4. (come, you, Will) with us? 너도 우리랑 같이 갈래?
➔ ____________________ with us?

5. (let me, My mom, won't). 우리 엄마는 허락하지 않으실 거야.
➔ ____________________.

6. That's too bad. (be interesting, It, will). 그거 안됐다. 재미있을 텐데.
➔ That's too bad. ____________________.

7. Don't worry. (bite, going to, The dog, not, is).
걱정 마. 그 개는 물지 않을 거야.
➔ Don't worry. ____________________.

정답과 해설 p.10

8. *Mother* : Please don't talk to strangers!
낯선 사람이랑 말하면 안 돼!

Little Red Riding Hood : Don't worry, Mommy. (careful, I'll, be).
빨간 모자 : 걱정 마세요, 엄마. 조심할게요.

➔ Don't worry, Mommy. ______________________.

9. (snow, will, It) tomorrow. 내일은 눈이 올 거야.

➔ ______________________ tomorrow.

10. (won't, I, you, tell). 나는 너에게 말해주지 않을 거야.

➔ ______________________.

11. I'm sure (will, you, pass the exam). 나는 네가 시험에 통과할 거라고 확신해.

➔ I'm sure ______________________.

12. (watch TV, She, is going to) after dinner.
그녀는 저녁식사 후에 TV를 볼 거야.

➔ ______________________
after dinner.

13. (go on a picnic, will, We) this Saturday. (*go on a picnic: 소풍가다)
우리는 이번 토요일에 소풍을 갈 거야.

➔ ______________________ this Saturday.

14. (read a book, am going to, I) this weekend. 나는 이번 주말에 책을 읽을 거야.

➔ ______________________ this weekend.

15. (are going to, have lunch, They) together. 그들은 함께 점심을 먹을 거야.

➔ ______________________ together.

정답과 해설 p.10

16. (will, He, wash the dishes) for his mom.
그는 그의 엄마를 위해 설거지를 할 거야.

➔ ____________________ for his mom.

17. (will, She, forgive me).
그녀는 나를 용서해 줄 거야.

➔ ____________________ ____________________.

18. (you, Will, listen to some music)? 너는 음악을 좀 들을 거니?
➔ ____________________________________?

19. I think (rain, it, will). 내 생각엔 비가 올 것 같아.
➔ I think ____________________.

20. (start, will, The class) at nine o'clock. 수업은 9시에 시작할 거야.
➔ ____________________ at nine o'clock.

CH 04

Cultural Tips
재미로 익히는 문화상식

형제자매는 영어로 어떻게 부를까요?

우리나라에서는 나이 많은 형제자매를 부를 때 '오빠, 형, 누나, 언니'로 부르죠?
미국에서는 그냥 이름을 부른답니다.
또, 우리나라는 나이와 성별에 따라 형제와 자매를 나타내는 말이 다르지만
미국에서는 성별에 상관없이 형, 오빠는'brother', 누나, 언니는 'sister'라고 해요.

정답과 해설 p.10

Practice 3 will과 be going to를 써서 문장을 써 보아요.

우리말 뜻을 참고하여 다음 주어진 표현을 사용해 문장을 완성해 보세요.

[1－10] 조동사 will을 써서 미래시제 문장을 완성해 보세요.

1. (Dinner, be ready soon) 저녁식사가 곧 준비될 거야.
   → Dinner will be ready soon.

2. (be right back) 걱정 마세요. 전 금방 돌아올 거예요.
   → Don't worry. ______________________.

3. (hold a party for her) 우리는 그녀를 위해 파티를 열 것이다.
   → ______________________.

4. (come) 너 올 거니?
   → ______________________?

5. (go to the party) 아니, 우린 싸웠어. 나는 파티에 가지 않을 거야.
   → No, we had a fight. ______________________.

6. (be better) 내일은 더 나을 것이다.
   → ______________________.

7. (be right back) 저희는 광고 후에 곧 돌아오겠습니다.
   → ______________________ after these commercials.
   (*commercial: 광고 (방송))

8. (play "League of Legends") 우리는 오늘 오후에 '리그 오브 레전드'를 할 것이다.
   → ______________________ this afternoon.

9. (join us) 너도 우리와 함께 할래?
   → ______________________?

10. (return this book) 알겠어. 하지만 난 먼저 이 책을 반납할 거야.
    → OK, but ______________________ first.

정답과 해설 p.10

[11 – 20] be going to 표현을 써서 미래시제 문장을 완성해 보세요.

11. (The baseball game, be fun) 야구경기는 재미있을 거야.

➔ The baseball game is going to be fun.

12. (go to the library) 나는 도서관에 갈 거야.

➔ ________________________________.

13. (enjoy the game) 같이 가자. 너도 경기를 즐기게 될 거야.

➔ Let's go together. ________________________, too.

14. (deliver your parcel) 저는 오늘 당신의 택배를 배달하려고 합니다.

➔ ________________________ today.

15. (stay at home) 당신은 집에 계실 건가요?

➔ ________________________________?

16. (be at school) 아니요, 저는 학교에 있을 거예요.

➔ No, ________________________________.

17. (go to a concert) 우리는 오늘 밤에 콘서트에 갈 거야.

➔ ________________________________ tonight.

18. (learn English) 나는 영어를 배울 거야.

➔ ________________________________.

19. (The final exam, be held) 기말고사가 내일 실시될 거야.

➔ ________________________________ tomorrow.

20. (ride a bicycle) 시후는 자전거를 탈거야.

➔ Sihu ________________________________.

정답과 해설 p.10

Let's Practice More!

SET 01

학습목표 1 | will과 be going to의 쓰임을 익혀보아요. 공부한 날 : 맞은 개수 : /12개

다음 ( ) 안에서 알맞은 것을 골라 보세요.

01. When will you (arrive / arriving)?
언제 도착하세요?

02. I think I will (arrived / arrive) around four.
전 4시쯤 도착할 것 같아요.

03. Nobody will (being / be) at home.
집에 아무도 없을 거에요.

04. Will anyone (is / be) there tomorrow?
내일은 거기 누군가 계신가요?

05. Suho and his friends will (play / playing) music.
수호와 그의 친구들은 음악을 연주할 것이다.

06. Mina and Sihu will (played / play) the recorder.
미나와 시후는 리코더를 연주할 것이다.

07. Taeyeon will (move / moving) to another school.
태연이는 다른 학교로 전학을 갈 것이다.

08. When will we (meet / meeting)?
우리 언제 만날 거야?

09. We will (watching / watch) a movie tonight.
우리는 오늘 밤에 영화를 볼 거야.

10. It will (is / be) interesting.
그것은 재미있을거야.

11. I'll (be / am) careful.
저 조심할게요.

12. It will (snow / snowing) tomorrow.
내일은 눈이 올 거야.

정답과 해설 p.11

Let's Practice More!

SET 02

학습목표 1 | will과 be going to의 쓰임을 익혀보아요. 공부한 날 : 맞은 개수 : /14개

다음 ( ) 안에서 알맞은 것을 골라 보세요.

01. What (are / will) we going to see?
우리 뭐 볼까?

02. We (are / will) going to see "Zootopia."
우리는 '주토피아'를 볼 거야.

03. Some students (be / are) going to dance.
몇몇 학생들은 춤을 출 것이다.

04. Jinwoo (be / is) going to do a magic show.
진우는 마술쇼를 할 것이다.

05. Suho is going to (playing / play) the triangle.
수호는 트라이앵글을 연주할 것이다.

06. He (is / will) going to sleep.
그는 잠을 잘 거야.

07. The final exam (is / are) going to be held tomorrow.
기말고사가 내일 실시될 거야.

08. The dog is not going to (bite / biting).
그 개는 물지 않을 거야.

09. She (is / will) going to watch TV after dinner.
그녀는 저녁식사 후에 TV를 볼 거야.

10. I am (go / going) to read a book this weekend.
나는 이번 주말에 책을 읽을 거야.

11. They (are / will) going to have lunch together.
그들은 함께 점심을 먹을 거야.

12. The baseball game is going to (be / being) fun.
그 야구 경기는 재미있을 거야.

13. I (will / am) going to go to the library.
나는 도서관에 갈 거야.

14. I am going to (deliver / delivering) your parcel today.
저는 오늘 당신의 택배를 배달하려고 합니다.

정답과 해설 p.11

Let's Practice More!

SET 03

학습목표 1 | will과 be going to의 쓰임을 익혀보아요. 공부한 날 : 맞은 개수 : /14개

다음 밑줄 친 부분이 맞으면 ○표, 틀리면 고쳐 써 보세요.

01. I am going to deliver a piece of registered mail soon. → ○
제가 곧 등기우편 한 통을 배달할 건데요.

02. I will studying at home tomorrow. → ______
내일은 제가 집에서 공부할 거에요.

03. I will delivering it tomorrow. → ______
제가 그것을 내일 배달할게요.

04. Dana and Jihye will play the piano. → ______
다나와 지혜는 피아노를 연주할 것이다.

05. Some of the students will have a farewell party. → ______
몇몇 학생들이 송별회를 할 것이다.

06. I will not go to the party. → ______
나는 파티에 가지 않을 것이다.

07. Will you come with us? → ______
너는 우리랑 같이 갈래?

08. I am go to deliver your parcel today. → ______
저는 오늘 당신의 택배를 배달하려고 합니다.

09. Are you go to stay at home? → ______
당신은 집에 계실 건가요?

10. I am going to being at school. → ______
저는 학교에 있을 거에요.

11. Will you joining us? → ______
너는 우리랑 함께 할래?

12. I will return this book first. → ______
난 먼저 이 책을 반납할거야.

13. The final exam will going to be held tomorrow. → ______
기말고사가 내일 실시될 거야.

14. Sihu will going to ride a bicycle. → ______
시후는 자전거를 탈거야.

정답과 해설 p.11

Let's Practice More!

SET 04

학습목표 2 | will과 be going to의 부정문과 의문문을 익혀보아요. 공부한 날 : 맞은 개수 : /12개

다음 문장을 ( ) 안의 지시대로 바꿔 보세요.

01. My mom will let me. (부정문)
➔ My mom will not[won't] let me.
우리 엄마는 허락하지 않으실 거야.

02. It will snow tomorrow. (의문문)
➔ ____________________?
내일은 눈이 올까?

03. You will pass the exam. (부정문)
➔ ____________________.
너는 시험에 통과하지 못할 거야.

04. We will go on a picnic this Saturday. (부정문)
➔ ____________________.
우리는 이번 토요일에 소풍을 가지 않을 거야.

05. He will wash the dishes. (의문문)
➔ ____________________?
그가 설거지를 할까?

06. She will forgive me. (의문문)
➔ ____________________?
그녀가 나를 용서해줄까?

07. You will listen to some music. (의문문)
➔ ____________________?
너는 음악을 좀 들을거니?

08. Anyone will be there tomorrow. (의문문)
➔ ____________________?
내일은 그곳에 누군가 계신가요?

09. You will join us. (의문문)
➔ ____________________?
너도 우리와 함께 할래?

10. Dinner will be ready. (부정문)
➔ ____________________.
저녁식사는 준비되지 않을 거야.

11. You will come. (의문문)
➔ ____________________?
너 올거니?

12. We will play games this afternoon. (부정문)
➔ ____________________.
우리는 오늘 오후에 게임을 하지 않을거야.

정답과 해설 p.11

Let's Practice More!

SET 05

학습목표 2 | will과 be going to의 부정문과 의문문을 익혀보아요. 공부한 날 : 맞은 개수 : /14개

다음 문장을 ( ) 안의 지시대로 바꿔 보세요.

01.

We are going to go to a concert tonight. (부정문)

➔ We are not[We're not /We aren't] going to go to a concert tonight.

우리는 오늘 밤에 콘서트에 가지 않을 거야.

02.

She is going to watch TV after dinner. (부정문)

➔ ______________________________.

그녀는 저녁식사 후에 TV를 보지 않을 거야.

03. I am going to go to the library. (부정문)

➔ ______________________________.

나는 도서관에 가지 않을 거야.

04. They are going to have lunch together. (의문문)

➔ ______________________________?

그들이 함께 점심을 먹을까?

05. I am going to deliver your parcel today. (부정문)

➔ ______________________________.

저는 오늘 당신의 택배를 배달하지 않을 것입니다.

06. They are going to stay at home. (의문문)

➔ ______________________________?

그들이 집에 있을까?

정답과 해설 p.11

07. He is going to be at school. (부정문)

➔ ____.

그는 학교에 있지 않을 거예요.

08. I am going to learn English. (부정문)

➔ ____.

나는 영어를 배우지 않을 거야.

09. The final exam is going to be held tomorrow. (의문문)

➔ ____?

기말고사가 내일 실시될까?

10. Sihu is going to ride a bicycle. (의문문)

➔ ____?

시후가 자전거를 탈까?

11. She is going to learn Japanese. (부정문)

➔ ____.

그녀는 일본어를 배우지 않을 거야.

12. I am going to read a book this weekend. (부정문)

➔ ____.

나는 이번 주말에 책을 읽지 않을 거야.

13.

You are going to enjoy the game. (의문문)

➔ ______________________

______________________?

너는 게임을 즐길거니?

14.

The baseball game is going to be fun. (의문문)

➔ ______________________

______________________?

그 야구 경기가 재미있을까?

정답과 해설 p.11

Let's Practice More!

SET 06

학습목표 3 | 동사의 현재, 과거시제와 미래시제를 비교해 보아요. 공부한 날 : 맞은 개수 : /14개

우리말 해석과 일치하도록 밑줄 친 부분을 알맞게 고쳐 문장을 다시 써 보세요. (단, 줄여서 쓰지 마세요.)

01. We saw "Zootopia."

➔ We will[are going to] see "Zootopia" .

우리는 '주토피아'를 볼 거야.

02. Dinner was ready.

➔ ______________________.

저녁식사는 준비될 거야.

03. Sihu rides a bicycle.

➔ ______________________.

시후는 자전거를 탈 거야.

04. I studied at home.

➔ ______________________.

나는 집에서 공부할 거야.

05. We held a school talent show.

➔ ______________________.

우리는 학예회를 개최할 것이다.

06. I delivered a piece of registered mail soon.

➔ ______________________.

제가 곧 등기우편 한 통을 배달할 거예요.

07. Jinwoo did a magic show.

➔ ______________________.

진우는 마술쇼를 할 것이다.

정답과 해설 p.11

08. Suho and his friends played music.

➜ ____.

수호와 그의 친구들은 음악을 연주할 것이다.

09. You passed the exam.

➜ ____.

너는 시험에 통과할 거야.

10. My mom doesn't let me.

➜ ____.

우리 엄마는 허락하지 않으실 거야.

11. It is interesting.

➜ ____.

재미있을 텐데.

12. The dog didn't bite.

➜ ____.

그 개는 물지 않을 거야.

13. 

We watched a movie

➜ ______________________

______________________.

우리는 영화 볼 거야.

14. 

He washes the dishes.

➜ ______________________

______________________.

그는 설거지를 할 거야.

정답과 해설 p.11

Let's Practice More!

SET 07

학습목표 4 | be going to 표현으로 다양한 문장을 만들어 보아요. 공부한 날 : 맞은 개수 : /20개

다음 문장을 ( ) 안의 지시대로 바꿔보세요.

01.

Suho is going to play the flute. (의문문)

→ Is Suho going to play the flute?

수호가 플루트를 연주할 거니?

02.

He is going to sleep. (의문문)

→ ____________________?

그가 잠을 잘 거니?

03. The baseball game is going to be fun. (부정문)

→ ____________________.

그 야구 경기는 재미있지 않을 거야.

04. I am going to go to the library. (부정문)

→ ____________________.

나는 도서관에 가지 않을 거야.

05. You are going to enjoy the game. (부정문)

→ ____________________.

너는 게임을 즐기지 않을 거야.

06. I am going to learn English. (부정문)

→ ____________________.

나는 영어를 배우지 않을 거야.

07. They are going to be right back. (부정문)

→ ____________________.

그들은 금방 돌아오지 않을 거야.

08. Tomorrow is going to be better. (의문문)

→ ____________________?

내일은 더 나을까?

정답과 해설 p.11

09. She is going to go to the party. (부정문)

➔ ____.

그녀는 파티에 가지 않을 거야.

10. The class is going to start at nine o'clock. (의문문)

➔ ____?

수업이 9시에 시작할까?

11. We are going to go on a picnic this Saturday. (부정문)

➔ ____.

우리는 이번 토요일에 소풍을 가지 않을 거야.

12. You are going to come with us. (의문문)

➔ ____?

너도 우리랑 같이 갈래?

13. It is going to snow tomorrow. (부정문)

➔ ____.

내일은 눈이 오지 않을 거야.

14. Jane is going to tell you. (의문문)

➔ ____?

Jane이 너에게 말해줄까?

15. Taeyeon is going to move to another school. (의문문)

➔ ____?

태연이가 다른 학교로 전학을 갈 거니?

16. It is going to rain. (부정문)

➔ ____.

비가 오지 않을 거야.

17. Jinwoo is going to do a magic show. (의문문)

➔ ____?

진우가 마술쇼를 할까?

18. I am going to deliver a piece of registered mail. (부정문)

➔ ____.

저는 등기우편 한 통을 배달하지 않을 것입니다.

19. Anyone is going to be there tomorrow. (의문문)

➔ ____?

내일은 거기 누군가 계신가요?

20. We are going to hold a school talent show. (부정문)

➔ ____.

우리는 학예회를 개최하지 않을 것입니다.

정답과 해설 p.12

Let's Practice More!

SET 08

학습목표 5 | 미래시제 표현으로 다양한 문장을 만들어 보아요. 공부한 날 : 맞은 개수 : /20개

주어진 문장을 ( ) 안의 표현을 이용하여 우리말 해석에 맞게 바꿔 써 보세요.

01.

I deliver your parcel. (be going to)

➔ I am[I'm] going to deliver your parcel.

저는 당신의 택배를 배달하려고 합니다.

02.

They stay at home. (will)

➔ ______________________.

그들은 집에 있을 것입니다.

03. Mina and Sihu play the recorder. (will)

➔ ______________________.

미나와 시후는 리코더를 연주할 것이다.

04. Some of the students don't have a farewell party. (will)

➔ ______________________.

몇몇 학생들은 송별회를 하지 않을 것이다.

05. I don't go to the party. (be going to)

➔ ______________________.

나는 파티에 가지 않을 것이다.

06. We watch a movie. (will)

➔ ______________________.

우리 영화 볼 거야.

07. I'm careful. (will)

➔ ______________________.

조심할게요.

08. She forgives me. (will)

➔ ______________________.

그녀는 나를 용서해 줄 거야.

정답과 해설 p.12

09. I am at school. (be going to)

➔ ________________________________.

저는 학교에 있을 거예요.

10. I think it rains. (will)

➔ ________________________________.

내 생각엔 비가 올 것 같아.

11. The class starts at nine o'clock. (be going to)

➔ ________________________________.

수업은 9시에 시작할 거야.

12. Dinner is ready. (be going to)

➔ ________________________________.

저녁 식사가 준비될 거야.

13. We hold a party for her. (will)

➔ ________________________________.

우리는 그녀를 위해 파티를 열 것이다.

14. We are right back. (will)

➔ ________________________________.

저희는 곧 돌아오겠습니다.

15. We don't play games. (will)

➔ ________________________________.

우리는 게임을 하지 않을 것이다.

16. I return this book. (be going to)

➔ ________________________________.

난 이 책을 반납할 거야.

17. I deliver it. (will)

➔ ________________________________.

제가 그것을 배달할게요.

18. I think I arrive. (will)

➔ ________________________________.

도착할 거 같아요.

19. Sihu rides a bicycle. (be going to)

➔ ________________________________.

시후는 자전거를 탈 거야.

20. Dana and I play the xylophone. (be going to)

➔ ________________________________.

다나와 나는 실로폰을 연주할 것이다.

정답과 해설 p.12

Chapter 05 현재진행시제

이 챕터에서는 현재 진행 중인 동작을 나타내는
동사의 '현재진행시제'의 용법에 대해 배워 보아요.

☆ 학습 방향 및 배울 내용 미리보기 ☆

☐ **Unit 01 : It is raining.**

현재진행시제

주어에 따라 달라지는 현재진행시제의 형태, 그리고 동사에 따라 다르게 바뀌는 -ing 형태에 대해 알아보아요.

▼

☐ **Unit 02 : I am not studying hard.**

현재진행시제의 부정문과 의문문

현재진행시제의 부정문과 의문문을 만드는 방법에 대해 알아보아요.

단어 미리보기

이 챕터에 나올 단어들 중 이미 알고 있는 단어가 있나요?
맞는 뜻을 골라 체크해 봐요.

날짜 : 이름 : 알고 있는 단어의 수 : /24개

No.	아는 단어	단어	품사	알맞은 뜻에 체크 표시해 봐요.			
1	☑	block	동사	공격하다	☐	가리다	☑
2	☐	wallet	명사	지갑	☐	장갑	☐
3	☐	ask	동사	묻다	☐	대답하다	☐
4	☐	win	동사	지다	☐	이기다	☐
5	☐	wear	동사	입다	☐	벗다	☐
6	☐	open	동사	닫다	☐	열다	☐
7	☐	raincoat	명사	우비	☐	우산	☐
8	☐	wait	동사	기다리다	☐	가다	☐
9	☐	think	동사	찾다	☐	생각하다	☐
10	☐	wet	형용사	젖은	☐	마른	☐
11	☐	send	동사	보내다	☐	받다	☐
12	☐	rose	명사	장미	☐	백합	☐
13	☐	actually	부사	미안하게도	☐	사실	☐
14	☐	cell phone	명사	세포	☐	핸드폰	☐
15	☐	ring	동사	울리다	☐	회전하다	☐
16	☐	download	동사	내려 받다	☐	올리다	☐
17	☐	wind	명사	습기	☐	바람	☐
18	☐	apologize	동사	용서하다	☐	사과하다	☐
19	☐	exercise	동사	운동하다	☐	연기하다	☐
20	☐	snack	명사	간식	☐	나물	☐
21	☐	mistake	명사	의도	☐	실수	☐
22	☐	lose	동사	잃다	☐	찾다	☐
23	☐	file	명사	종이	☐	파일	☐
24	☐	battery	명사	배터리	☐	막대	☐

UNIT 현재진행시제

01 It is raining.

❖ POiNT 1 ❖

현재진행시제는 **현재 진행 중인 동작을 나타내고 '~하고 있다'라는 의미가 있어요.**

I	clean	my room.
나는	청소한다	내 방을
I	**am cleaning**	my room.
나는	청소하고 있다	내 방을

❖ POiNT 2 ❖

주어 + am/are/is + 동사원형 + −ing	
I **am**	I **am** read**ing** a book. 난 책을 읽고 있어.
You/We/They **are**	You **are** block**ing** the camera. 넌 카메라를 가리고 있어. We **are** look**ing** for Junwoo's wallet. 우리는 준우의 지갑을 찾고 있어.
She/He/It **is**	She **is** talk**ing** in her sleep. 그녀는 잠꼬대를 하고 있어. It **is** rain**ing**. 비가 오고 있어.

❖ POiNT 3 ❖

[동사원형 + −ing]는 어떻게 바뀔까요?

대부분의 동사	동사원형에 -ing를 붙여요.	**sing**(노래하다)+ing=**singing** **clean**(청소하다)+ing=**cleaning**
[자음 + -e]로 끝나는 동사	마지막 e를 없애고 -ing를 붙여요.	**make**(만들다)+ing=**making** **come**(오다)+ing=**coming**
[단모음 + 단자음]으로 끝나는 동사	마지막 자음을 한 번 더 쓰고 -ing를 붙여요.	**swim**(수영하다)+ing=**swimming** **stop**(멈추다)+ing=**stopping**
-ie로 끝나는 동사	-ie를 -y로 바꾸고 -ing를 붙여요.	**lie**(눕다)+ing=**lying** **die**(죽다)+ing=**dying**

Check and Write

다음 밑줄 친 동사를 현재진행시제로 바꿔서 전체 문장을 다시 써 보세요.

1. The cat sleeps.

➔ The cat is sleeping.

그 고양이는 자고 있어.

2. They lie on the beach.

➔ ______________.

그들은 해변에 누워 있어.

3. You take a shower.

➔ ______________.

너는 샤워를 하고 있어.

4. I listen to music.

➔ ______________.

나는 음악을 듣고 있어.

정답과 해설 p.12

UNIT 02 I am not studying hard.

현재진행시제의 부정문과 의문문

❖ POiNT 1 ❖

현재진행 부정문은 '~하고 있지 않다'의 의미로, '주어 + am/are/is + not + 동사원형 + -ing'로 표현해요.

My mother **is not** watching TV.
우리 엄마는 TV를 보고 있지 않아.

She is on the phone.
엄마는 전화 통화 중이야.

I have a math test tomorrow.
나 내일 수학시험이 있어.

But I **am not** studying hard.
하지만 난 열심히 공부하고 있지 않아.

❖ POiNT 2 ❖

현재진행 의문문은 '~하고 있니?'의 의미로, 'Am/Are/Is + 주어 + 동사원형 + -ing ~?'로 표현해요.

Am I bothering you?
내가 널 귀찮게 하고 있니?

Is it snowing outside?
밖에 눈이 오고 있어?

Check and Write

우리말 뜻을 참고하여 다음 주어진 문장을 현재진행시제의 부정문 또는 의문문으로 만들어 보세요.

1. He is going home.

→ Is he going home?

그는 집에 가는 중이니?

2. I am playing.

→ ______.

나는 놀고 있지 않아.

3. The dog is playing with a ball.

→ ______.

그 개는 공을 가지고 놀고 있지 않아.

4. You are swimming.

→ ______?

너 수영하고 있니?

정답과 해설 p.12

Practice 1 현재진행시제의 쓰임을 익혀 보아요.

다음 문장에 알맞은 단어를 보기에서 골라 빈칸에 써 보세요. (단, 한 단어를 여러 번 쓸 수 있어요.)

A What happened to my phone?

보기 am is are trying working doing not

1. What __are__ you __doing__?
너 뭐 하고 있어?

2. I ________ ________ to turn on my phone.
나는 휴대폰을 켜려고 하고 있어.

3. But it ________ ________ ________.
그런데 그것은 작동을 하지 않고 있어.

B Toilet paper

보기 asking am coming watching

1. *Mom* : Mina, can you bring me some toilet paper?
미나야, 나한테 휴지 좀 갖다 줄 수 있겠니?
Mina : But I ________ ________ TV now.
하지만 전 지금 TV를 보고 있는데요.

2. *Mom* : I ________ ________ you.
내가 부탁하고 있잖니.

3. *Mina* : OK, Mom. I ________ ________.
알겠어요, 엄마. 가요.

정답과 해설 p.12

C It is pouring down!

보기				
am	Is[is]	are	doing	raining
making	watching	baking	pouring	

1. *Sihu* : I'm home.
   다녀왔습니다.

   Mom : __________ it __________ outside?
   밖에 비가 오고 있니?

2. *Sihu* : Yes. The rain __________ __________ down!
   네. 비가 쏟아지고 있어요!

3. *Sihu* : What __________ Mina __________?
   미나는 무엇을 하고 있어요?

4. *Mom* : She __________ __________ TV.
   그녀는 TV를 보고 있어.

5. *Sihu* : What __________ you __________, Mom?
   엄마는 뭘 만들고 계세요?

6. *Mom* : I __________ __________ cookies.
   난 쿠키를 굽고 있단다.

정답과 해설 p.12

D On the phone

보기 am waiting checking

1. *Mina* : Hello.

   여보세요.

   Yuri : Hello, Mina. Do you know Sihu's phone number?

   여보세요, 미나야. 너 시후 전화번호 아니?

   Mina : Hold on. I __________ __________ my contact list.

   잠시만. 내 연락처 목록을 확인 중이야(확인해볼게).

2. *Yuri* : OK. I __________ __________.

   알았어. 기다리고 있어.

E I have a quiz tomorrow.

보기 am are not playing studying winning

1. I have an English quiz tomorrow.

   나는 내일 영어 시험이 있다.

   But I __________ __________ __________.

   하지만 나는 공부를 하고 있지 않다.

2. I __________ __________ computer games.

   나는 컴퓨터 게임을 하고 있다.

3. I __________ __________ with Jinwoo and Sihu.

   나는 진우와 시후와 함께 게임을 하고 있다.

4. And now, we __________ __________!

   그리고 지금, 우리가 이기고 있다!

정답과 해설 p.12

Practice 2 현재진행시제를 써서 문장을 완성해 보아요.

다음 우리말 뜻과 같도록 주어진 표현을 순서에 맞게 배열하여 문장을 완성하세요.

1. *Mom* : Yuri, come and have a snack.
   유리야, 와서 간식 먹으렴.
   Yuri : (I, studying, am) now.
   지금 저 공부하고 있어요.
   ➔ *Yuri:* I am studying now.

2. (having, We, chocolate ice cream, are).
   우리는 초콜릿 아이스크림을 먹고 있어.
   ➔ ______________________.

3. Yes, (coming, am, I) now!
   네, 저 지금 가고 있어요!
   ➔ Yes, ______________________ now!

4. (is, It, raining) hard.
   비가 많이 내리고 있다.
   ➔ ______________________ hard.

5. (their umbrellas, opening, People, are).
   사람들은 우산을 펼치고 있다.
   ➔ ______________________.

6. (am, wearing, my raincoat, I).
   나는 비옷을 입고 있다.
   ➔ ______________________.

정답과 해설 p.13

7. (getting wet, are, My sneakers).

내 운동화가 젖고 있다.

➜ ____.

8. (I, shaking, am) now.

나 지금 떨고 있어.

➜ ____________________

____________________ now.

9. (am, thinking, I).

난 생각하는 중이야.

➜ ____________________

____________________.

10. (We, going to a concert, are).

우리는 콘서트에 가는 중이야.

➜ ____.

11. As usual, (am, I, following, not) you.

늘 그렇듯이, 나는 네 말을 못 따라가겠어(이해를 못하겠어).

➜ As usual, ______________________________ you.

12. (are, driving me crazy, You)! (*drive ~ crazy: ~를 미치게 하다)

네가 나를 미치게 하고 있어(너 때문에 미치겠다)!

➜ ____!

13. (I, crying, am), but nobody cares!

난 울고 있는데 아무도 신경 쓰지 않아!

➜ ______________________________, but nobody cares!

정답과 해설 p.13

14. (am, I, calling) to apologize for my mistake.
난 내 잘못에 대해 사과하려고 전화하는 거야.

➔ ______________________________ to apologize for my mistake.

15. (you, Are, saying) I am stupid?
너 내가 멍청하다고 말하는 거니?

➔ ______________________________ I am stupid?

CH 05

16. (I, daydreaming, am).
나는 공상 중이야. (*daydream: 공상하다)

➔ ______________________________
______________________________.

17. (exercising, Are, they)?
그들은 운동하고 있니?

➔ ______________________________
______________________________?

18. (am, I, not, kidding).
나 농담하고 있는 거 아니야.

➔ ______________________________.

19. (having a good time, are, They).
그들은 좋은 시간을 보내고 있어.

➔ ______________________________.

20. (He, not, exercising, is).
그는 운동하고 있지 않아.

➔ ______________________________.

정답과 해설 p.13

Practice 3 현재진행시제를 써서 문장을 써 보아요.

우리말 뜻을 참고하여 다음 주어진 표현을 활용해 문장을 완성해 보세요.
(주어진 동사원형을 현재진행시제로 알맞게 변형하세요.)

1. (send an e-mail)
시후는 이메일을 보내고 있어.

➔ Sihu is sending an e-mail.

2. (The rain, pour down)
비가 쏟아지고 있어.

➔ ______________________________
______________________________.

3. (It, snow) 눈이 오고 있지 않아.

➔ ______________________________.

4. (plant trees) 우리는 나무를 심고 있어.

➔ ______________________________.

5. (study) 내가 공부하고 있을 때는 나를 방해하지 말아 주세요.

➔ Don't bother me when ______________________________.

6. (charge a battery)
그는 배터리를 충전하는 중이야.

➔ ______________________________
______________________________.

7. (My roses, die)
내 장미들이 죽어가고 있어.

➔ ______________________________
______________________________.

정답과 해설 p.13

8. (The wind, blow) 바람이 강하게 불고 있어.

➔ ______________________________ hard.

9. (download a file)
그는 파일을 다운로드하고 있어.

➔ ______________________
______________________.

10. (cook, in the kitchen)
그녀는 부엌에서 요리하는 중이야.

➔ ______________________
______________________.

11. (play soccer) 우리는 축구를 하고 있어.

➔ ______________________________.

12. (Our team, lose) 우리 팀이 지고 있어.

➔ ______________________________.

13. (Your phone, ring) 네 전화가 울리고 있어.

➔ ______________________________.

14. (waste your time) 너는 네 시간을 낭비하고 있는 거야.

➔ ______________________________.

정답과 해설 p.13

15. (chat) 그는 그의 친구들과 수다를 떨고 있어.

➔ ______________________ with his friends.

16. (look for, his cell phone) (*look for: ~을 찾다, 구하다)

수호는 그의 핸드폰을 찾고 있어.

➔ Suho ______________________.

17. (his mother, use his phone)

사실, 그의 어머니가 그의 전화기를 쓰고 있어.

➔ Actually, ______________________

______________________.

18. (sit)

그들은 앉아있니?

➔ ______________________

______________________?

19. (do their homework) 그들은 숙제를 하고 있니?

➔ ______________________?

20. (tease) 너 나를 놀리고 있는 거야?

➔ ______________________?

정답과 해설 p.13

Let's Practice More!

SET 01

학습목표 1 | 현재진행시제의 형태를 연습해 보아요. 공부한 날 : 맞은 개수 : /12개

다음 동사원형을 '-ing' 형태로 바꿔 보세요.

01. make 만들다 → making

02. clean 청소하다 → ______

03. stop 멈추다 → ______

04. talk 말하다 → ______

05. rain 비가 오다 → ______

06. swim 수영하다 → ______

07. lie 눕다 → ______

08. sing 노래하다 → ______

09. read 읽다 → ______

10. look 보다 → ______

11. come 오다 → ______

12. die 죽다 → ______

정답과 해설 p.13

Let's Practice More!

SET 02

학습목표 1 | **현재진행시제의 형태를 연습해 보아요.** 공부한 날 : 맞은 개수 : /14개

다음 ( ) 안에서 알맞은 것을 골라 보세요.

01. She is (lying / lieing) on the ground. 그녀는 땅바닥에 누워 있어.

02. I (am / is) playing soccer. 나는 축구를 하고 있어.

03. I am (makeing / making) cookies. 난 쿠키를 만들고 있어.

04. My brother (was / is) not studying. 내 남동생은 공부를 하고 있지 않아.

05. They are (shopping / shoping) together. 그들은 함께 쇼핑하고 있어.

06. And now, we are (wining / winning)! 그리고 지금, 우리가 이기고 있어!

07. People are (openning / opening) their umbrellas. 사람들은 우산을 펼치고 있다.

08. You (is / are) driving me crazy! 네가 나를 미치게 하고 있어(너 때문에 미치겠다)!

09. I am not (kiding / kidding). 나 농담하고 있는 거 아니야.

10. I am (taking / takeing) a shower. 난 샤워중이야.

11. You are (wasted / wasting) your time. 너는 네 시간을 낭비하고 있는 거야.

12. They are (sitting / siting) on the chair. 그들은 의자에 앉아 있어.

13. (Is / Are) you teasing me? 너 나를 놀리고 있는 거야?

14. Actually, his mother is (use / using) his phone.
사실, 그의 어머니가 그의 전화기를 쓰고 있어.

정답과 해설 p.13

Let's Practice More!

SET 03

학습목표 1 | 현재진행시제의 형태를 연습해 보아요.　　공부한 날 :　　맞은 개수 :　　/14개

다음 밑줄 친 부분이 맞으면 ○표, 틀리면 고쳐 써 보세요.

01. She is makeing a cake. 그녀는 케이크를 만들고 있어. → making

02. They are haveing a good time. 그들은 좋은 시간을 보내고 있어. → ______

03. He is not exercising. 그는 운동하고 있지 않아. → ______

04. Are you swiming? 너 수영하고 있니? → ______

05. The wind is blowing hard. 바람이 강하게 불고 있어. → ______

06. I am comming. 난 가고 있어요. → ______

07. Sihu is downloading a file. 시후는 파일을 다운로드하고 있어. → ______

08. My roses are dieing. 내 장미들이 죽어가고 있어. → ______

09. My mother is cuting the cake. 우리 엄마가 케이크를 자르고 있어. → ______

10. She is cooking in the kitchen. 그녀는 부엌에서 요리하는 중이야. → ______

11. Our team is loseing. 우리 팀이 지고 있어. → ______

12. It is rainning hard. 비가 많이 내리고 있다. → ______

13. He is chatting with his friends. 그는 그의 친구들과 수다를 떨고 있어. → ______

14. He is runing in the race. 그는 경주에서 뛰고 있어. → ______

정답과 해설 p.13

Let's Practice More!

SET 04

학습목표 1 | 현재진행시제의 형태를 연습해 보아요.　　공부한 날 :　　맞은 개수 :　　/12개

다음 밑줄 친 부분이 맞으면 ○표, 틀리면 고쳐 써 보세요.

01. You is blocking the camera. 너는 카메라를 가리고 있어. → are

02. What are you make, Mom? 뭘 만들고 계세요, 엄마? → ____________

03. We are having chocolate ice cream. 우리는 초콜릿 아이스크림을 먹고 있어. → ____________

04. It is raining hard. 비가 많이 내리고 있다. → ____________

05. My sneakers are got wet. 내 운동화가 젖고 있다. → ____________

06. People is opening their umbrellas. 사람들은 우산을 펼치고 있다. → ____________

07. I am shaking now. 나 지금 떨고 있어. → ____________

08. We are go to a concert. 우리는 콘서트에 가는 중이야. → ____________

09. I are thinking about my future. 난 나의 미래에 대해 생각하는 중이야. → ____________

10. He is takes a shower. 그는 샤워 중이야. → ____________

11. You are driving me crazy! 네가 나를 미치게 하고 있어(너 때문에 미치겠다)! → ____________

12. I am daydream. 나는 공상중이야. → ____________

정답과 해설 p.13

Let's Practice More!

SET 05

학습목표 2 | 현재진행시제의 긍정문, 부정문, 그리고 의문문을 연습해 보아요.

공부한 날 : 맞은 개수 : /14개

CH 05

다음 문장을 ( ) 안의 지시대로 고쳐 써 보세요.

01. 

My mother is watching TV. (부정문으로)

➔ My mother is not[isn't] watching TV.

나의 엄마는 TV를 보고 계시지 않아.

02. 

She is doing the dishes. (의문문으로)

➔ ____________________ ?

그녀는 설거지를 하고 있니?

03. The computer is working. (부정문으로)

➔ ____________________ .

그 컴퓨터는 작동하지 않고 있어.

04. It is snowing a lot outside. (의문문으로)

➔ ____________________ ?

밖에 눈이 많이 오고 있니?

05. Is it raining outside? (긍정문으로)

➔ ____________________ .

밖에 비가 오고 있어.

06. I am asking you. (부정문으로)

➔ ____________________ .

나는 너에게 물어보고 있지 않아.

정답과 해설 p.13

07. You are baking cookies. (의문문으로)

➔ ______________________________?

너는 쿠키를 굽고 있니?

08. He is studying now. (부정문으로)

➔ ______________________________.

그는 지금 공부하고 있지 않아.

09. They are lying on the beach. (의문문으로)

➔ ______________________________?

그들은 해변 위에 누워 있니?

10. Sihu is sending an e-mail. (부정문으로)

➔ ______________________________.

시후는 이메일을 보내고 있지 않아.

11. I am shaking now. (부정문으로)

➔ ______________________________.

나는 지금 떨고 있지 않아.

12. They are having a good time. (의문문으로)

➔ ______________________________?

그들은 좋은 시간을 보내고 있니?

13.

He is wearing his raincoat.
(의문문으로)

➔ ______________________________

______________________________?

그는 그의 우비를 입고 있니?

14.

Is he planting trees?
(긍정문으로)

➔ ______________________________

______________________________.

그는 나무를 심고 있어.

정답과 해설 p.13

Let's Practice More!

SET 06

학습목표 3 | **현재진행시제를 동사의 다른 시제와 비교해 보아요.** 공부한 날 : 맞은 개수 : /14개

다음 밑줄 친 부분의 우리말 해석으로 옳은 것을 고르세요.

01. She is talking to her mom. (말하고 있다 / 말했다)

02. I am washing my hair. (씻고 있다 / 씻는다)

03. I watched TV yesterday. (보고 있다 / 보았다)

04. She is coming. (오고 있다 / 왔다)

05. I will check my contact list. (확인할 것이다 / 확인하는 중이다)

06. I am waiting for my mother. (기다릴 거야 / 기다리고 있다)

07. Is it raining outside? (비가 오고 있니? / 비가 왔었니?)

08. I baked cookies. (굽고 있다 / 구웠다)

09. Sihu is sending an e-mail. (보낸다 / 보내고 있다)

10. He exercises every day. (운동한다 / 운동하고 있다)

11. The rain is pouring down. (쏟아지는 중이다 / 쏟아졌다)

12. We are going to plant trees. (심을 것이다 / 심고 있다)

13. Our team is winning! (이기고 있다 / 이겼다)

14. They are lying on the beach. (누웠다 / 누워 있다)

정답과 해설 p.14

Let's Practice More!

SET 07

학습목표 4 | 현재진행시제를 이용해 다양한 표현을 만들어 보아요. 공부한 날 : 맞은 개수 : /20개

다음 문장을 현재진행시제로 고쳐 보세요.

01. 

She cooks in the kitchen.

➜ She is[She's] cooking in the kitchen.

그녀는 부엌에서 요리를 하고 있어.

02. 

He chats with his friends.

➜ ______________________.

그는 그의 친구들과 잡담을 하고 있어.

03. She looks for her wallet.

➜ ______________________.

그녀는 그녀의 지갑을 찾고 있어.

04. We play soccer.

➜ ______________________.

우리는 축구를 하고 있어.

05. Our team loses.

➜ ______________________. 우리 팀은 지고 있어.

06. Your phone rings.

➜ ______________________. 너의 전화기가 울리고 있어.

07. You waste your time.

➜ ______________________.

너는 너의 시간을 낭비하고 있어.

08. His mother uses his phone.

➜ ______________________.

그의 엄마는 그의 전화를 사용하고 계셔.

09. Do they sit?

➜ ______________________?

그들이 앉아 있니?

정답과 해설 p.14

10. Do you tease me?

➔ ______________________________?

너는 나를 놀리고 있는 거니?

11. I wash my hair.

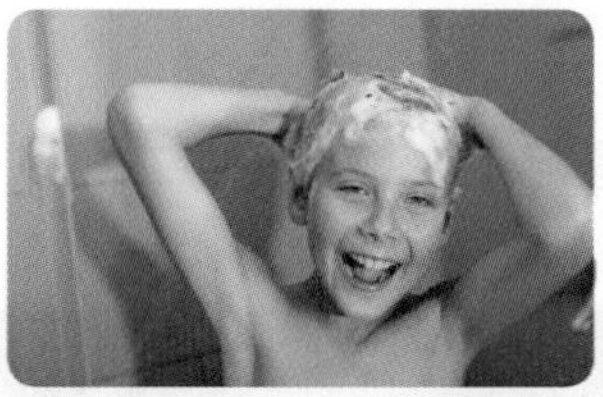

➔ ______________________________.

나는 머리를 감고 있어.

12. The wind blows hard.

➔ ______________________________.

바람이 세게 불고 있어.

13. He downloads a file.

➔ ______________________________.

그는 파일을 다운 받고 있어.

14. My roses die.

➔ ______________________________.

내 장미들은 죽어가고 있어.

15. He charges a battery.

➔ ______________________________.

그는 배터리를 충전하고 있어.

16. I check my contact list.

➔ ______________________________.

나는 내 연락망을 확인하고 있어.

17. We have chocolate ice cream.

➔ ______________________________.

우리는 초콜릿 아이스크림을 먹고 있어.

18. People open their umbrellas.

➔ ______________________________.

사람들은 그들의 우산을 펴고 있어.

19. My sneakers get wet.

➔ ______________________________.

내 운동화는 젖고 있어.

20. We go to a concert.

➔ ______________________________.

우리는 콘서트에 가고 있어.

정답과 해설 p.14

Let's Practice More!

SET 08

학습목표 4 | 현재진행시제를 이용해 다양한 표현을 만들어 보아요. 공부한 날 : 맞은 개수 : /20개

다음 우리말 해석을 보고 ( ) 안의 단어를 이용해 문장을 완성해 보세요.

01.

He ___is___ ___writing___ a letter. (write) 그는 편지를 쓰고 있어.

02.

It __________ __________ heavily. (snow) 눈이 많이 내리고 있어.

03. I __________ __________ my contact list. (check)
나는 내 연락처 목록을 확인 중이야.

04. I __________ __________ for my mother. (wait)
난 우리 엄마를 기다리고 있어.

05. The rain __________ __________ down! (pour)
비가 쏟아지고 있어요!

06. They __________ __________ games with me. (play)
그들은 나와 함께 게임을 하고 있어.

07. __________ they __________? (exercise)
그들은 운동하고 있니?

08. I __________ not __________ you. (follow)
나는 네 말을 못 따라가겠어(이해를 못하겠어).

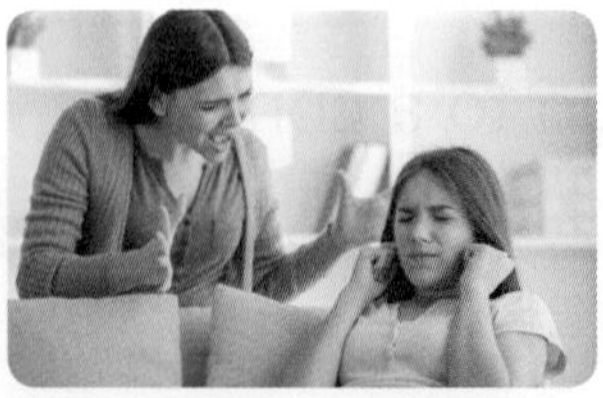

09. You __________ __________ me crazy! (drive)
네가 나를 미치게 하고 있어(너 때문에 미치겠다)!

정답과 해설 p.14

10. She __________ __________, but nobody cares! (cry)
그녀가 울고 있는데 아무도 신경 쓰지 않아!

11. I __________ __________ to apologize for my mistake. (call)
난 내 잘못에 대해 사과하려고 전화하는 거야.

12. __________ you __________ I am stupid? (say)
너 내가 멍청하다고 말하는 거니?

13. We __________ __________ trees. (plant)
우리는 나무를 심고 있어.

14. Sihu __________ __________ now. (study)
시후는 지금 공부하고 있어요.

15. I __________ not __________. (kid)
나 농담하고 있는 거 아니야.

16. Finally, we __________ __________! (win)
드디어, 우리가 이기고 있어!

17. I __________ __________ in the company now. (work)
난 지금 회사에서 일하고 있어.

18. Mina __________ __________ her raincoat. (wear)
미나는 그녀의 우비를 입고 있다.

19. I __________ __________ to turn on my phone. (try)
나는 휴대폰을 켜려고 하고 있어.

20. They __________ __________ TV now. (watch)
그들은 지금 TV를 보고 있어.

정답과 해설 p.14

Chapter 06 과거진행시제

이 챕터에서는 과거의 특정 시점에 진행 중이었던
동작을 나타내는 동사의 '과거진행시제'의 용법에 대해 배워 보아요.

☆ 학습 방향 및 배울 내용 미리보기 ☆

☐ **Unit 01 : I was sleeping at 3 o'clock.**

과거진행시제

주어에 따라 달라지는 과거진행시제의 형태, 그리고 과거시제와 과거진행시제의 차이에 대해 알아보아요.

▼

☐ **Unit 02 : I was not talking on my cell phone.**

과거진행시제의 부정문과 의문문

과거진행시제의 부정문과 의문문을 만드는 방법에 대해 알아보아요.

단어 미리보기

이 챕터에 나올 단어들 중 이미 알고 있는 단어가 있나요?
맞는 뜻을 골라 체크해 봐요.

날짜 : 이름 : 알고 있는 단어의 수 : /24개

No.	아는 단어	단어	품사	알맞은 뜻에 체크 표시해 봐요.			
1	✔	guitar	명사	기타	✔	피아노	☐
2	☐	hug	동사	앉다	☐	안다	☐
3	☐	late	형용사	이른	☐	늦은	☐
4	☐	shop	동사	쇼핑하다	☐	팔다	☐
5	☐	cousin	명사	사촌	☐	언니	☐
6	☐	work	동사	고장나다	☐	일하다	☐
7	☐	slide	명사	미끄럼틀	☐	그네	☐
8	☐	seesaw	명사	회전목마	☐	시소	☐
9	☐	front	형용사	앞의	☐	뒤의	☐
10	☐	walk	동사	걷다	☐	달리다	☐
11	☐	hair	명사	뇌	☐	머리카락	☐
12	☐	answer	동사	대답하다	☐	질문하다	☐
13	☐	drink	동사	덮다	☐	마시다	☐
14	☐	lion	명사	사자	☐	호랑이	☐
15	☐	green	형용사	초록의	☐	노란	☐
16	☐	climb	동사	오르다	☐	내려가다	☐
17	☐	forest	명사	숲	☐	나무	☐
18	☐	crosswalk	명사	가로등	☐	횡단보도	☐
19	☐	brush	동사	닦다	☐	찢다	☐
20	☐	wait for	동사	기다리다	☐	버리다	☐
21	☐	radio	명사	라디오	☐	텔레비전	☐
22	☐	between	전치사	~사이에	☐	~앞에	☐
23	☐	laugh	동사	눕다	☐	웃다	☐
24	☐	hand	명사	손	☐	발	☐

과거진행시제

UNIT 01 I was sleeping at 3 o'clock.

❖ POiNT 1 ❖

과거진행은 과거의 특정 시점에 진행 중이었던 동작을 나타내며 '~하고 있었다'는 의미이고, 주어+was/were+동사원형+-ing로 표현해요.

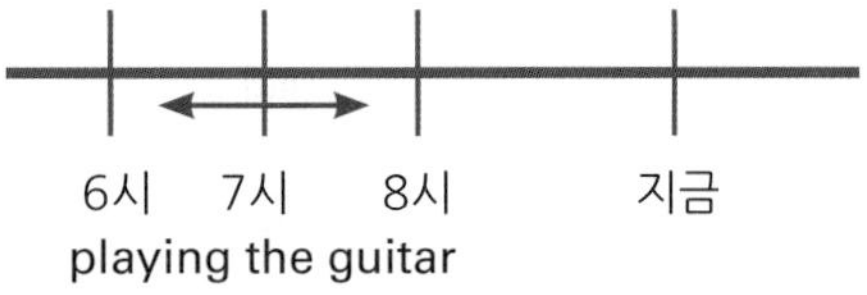

What **were** you do**ing** at 7 p.m.?
너 7시에 뭐하고 있었어?

I **was** play**ing** the guitar.
난 기타치고 있었어.

❖ POiNT 2 ❖

주어+was/were(be동사의 과거형)+동사원형+-ing	
I/He/She/It **was**	I **was** sleep**ing** at 3 o'clock. 난 3시에 자고 있었어. He **was** wait**ing** for me. 그는 날 기다리고 있었어. She **was** listen**ing** to Twice's song. 그녀는 트와이스의 노래를 듣고 있었어. It **was** snow**ing** then. 그때 눈이 오고 있었어. 
You/We/They **were**	You **were** swimm**ing** in the pool. 넌 수영장에서 수영하고 있었어. We **were** fight**ing**. 우린 싸우고 있었어. They **were** look**ing** for you. 그들은 널 찾고 있었어. 

❖ POiNT 3 ❖

과거와 과거진행의 차이

과거	끝난 동작, 과거의 습관이나 사실을 표현할 때 사용해요. I **went** to the movies yesterday. 난 어제 영화 보러 갔다.
과거진행	과거 특정 시점에 진행된 일을 표현할 때 사용해요. Jack **was reading** a book. Then, the phone rang. Jack은 책을 읽고 있었다. 그때 전화가 울렸다.

Check and Write

다음 밑줄 친 동사를 과거진행시제로 바꿔 전체 문장을 다시 써 보세요.

1. They lie on the ground.
   → They were lying on the ground.
   그들은 땅 위에 누워 있었어.

2. She hugs her dog.
   → ______.
   그녀는 그녀의 개를 안고 있었어.

3. We look at the camera.
   → ______.
   우리는 카메라를 보고 있었어.

4. I tell my secret.
   → ______.
   나는 내 비밀을 말하고 있었어.

정답과 해설 p.14

UNIT 과거진행시제의 부정문과 의문문

02 I was not talking on my cell phone.

❖ POiNT 1 ❖

과거진행 부정문

'~하고 있지 않았다'는 의미이고, **주어+was/were+not+동사원형+-ing**로 표현해요.

I/He/She/It	**was not (=wasn't)**	I **was not(=wasn't)** talk**ing** on my cell phone. 전 핸드폰으로 통화하고 있지 않았어요. I **was not(=wasn't)** watch**ing** a TV show on my iPad. 전 아이패드로 TV쇼를 보고 있지 않았어요.
You/We/ They	**were not (=weren't)**	*Jina*: Sorry, I'm late. 늦어서 미안해.  *Minjun*: Don't worry. We **were not(=weren't)** wait**ing** for long. 걱정하지 마. 우린 오래 기다리고 있지 않았어.

❖ POiNT 2 ❖

과거진행 의문문

'~하고 있었니?'의 의미로, **Was/Were+주어+동사원형+-ing ~?**로 표현해요.

대답은 긍정이면 'Yes, 주어+was/were.'

부정이면 'No, 주어+was not[wasn't]/were not[weren't].'로 해요.

Was	**I/he/she/it**	**Was** she **doing** the dishes? 그녀가 설거지하고 있었니?  **Yes,** she **was.** 응, 설거지하고 있었어. **No,** she **was not[wasn't].** 아니, 설거지하고 있지 않았어.
Were	**you/we/they**	**Were** they **shopping**? I saw them at the mall yesterday. 걔네들 쇼핑하고 있었어? 나 어제 쇼핑몰에서 걔네들 봤어. **Yes,** they **were.** 응, 걔네들 쇼핑하고 있었어. **No,** they **were not[weren't].** 아니, 걔네들 쇼핑하고 있지 않았어.

Check and Write

다음 과거진행시제 문장을 의문문과 부정문으로 만들어 보세요.

1. The baby was sleeping.

➔ Was the baby sleeping ?

그 아기는 자고 있었니?

➔ The baby was not sleeping .

➔ The baby wasn't sleeping .

그 아기는 자고 있지 않았어.

2. The cow was looking at us.

➔ ?

그 소가 우리를 쳐다보고 있었니?

➔ .

➔ .

그 소는 우리를 쳐다보고 있지 않았어.

3. They were smiling.

➔ ?

그들은 웃고 있었니?

➔ .

➔ .

그들은 웃고 있지 않았어.

정답과 해설 p.14

Practice 1 과거진행시제를 익혀 보아요.

다음 문장에 알맞은 말을 보기에서 골라 빈칸에 써 보세요. (단, 한 번 쓴 말을 여러 번 쓸 수 있어요.)

A Working at a cafe

보기 was were doing meeting talking

1. I saw you at the cafe yesterday. What were you doing?
   나 어제 카페에서 널 봤어. 넌 무엇을 하고 있었니?

2. I ________ ________ to my cousin. She works there. And you?
   난 사촌에게 이야기하고 있었어. 그녀는 거기서 일하거든. 너는?

3. I ________ ________ my friends.
   난 친구들을 만나고 있었어.

B In the playground

보기 was playing were playing was walking was crossing

1. Your friends ________ ________ in the playground.
   네 친구들은 놀이터에서 놀고 있었어.

2. Sihu ________ ________ on the slide. 시후는 미끄럼틀을 타고 있었어.

3. Junwoo ________ ________ the monkey bars.
   준우는 구름사다리를 건너고 있었어.

4. Yuri and Taeyeon ________ ________ on the seesaw.
   유리와 태연이는 시소를 타고 있었어.

5. Mina and Suji ________ ________ on the swings. 미나와 수지는 그네를 타고 있었어.

6. Suho ________ ________ his dog.
   수호는 그의 개를 산책시키고 있었어.

정답과 해설 p.14

C In the car

보기				
sleeping	singing	listening	going	feeling
blowing	driving			

1. We were __________ to my grandparents' house. 우리는 할아버지, 할머니 댁으로 가고 있었다.

2. My father was __________ the car. 아버지는 차를 운전하고 계셨다.
3. My mother was __________ in the front seat.
어머니는 앞좌석에서 주무시고 계셨다.
4. My sister was __________ to music. 여동생은 음악을 듣고 있었다.
5. She was __________ along with the songs.
그녀는 노래들을 따라 부르고 있었다.

6. I was __________ the wind in my hair.
나는 머리가 바람에 날리는 것을 느끼고 있었다.
7. The wind was __________. 바람이 불고 있었다.

D You didn't answer my call.

보기			
was	Were	sleeping	taking

1. You didn't answer my call. __________ you __________?
너 내 전화 안 받더라. 너 자고 있었니?
2. No. I __________ not __________. 아니요. 전 자고 있지 않았어요.
3. I __________ __________ a shower. 저는 샤워를 하고 있었어요.

정답과 해설 p.14

Practice 2 과거진행시제를 써서 문장을 완성해 보아요.

다음 우리말 뜻과 같도록 주어진 표현을 순서에 맞게 배열하여 문장을 완성하세요.

1. (was, drinking juice, He).
그는 주스를 마시고 있었다.

➔ He was drinking juice
________________.

2. (sleeping, The lion, was) in a tree.
사자가 나무에서 자고 있었다.

➔ ________________ in a tree.

3. (playing, The kids, were) in the playground. 아이들이 놀이터에서 놀고 있었다.
➔ ________________ in the playground.

4. (was, Sihu, going down the slide). (*slide: 미끄럼틀)
시후는 미끄럼틀을 타고 내려오고 있었다.
➔ ________________.

5. (Taeyeon, playing on the swing, was). 태연이는 그네를 타고 있었다.
➔ ________________.

6. (Suho, climbing the jungle gym, was). (*climb: 오르다, 올라가다)
수호는 정글짐을 오르고 있었다.
➔ ________________.

7. (playing on the seesaw, were, Mina and Yuri). 미나와 유리는 시소를 타고 있었다.
➔ ________________.

8. (Mike, hanging, was) upside down from the monkey bars.
Mike는 구름사다리에 거꾸로 매달려 있었다. (*hang: 걸다, 매달리다 *upside down: 거꾸로)
➔ ________________ upside down from the monkey bars.

9. (was, The merry-go-round, spinning). (*merry-go-round: 회전목마) 회전목마가 돌아가고 있었다.
➔ ________________.

정답과 해설 p.14

10. (What, you, doing, were) there? 너는 거기서 무엇을 하고 있었니?

➔ ______________________________ there?

11. (was, doing my homework, I). 나는 숙제하고 있었어.

➔ ______________________________.

12. (waiting for the green light, She, was) at the crosswalk.
그녀는 횡단보도에서 녹색등을 기다리고 있었다.

➔ ______________________________ at the crosswalk.

13. (was, feeling well, He, not). 그는 몸이 좋지 않았다.

➔ ______________________________.

14. (was, singing, He) loudly.
그는 큰 소리로 노래를 부르고 있었다.

➔ ______________ loudly.

15. (brushing her teeth, was, She).
그녀는 양치하고 있었다. (*brush one's teeth: 양치하다)

➔ ______________.

16. (rising, The evening moon, was). 저녁달이 떠오르고 있었다.

➔ ______________________________.

17. (looking for, My parents, were) a new house. 나의 부모님은 새 집을 찾고 있었다.

➔ ______________________________ a new house.

18. (waiting for me, Mom, was). (*wait for: ~를 기다리다) 엄마가 나를 기다리고 계셨다.

➔ ______________________________.

19. (thinking about it, I, was). 나는 그것에 대해 생각하고 있었다.

➔ ______________________________.

20. (washing his hands, was, He). 그는 손을 씻고 있었다.

➔ ______________________________.

정답과 해설 p.15

Practice 3 과거진행시제를 써서 문장을 써 보아요.

우리말 뜻을 참고하여 다음 주어진 표현을 활용해 문장을 완성해 보세요.
(주어진 동사를 과거진행시제로 알맞게 바꾸세요.)

1. (wash her face)

그녀는 세수하고 있었다.

➔ She was washing her face.

2. (walk in the forest)

그들은 숲 속을 걷고 있었다.

➔ ______________________.

3. (play with your friends) 너는 친구들과 놀고 있었니?

➔ ______________________?

4. (watch TV) 나는 TV를 보고 있지 않았어.

➔ ______________________.

5. (walk my dog) 나는 내 개를 산책시키고 있었어.

➔ ______________________.

6. (What, do) 너는 내 전화를 받지 않았어. 너는 무엇을 하고 있었니?

➔ You didn't answer my call. ______________________?

정답과 해설 p.15

7. (sleep) 미안, 전화벨을 못 들었어. 나는 자고 있었어.

→ Sorry, I didn't hear the phone. ______________________.

8. (Suho, go to his grandparents' house)

수호는 가족과 함께 그의 할아버지, 할머니 댁에 가고 있었다.

→ ______________________ with his family.

9. (feel dizzy) (*dizzy: 어지러운)

나는 어지러웠다.

→ ______________________

______________________.

10. (eat popcorn)

그들은 팝콘을 먹고 있었다.

→ ______________________

______________________.

11. (His father, look at) 그의 아버지는 GPS를 보고 있었다.

→ ______________________ the GPS.

12. (feel well) 나는 어제 수업 중에 몸이 좋지 않았다.

→ ______________________ in class yesterday.

13. (The host, talk about) 진행자는 케이팝에 대해 말하고 있었다.

→ ______________________ K-pop.

CH 06

정답과 해설 p.15

14. (roll a pencil) 그는 손가락 사이로 연필을 돌리고 있었다.

➔ ______________________ between his fingers.

15. (cut vegetables)

그녀는 야채를 자르고 있었다.

➔ ______________________

______________________.

16. (take a break)

그들은 휴식을 취하고 있었다.

➔ ______________________

______________________.

17. (His grandparents, wait for him) 그의 할아버지, 할머니가 그를 기다리고 계셨다.

➔ ______________________.

18. (laugh) (*laugh: (크게) 웃다) 그는 웃고 있었다.

➔ ______________________.

19. (His mother, listen to the radio)

그의 어머니는 라디오를 듣고 있었다.

➔ ______________________

______________________.

20. (Suho, sleep)

수호는 뒷좌석에서 자고 있었다.

➔ ______________________

in the back seat.

정답과 해설 p.15

Let's Practice More!

SET 01

학습목표 1 | 과거진행시제의 형태를 연습해 보아요. 공부한 날 : 맞은 개수 : /12개

다음 단어를 '-ing' 형태로 바꿔 보세요.

01. study 공부하다 → studying

02. wait 기다리다 → ____

03. sleep 자다 → ____

04. cut 자르다 → ____

05. play 놀다 → ____

06. drive 운전하다 → ____

07. snow 눈이 오다 → ____

08. fight 싸우다 → ____

09. visit 방문하다 → ____

10. run 달리다 → ____

11. watch 보다 → ____

12. listen 듣다 → ____

정답과 해설 p.15

Let's Practice More!

SET 02

학습목표 1 | 과거진행시제의 형태를 연습해 보아요. 공부한 날 : 맞은 개수 : /14개

다음 우리말 해석을 읽고 ( ) 안에서 알맞은 것을 골라 보세요.

01. I (were / was) playing soccer. 나는 축구를 하고 있었어.

02. What (were / was) you doing? 넌 무엇을 하고 있었니?

03. Your friends (were / was) playing in the playground.
네 친구들은 놀이터에서 놀고 있었어.

04. They (are / were) playing on the seesaw.
그들은 시소를 타고 있었어.

05. Junwoo (was / were) crossing the monkey bars. 준우는 구름사다리를 건너고 있었어.

06. Sihu (is / was) reading a comic book. 시후는 만화책을 읽고 있었어.

07. Mina and Suji (were / was) brushing their teeth. 미나와 수지는 양치를 하고 있었어.

08. We (are / were) going to my grandparents' house.
우리는 할아버지, 할머니 댁으로 가고 있었어.

09. My father was (driving / drove) the car.
나의 아버지는 차를 운전하고 계셨어.

10. My sister was (listen / listening) to music. 나의 여동생은 음악을 듣고 있었어.

11. She (is / was) singing along with the songs. 그녀는 노래들을 따라 부르고 있었어.

12. The wind (was / were) blowing. 바람이 불고 있었어.

13. Was she (sleeps / sleeping)? 그녀는 자고 있었니?

14. You (was / were) swimming in the pool.
넌 수영장에서 수영하고 있었어.

정답과 해설 p.15

Let's Practice More!

SET 03

학습목표 1 | **과거진행시제의 형태를 연습해 보아요.** 공부한 날 : 맞은 개수 : /14개

다음 우리말 해석을 보고 밑줄 친 부분이 맞으면 ○표, 틀리면 고쳐 써 보세요.

01. She were reading a book. 그녀는 책을 읽고 있었어. → was reading

02. I was doing my homework. 나는 숙제하고 있었어. → ______

03. She is waiting for the green light at the crosswalk. → ______
그녀는 횡단보도에서 녹색등을 기다리고 있었어.

04. They was walking in the forest. 그들은 숲 속을 걷고 있었다. → ______

05. He was feel well. 그는 기분이 좋았었어. → ______

06. The evening moon was rising. 저녁달이 떠오르고 있었다. → ______

07. My parents are looking for a new house. → ______
나의 부모님은 새 집을 찾고 계셨다.

08. He were singing loudly. 그는 큰 소리로 노래를 부르고 있었다. → ______

09. She was brushed her teeth. 그녀는 양치하고 있었다. → ______

10. Was you playing with your friends? 너는 친구들과 놀고 있었니? → ______

11. Mom was waiting for me. 엄마가 나를 기다리고 계셨다. → ______

12. I was thought about it. 나는 그것에 대해 생각하고 있었다. → ______

13. We was eating popcorn. 우리는 팝콘을 먹고 있었다. → ______

14. She was washed her face. 그녀는 세수하고 있었다. → ______

정답과 해설 p.15

Let's Practice More!

SET 04

학습목표 2 | 과거진행시제의 부정문과 의문문을 연습해 보아요. 공부한 날 : 맞은 개수 : /14개

다음 문장을 ( ) 안의 지시대로 고쳐 써 보세요.

01. It was raining outside. (의문문)

→ Was it raining outside

______________________?

바깥에는 비가 오고 있었니?

02. The lion was sleeping in a tree. (의문문)

→ ______________________

______________________?

사자가 나무에서 자고 있었니?

03. Mina and Yuri were playing board games. (부정문)

→ ______________________.

미나와 유리는 보드게임을 하고 있지 않았다.

04. The merry-go-round was spinning. (의문문)

→ ______________________?

회전목마가 돌아가고 있었니?

05. My mother was meeting her friends. (부정문)

→ ______________________.

어머니는 그녀의 친구들을 만나고 계시지 않았어.

06. The kids were playing in the playground. (부정문)

→ ______________________.

아이들이 놀이터에서 놀고 있지 않았어.

정답과 해설 p.15

07. He was going down the slide. (의문문)

➔ ____?

그는 미끄럼틀을 타고 내려오고 있었니?

08. Taeyeon was playing on the swing. (부정문)

➔ ____.

태연이는 그네를 타고 있지 않았어.

09. He was climbing the jungle gym. (의문문)

➔ ______________________

______________________?

그는 정글짐을 오르고 있었니?

10. They were taking a break. (의문문)

➔ ______________________

______________________?

그들은 쉬고 있었니?

11. She was cutting vegetables. (의문문)

➔ ____?

그녀는 야채를 자르고 있었니?

12. She was hanging upside down from the monkey bars. (부정문)

➔ ____.

그녀는 구름사다리에 거꾸로 매달려 있지 않았어.

13. His grandparents were waiting for him. (부정문)

➔ ____.

그의 할아버지, 할머니는 그를 기다리고 계시지 않았어.

14. He was laughing loudly. (부정문)

➔ ____.

그는 크게 웃고 있지 않았어.

정답과 해설 p.15

Let's Practice More!

SET 05

학습목표 3 | 과거진행시제의 의문문에 대한 대답을 연습해 보아요.　　공부한 날 :　　맞은 개수 :　　/12개

다음 질문에 대해 빈칸에 알맞은 대답을 써 보세요.

01. Was she doing the dishes?
➜ Yes, ______she was______.

02. Were you talking to your cousin?
➜ Yes, ____________.

03. Were they meeting their teacher?
➜ No, ____________.

04. Were you feeling the wind in your hair?
➜ Yes, ____________.

05. Were your dogs sleeping?
➜ Yes, ____________.

06. Was she playing with her friends?
➜ No, ____________.

07. Was he drinking juice?
➜ No, ____________.

08. Were they walking in the forest?
➜ No, ____________.

09. Was she singing along with the songs?
➜ No, ____________.

10. Were you taking a shower?
➜ Yes, ____________.

11. Was the wind blowing?
➜ No, ____________.

12. Was your sister walking your puppy?
➜ Yes, ____________.

정답과 해설 p.16

Let's Practice More!

SET 06

학습목표 4 | **현재진행시제와 과거진행시제를 비교해 보아요.** 공부한 날 : 맞은 개수 : /14개

( ) 안의 단어를 이용해 우리말 뜻과 같아지도록 빈칸을 완성하세요.

01. I ____am____ ____studying____ hard. (study) 나는 공부를 열심히 하고 있어.

02. Suho __________ __________ his dog. (walk) 수호는 그의 개를 산책시키고 있었어.

03. We __________ __________ to our grandparents' house. (go)
우리는 할아버지, 할머니 댁으로 가고 있어.

04. My sister __________ __________ to music. (listen) 나의 여동생은 음악을 듣고 있었어.

05. She __________ __________ along with the songs. (sing)
그녀는 노래들을 따라 부르고 있다.

06. I __________ __________ the wind in my hair. (feel)
나는 머리가 바람에 날리는 것을 느끼고 있었다.

07. The wind __________ __________. (blow) 바람이 불고 있다.

08. I __________ __________. (sleep) 난 자고 있었어.

09. I __________ __________ a shower. (take) 저는 샤워를 하고 있어요.

10. He __________ __________ juice. (drink) 그는 주스를 마시고 있다.

11. The lion __________ __________ in a tree. (sleep) 사자가 나무에서 자고 있었다.

12. You __________ __________ in the pool. (swim) 넌 수영장에서 수영하고 있었어.

13. My father __________ __________ the car. (drive)
아버지는 차를 운전하는 중이시다.

14. My mother __________ __________ in the kitchen. (cook)
어머니는 부엌에서 요리하고 계셨어.

정답과 해설 p.16

Let's Practice More!

SET 07

학습목표 5 | 과거시제와 과거진행시제를 비교해 보아요. 공부한 날 : 맞은 개수 : /20개

( ) 안의 단어를 이용해 우리말 뜻과 같아지도록 빈칸을 완성하세요.

01. Jack ___was crossing___ the monkey bars. (cross)

Jack은 구름 사다리를 건너고 있었다.

02. The merry-go-round ____________. (spin)

회전목마가 돌아가고 있었다.

03. Suho ____________ the jungle gym. (climb)

수호는 정글짐을 올랐다.

04. Mina and Yuri ____________ a board game. (play)

미나와 유리는 보드게임을 했다.

05. The kids ____________ in the playground. (play)

아이들이 놀이터에서 놀고 있었다.

06. I ____________ to the movies yesterday. (go)

나는 어제 영화를 보러 갔다.

07. I ____________ to my cousin. (talk)

난 나의 사촌에게 이야기했어.

08. He ____________ his hands. (wash)

그는 손을 닦고 있었어.

정답과 해설 p.16

09. They ______________________ in the forest. (walk)

그들은 숲 속을 걷고 있었다.

10. I ______________________ with my friends. (play)

나는 친구들과 놀고 있었어.

11. I ______________________ my puppy. (walk)

나는 내 강아지를 산책시켰다.

12. He ______________________ lunch. (have)

그는 점심을 먹고 있었다.

13. They ______________________ popcorn. (eat)

그들은 팝콘을 먹었다.

14. Suho ________________ to his grandparents' house with his family. (go)

수호는 가족과 함께 그의 할아버지, 할머니 댁에 가고 있었다.

15. His father ______________________ at the GPS. (look)

그의 아버지는 GPS를 보고 있었다.

16. I ______________________ my friends. (meet)

난 친구들을 만났어.

17. They ______________________ on the seesaw. (play)

그들은 시소를 타고 있었어.

18. Junwoo ________________ upside down from the monkey bars. (hang)

준우는 구름 사다리에 거꾸로 매달려 있었다.

19. Sumi ______________________ the dishes. (do)

수미는 설거지하고 있었어.

20. I ______________________ TV. (watch)

나는 TV를 봤다.

정답과 해설 p.16

Let's Practice More!

SET 08

학습목표 6 | 과거진행시제를 이용해 다양한 표현을 만들어 보아요. 공부한 날 : 맞은 개수 : /20개

( ) 안의 단어를 이용해 우리말 뜻과 같아지도록 빈칸을 완성하세요. (단, 시제는 과거진행시제가 되게 하세요.)

01. She ___was___ ___brushing___ her teeth. (brush)
그녀는 양치하고 있었다.

02. She __________ __________ vegetables. (cut)
그녀는 야채를 자르고 있었다.

03. She __________ __________ for the green light at the crosswalk. (wait)
그녀는 횡단보도에서 녹색등을 기다리고 있었다.

04. He __________ __________ __________ well. (feel) 그는 몸이 좋지 않았다.

05. The evening moon __________ __________. (rise) 저녁달이 떠오르고 있었다.

06. We __________ __________ loudly. (sing) 우리는 큰 소리로 노래를 부르고 있었다.

07. He __________ __________ on the street. (run) 그는 길 위에서 뛰고 있었어.

08. My parents __________ __________ for a new house. (look)
나의 부모님은 새 집을 찾고 있었다.

09. They __________ __________ popcorn. (eat) 그들은 팝콘을 먹고 있었다.

정답과 해설 p.16

10. I __________ __________ about it. (think) 나는 그것에 대해 생각하고 있었다.

11. He __________ __________ his hands. (wash) 그는 손을 씻고 있었다.

12. His father __________ __________ at the GPS. (look)
그의 아버지는 GPS를 보고 있었다.

13. His mother __________ __________ to the radio. (listen)
그의 어머니는 라디오를 듣고 있었다.

14. The host __________ __________ about K-pop. (talk)
진행자는 케이팝에 대해 말하고 있었다.

15. You __________ __________ in the back seat. (sleep)
너는 뒷좌석에서 자고 있었다.

16. They __________ __________ their homework. (do) 그들은 숙제하고 있었어.

17. They __________ __________ a break. (take) 그들은 휴식을 취하고 있었다.

18. He __________ __________. (laugh) 그는 웃고 있었다.

19. I __________ __________ __________ TV. (watch)
나는 TV를 보고 있지 않았어.

20. He __________ __________ a pencil between his fingers. (roll)
그는 손가락 사이로 연필을 돌리고 있었다.

정답과 해설 p.16

실전테스트

CHAPTER 03~06

공부한 날 :

복습한 날 :

부모님 확인 :

CHAPTER 03 현재시제 / 과거시제　CHAPTER 04 미래시제　CHAPTER 05 현재진행시제　CHAPTER 06 과거진행시제

● 정답과 해설은 별책 16쪽에서 확인하세요!!

01

다음 문장의 밑줄 친 부분을 현재진행형으로 바르게 고쳐 쓴 것을 고르세요.

He listens to the music.

① listening　② is listening
③ is going to listen　④ was listening

02

다음 표의 빈칸에 [보기]의 단어를 알맞게 분류해서 골라 쓰세요.

[보기] took / liked / studied / went / watched / felt

불규칙 동사(과거형)	규칙 동사(과거형)

[03~04] 다음 그림을 보고, 괄호 안의 동사를 이용하여 우리말 해석과 같도록 빈칸을 채우세요.

03

It ________ ________ outside. (snow)

(밖에 눈이 오고 있는 중이다.)

04

______ the dog ______ with a ball? (play)

(개가 공을 가지고 놀고 있습니까?)

05

다음 문장이 완성되도록 관계있는 것끼리 연결하세요.

① Amy went •　　• ⓐ her cousins.
② Sarah will meet •　　• ⓑ steak and rice.
③ Henry ate •　　• ⓒ to school.

06

다음 동사의 현재형과 과거형이 바르게 짝지어지지 않은 것을 고르세요.

	현재형	과거형
①	drink	drank
②	walk	walked
③	break	breaked
④	have	had

07

다음 그림을 보고, 빈칸에 들어갈 알맞은 단어를 고르세요.

I ____________ play basketball tomorrow.

① was　② am
③ did　④ will

08

다음 중 과거시제 문장을 두 개 고르세요.

① He bought three pears.
② He will finish his homework.
③ I saw your new car.
④ I am from Australia.

[09~10] 다음 문장의 빈칸에 공통으로 들어갈 알맞은 말을 쓰세요.

09 ____________

• Sam was ____________ a song.
Sam은 노래를 부르고 있었다.
• He is ____________ loudly.
그는 큰 소리로 노래를 부르고 있는 중이다.

10 ____________

• I ____________ fishing yesterday.
나는 어제 낚시를 하러 갔다.
• She ____________ to church last week.
그녀는 지난주 교회에 갔다.

11

다음 문장의 시제를 [보기]에서 골라 쓰세요.

[보기] 미래시제　과거시제
과거진행시제　현재시제

• I am very happy. (　　　　)
• He will jog with her. (　　　　)
• I saw that program. (　　　　)
• She was sleeping. (　　　　)

12

다음 그림에 맞는 대화가 되도록 주어진 글자로 시작하는 단어를 쓰세요.

A: Are you (1) g____________ ____________ play soccer?
B: Yes, do you want to join us?
A: Yes! When (2) w____________ you play soccer?

[13~14] 다음 우리말 뜻과 같도록 알파벳을 배열하여 과거형 단어를 쓰고 그 단어의 동사원형을 쓰세요.

13

o　h　u
b　t　g

____
뜻 : 샀다
동사원형 :

14

r　i　v　r

a　d　e

____

뜻 : 도착했다

동사원형 :

[15~16] 다음 그림을 참고하여 우리말 해석과 같도록 빈칸에 알맞은 말을 쓰세요.

15

He is __________ milk.
(그는 우유를 마시고 있다.)

16

He is __________ a winter coat.
(그는 겨울 코트를 입고 있다.)

[17~18] 다음 그림을 보고 괄호 안의 시제에 맞는 말을 빈칸에 쓰세요.

17

I ______ ______ a book now. (현재진행형)

18

I ______ ______ a picture. (과거진행형)

19

다음 중 미래시제 문장을 고르세요.

① I was riding a bike.
② I will go to the park.
③ He went to the zoo.
④ I am walking on the street.

20

다음 중 [보기]의 밑줄 친 부분과 시제가 같은 것을 고르세요.

[보기] I <u>was sleeping</u> in my room.

① The weather <u>was</u> sunny.
② There <u>is</u> a running man on the street.
③ He <u>was doing</u> his homework.
④ I <u>am going to</u> visit her house next week.

[21~25] 다음 중 과거시제 문장에는 '과', 현재시제 문장에는 '현'이라고 쓰세요.

21

They played hide-and-seek. ( )

22

My homeroom teacher comes. ( )

23

We studied English in the library. ( )

24

I dance with her on the stage. ( )

25

My sister is not at home. ( )

26

다음 그림에 맞게 대화에 들어갈 말을 [보기]에서 골라 쓰세요.

[보기] did do looked looking

A: What (1) ______ you do yesterday?

B: I was (2) ______ for my dog all day.

27

다음 문장의 동사를 과거시제로 바르게 고쳐 다시 쓰세요.

I goed to an English lesson last week.

[28~30] 다음 단어들을 순서에 맞게 배열하여 문장을 완성하세요.

28

(sitting / I / on the bench / was).

⇨ ______

29

(I / play baseball / next weekend / will).

⇨ ______

30

(did / you / What / yesterday / do)?

⇨ ______

실전테스트

정답 p. 16

Game

아래 그림에 해당하는 단어를 찾아 동그라미 하세요.

T	A	M	P	E	K	B	D	X
L	I	O	N	J	Y	A	F	J
R	Q	O	E	H	U	S	I	U
A	B	N	C	A	K	E	W	T
X	P	W	G	N	T	B	A	C
C	N	T	R	D	P	A	E	R
W	F	D	M	K	X	L	Z	U
G	U	M	B	R	E	L	L	A

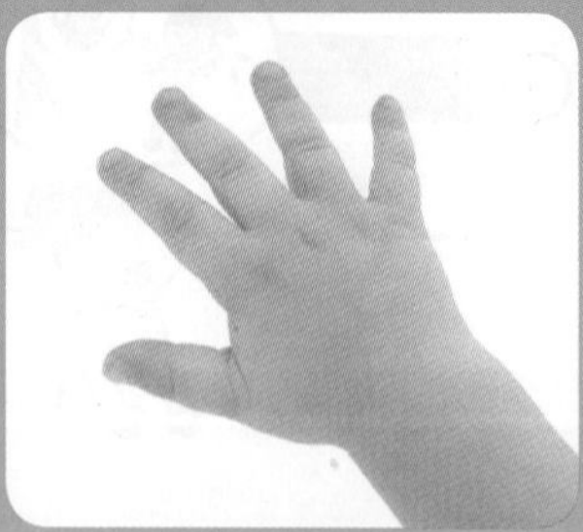

초등영문법3800제 LEVEL 4

워크북

WORKBOOK

1. **단어 쓰기 연습** mp3 음성 파일을 듣고 들려주는 단어를 세 번씩 써 보아요.
2. **Dictation Test** mp3 음성 파일을 듣고 빈칸을 채워 보세요.
3. **단어테스트** 단어 쓰기 연습을 하며 암기한 단어들을 제대로 외웠는지 확인해 보아요.
4. **워크북 정답** Dictation Test와 단어테스트의 정답

초등영문법3800제 MP3 파일 이용 방법

1. 홈페이지에서 다운로드

① 마더텅 홈페이지(www.toptutor.co.kr) 접속 → 상단 메뉴 중 [초등 · 유아]의 [교재 소개] 선택
→ 교재 목록에서 해당 교재명 찾아 선택 → 학습자료의 [mp3] 선택 후 다운로드

② 마더텅 홈페이지(www.toptutor.co.kr) 접속 → 상단 메뉴 중 [초등 · 유아] 의 [교재자료실] 선택
→ 자료실 상단의 [교재를 선택하세요.] 에서 해당 교재명 선택
→ 자료 목록에서 mp3 게시물 선택 후 다운로드

2. 모바일 스트리밍 / 다운로드

① 스마트폰으로 교재 뒷면의 QR코드 스캔 → MP3 스트리밍 or 다운로드

② 주소창에 m.toptutor.co.kr 또는 포털에서 '마더텅' 검색 → [MP3 자료실] 선택
→ 상단 메뉴 중 [초등 · 유아] 선택 → 해당 교재명 찾아 선택 후 MP3 스트리밍 or 다운로드

단어 쓰기 연습 1

초3800_4_w1

들려주는 단어를 잘 듣고, 세 번씩 써 보세요.

MP3 4권 단어 **01**

01 **lazy** (형) 게으른	lazy			
02 **surprised** (형) 놀란	surprised			
03 **classroom** (명) 교실	classroom			
04 **ago** (부) 전에	ago			
05 **evening** (명) 저녁	evening			
06 **hour** (명) 시간	hour			
07 **then** (부) 그때	then			
08 **preschool student** (명) 유치원생	preschool student			
09 **elementary** (형) 초급의	elementary			
10 **now** (부) 지금	now			
11 **playground** (명) 운동장	playground			
12 **age** (명) 나이	age			
13 **small** (형) 작은	small			

들려주는 단어를 잘 듣고, 세 번씩 써 보세요.

MP3 4권 단어 01

14 **shy** ⓗ 수줍은	shy		
15 **crybaby** ⓜ 울보	crybaby		
16 **preschool** ⓜ 유치원	preschool		
17 **kid** ⓜ 아이	kid		
18 **older brother** ⓜ 형, 오빠	older brother		
19 **busy** ⓗ 바쁜	busy		
20 **kind** ⓗ 다정한	kind		
21 **nurse** ⓜ 간호사	nurse		
22 **housewife** ⓜ 가정주부	housewife		
23 **team** ⓜ 팀, 단체	team		
24 **America** ⓜ 미국	America		
25 **from** ⓙ ~출신의	from		
26 **bank** ⓜ 은행	bank		

단어 쓰기 연습 2

초3800_4_w2

들려주는 단어를 잘 듣고, 세 번씩 써 보세요. MP3 4권 단어 **02**

27 **couch** ㉮ 소파	couch		
28 **near** ㉠ ~에서 가까이	near		
29 **library** ㉮ 도서관	library		
30 **China** ㉮ 중국	China		
31 **last** ㉯ 지난	last		
32 **vacation** ㉮ 방학	vacation		
33 **fantastic** ㉯ 환상적인	fantastic		
34 **worried** ㉯ 걱정하는	worried		
35 **really** ㉰ 정말	really		
36 **strange** ㉯ 이상한	strange		
37 **backpack** ㉮ 배낭	backpack		
38 **final** ㉯ 마지막의	final		
39 **aunt** ㉮ 이모	aunt		

들려주는 단어를 잘 듣고, 세 번씩 써 보세요.

MP3 4권 단어 02

40 **hospital** 명 병원	hospital		
41 **cheap** 형 (가격이) 싼	cheap		
42 **quiet** 형 조용한	quiet		
43 **garden** 명 정원	garden		
44 **tired** 형 힘든, 지친	tired		
45 **birthday** 명 생일	birthday		
46 **great** 형 멋진	great		
47 **Friday** 명 금요일	Friday		
48 **neighbor** 명 이웃	neighbor		
49 **dish** 명 접시	dish		
50 **break** 동 깨뜨리다	break		
51 **police officer** 명 경찰관	police officer		
52 **person** 명 사람	person		

단어 쓰기 연습 3

초3800_4_w3

들려주는 단어를 잘 듣고, 세 번씩 써 보세요.

MP3 4권 단어 **03**

01 **happy** ㉠ 행복한	happy		
02 **yesterday** ㉮ 어제	yesterday		
03 **friend** ㉢ 친구	friend		
04 **student** ㉢ 학생	student		
05 **bored** ㉠ 지루해 하는	bored		
06 **classroom** ㉢ 교실	classroom		
07 **player** ㉢ 선수	player		
08 **minute** ㉢ 분	minute		
09 **ago** ㉮ 전에	ago		
10 **actress** ㉢ 여배우	actress		
11 **rainy** ㉠ 비가 오는	rainy		
12 **glad** ㉠ 기쁜	glad		
13 **tall** ㉠ 키가 큰	tall		

들려주는 단어를 잘 듣고, 세 번씩 써 보세요.

MP3 4권 단어 03

14 **healthy** ⓗ 건강한	healthy		
15 **cry** ⓓ 울다	cry		
16 **sick** ⓗ 아픈	sick		
17 **hungry** ⓗ 배고픈	hungry		
18 **problem** ⓜ 문제	problem		
19 **alike** ⓗ 비슷한	alike		
20 **different** ⓗ 다른	different		
21 **same** ⓗ 같은	same		
22 **cook** ⓜ 요리사	cook		
23 **food** ⓜ 음식	food		
24 **tasty** ⓗ 맛있는	tasty		
25 **Internet cafe** ⓜ 피시방	Internet cafe		
26 **know** ⓓ 알다	know		

단어 쓰기 연습 4

초3800_4_w4

들려주는 단어를 잘 듣고, 세 번씩 써 보세요.

MP3 4권 단어 04

27 **late** 형 늦은	late		
28 **cute** 형 귀여운	cute		
29 **where** 부 어디에	where		
30 **teachers' room** 명 교무실	teachers' room		
31 **fault** 명 잘못	fault		
32 **how** 부 어떻게, 어떠하여	how		
33 **delicious** 형 맛있는	delicious		
34 **interesting** 형 재미있는	interesting		
35 **twins** 명 쌍둥이	twins		
36 **boring** 형 지루한	boring		
37 **smaller** 형 더 작은	smaller		
38 **big** 형 큰	big		
39 **with** 전 ~와 함께	with		

들려주는 단어를 잘 듣고, 세 번씩 써 보세요.

MP3 4권 단어 04

40 **clear** ⓗ 맑은	clear		
41 **snowy** ⓗ 눈이 오는	snowy		
42 **close** ⓗ 친한	close		
43 **math** ⓜ 수학	math		
44 **difficult** ⓗ 어려운	difficult		
45 **absent** ⓗ 결석한	absent		
46 **stomachache** ⓜ 복통	stomachache		
47 **salad** ⓜ 샐러드	salad		
48 **fresh** ⓗ 신선한	fresh		
49 **easy** ⓗ 쉬운	easy		
50 **good** ⓗ 잘하는	good		
51 **bike** ⓜ 자전거	bike		
52 **old** ⓗ 낡은	old		

초3800_4_w5

단어 쓰기 연습 5

들려주는 단어를 잘 듣고, 세 번씩 써 보세요.

MP3 4권 단어 05

01 **skateboard** 명 스케이트보드	skateboard			
02 **help** 동 돕다	help			
03 **like** 동 좋아하다	like			
04 **die** 동 죽다	die			
05 **study** 동 공부하다	study			
06 **enjoy** 동 즐기다	enjoy			
07 **stay** 동 머무르다	stay			
08 **hard** 부 열심히	hard			
09 **take** 동 데리고 가다	take			
10 **eat** 동 먹다	eat			
11 **drink** 동 마시다	drink			
12 **get** 동 얻다	get			
13 **hear** 동 듣다	hear			

들려주는 단어를 잘 듣고, 세 번씩 써 보세요.

MP3 4권 단어 05

14 **fall** ⓢ 떨어지다	fall		
15 **feel** ⓢ 느끼다	feel		
16 **cut** ⓢ 자르다	cut		
17 **put** ⓢ 놓다	put		
18 **hit** ⓢ 치다	hit		
19 **hurt** ⓢ 상처 입히다, 아프다	hurt		
20 **let** ⓢ ~하게 하다	let		
21 **many** ⓗ 많은	many		
22 **mouse** ⓜ 쥐	mouse		
23 **cake** ⓜ 케이크	cake		
24 **goal** ⓜ 골	goal		
25 **laugh** ⓢ 웃다	laugh		
26 **loudly** ⓑ 크게	loudly		

초3800_4_w6

단어 쓰기 연습 6

들려주는 단어를 잘 듣고, 세 번씩 써 보세요.

MP3 4권 단어 **06**

27 **because** ⓙ 왜냐하면 ~때문에	because		
28 **funny** ⓗ 웃긴	funny		
29 **call** ⓓ 부르다	call		
30 **scold** ⓓ 혼내다	scold		
31 **letter** ⓜ 편지	letter		
32 **apology** ⓜ 사과	apology		
33 **arm** ⓜ 팔	arm		
34 **much** ⓑ 많이	much		
35 **tease** ⓓ 괴롭히다	tease		
36 **Saturday** ⓜ 토요일	Saturday		
37 **later** ⓑ 나중에, 후에	later		
38 **worry** ⓓ 걱정하다	worry		
39 **with** ⓙ ~로	with		

들려주는 단어를 잘 듣고, 세 번씩 써 보세요.

MP3 4권 단어 06

40 **scissors** ⑲ 가위	scissors		
41 **test paper** ⑲ 시험지	test paper		
42 **face** ⑲ 얼굴	face		
43 **watch** ⑧ 보다	watch		
44 **comedy film** ⑲ 코미디 영화	comedy film		
45 **shoe** ⑲ 신발	shoe		
46 **box** ⑲ 상자	box		
47 **chess** ⑲ 체스	chess		
48 **favorite** ⑱ 가장 좋아하는	favorite		
49 **Sunday** ⑲ 일요일	Sunday		
50 **visit** ⑧ 방문하다	visit		
51 **fruit** ⑲ 과일	fruit		
52 **city hall** ⑲ 시청	city hall		

단어 쓰기 연습 7

초3800_4_w7

들려주는 단어를 잘 듣고, 세 번씩 써 보세요. MP3 4권 단어 07

01 **sleep** ⓢ 자다	sleep		
02 **well** ⓟ 잘	well		
03 **these** ⓗ 이(것)들의	these		
04 **homework** ⓜ 숙제	homework		
05 **light** ⓜ 불	light		
06 **buy** ⓢ 사다	buy		
07 **popcorn** ⓜ 팝콘	popcorn		
08 **melt** ⓢ 녹다	melt		
09 **talk** ⓢ 말하다	talk		
10 **again** ⓟ 다시	again		
11 **answer** ⓢ (전화를) 받다	answer		
12 **understand** ⓢ 이해하다	understand		
13 **win** ⓢ 이기다	win		

들려주는 단어를 잘 듣고, 세 번씩 써 보세요.

MP3 4권 단어 07

14 **remember** ⓢ 기억하다	remember		
15 **lunch** 명 점심식사	lunch		
16 **get** ⓢ 받다	get		
17 **call** 명 전화	call		
18 **nightmare** 명 악몽	nightmare		
19 **basketball** 명 농구	basketball		
20 **yet** 부 아직	yet		
21 **ill** 형 아픈	ill		
22 **shine** ⓢ 빛나다	shine		
23 **dry** ⓢ 마르다	dry		
24 **window** 명 창문	window		
25 **clean** ⓢ 청소하다	clean		
26 **exercise** ⓢ 운동하다	exercise		

초3800_4_w8

단어 쓰기 연습 8

들려주는 단어를 잘 듣고, 세 번씩 써 보세요.

MP3 4권 단어 08

27 **push** ⓓ 누르다	push		
28 **button** ⓜ 버튼	button		
29 **street** ⓜ 길	street		
30 **bring** ⓓ 가져오다	bring		
31 **umbrella** ⓜ 우산	umbrella		
32 **soup** ⓜ 수프	soup		
33 **taste** ⓓ ~한 맛이 나다	taste		
34 **raise** ⓓ 올리다	raise		
35 **hand** ⓜ 손	hand		
36 **family** ⓜ 가족	family		
37 **pencil case** ⓜ 필통	pencil case		
38 **alarm** ⓜ 알람(시계)	alarm		
39 **bed** ⓜ 침대	bed		

들려주는 단어를 잘 듣고, 세 번씩 써 보세요.

MP3 4권 단어 08

40 **wake up** ⓢ 깨우다	wake up		
41 **textbook** ⓜ 교과서	textbook		
42 **store** ⓜ 가게	store		
43 **sell** ⓢ 팔다	sell		
44 **respect** ⓢ 존경하다	respect		
45 **notebook** ⓜ 공책	notebook		
46 **arrive** ⓢ 도착하다	arrive		
47 **early** ⓑ 일찍	early		
48 **write** ⓢ 쓰다	write		
49 **secret** ⓜ 비밀	secret		
50 **report card** ⓜ 성적표	report card		
51 **happen** ⓢ 일어나다	happen		
52 **keep** ⓢ 지키다	keep		

단어 쓰기 연습 9

초3800_4_w9

들려주는 단어를 잘 듣고, 세 번씩 써 보세요.

MP3 4권 단어 09

01 **fever** 명 열	fever		
02 **until** 전 ~까지	until		
03 **temper** 명 성질	temper		
04 **rise** 동 뜨다	rise		
05 **east** 명 동쪽	east		
06 **fall** 동 떨어지다	fall		
07 **autumn** 명 가을	autumn		
08 **stitch** 명 (바느질) 땀	stitch		
09 **save** 동 아끼다	save		
10 **yawn** 동 하품하다	yawn		
11 **swan** 명 백조	swan		
12 **form** 동 만들다, 형성하다	form		
13 **heart** 명 심장, 가슴, 하트모양	heart		

들려주는 단어를 잘 듣고, 세 번씩 써 보세요.

MP3 4권 단어 09

14 **shape** ⓜ 모양	shape		
15 **take** ⓢ (사진을) 찍다	take		
16 **funny** ⓗ 웃긴	funny		
17 **sleepy** ⓗ 졸린	sleepy		
18 **church** ⓜ 교회	church		
19 **those** ⓗ 그것들의	those		
20 **discover** ⓢ 발견하다	discover		
21 **October** ⓜ 10월	October		
22 **mind** ⓢ 신경쓰다	mind		
23 **paint** ⓢ 칠하다	paint		
24 **together** ⓑ 함께	together		
25 **upset** ⓗ 화난	upset		
26 **fun** ⓗ 재밌는	fun		

단어 쓰기 연습 10

초3800_4_w10

들려주는 단어를 잘 듣고, 세 번씩 써 보세요.

MP3 4권 단어 10

27 **late** ⓟ 늦게	late		
28 **search** ⓜ 검색	search		
29 **catch** ⓓ 잡다	catch		
30 **also** ⓟ 또한	also		
31 **possible** ⓗ 가능한	possible		
32 **close** ⓗ 친한	close		
33 **cut** ⓓ 자르다	cut		
34 **finger** ⓜ 손가락	finger		
35 **break** ⓓ 부러뜨리다	break		
36 **truth** ⓜ 진실	truth		
37 **idea** ⓜ 생각	idea		
38 **regret** ⓓ 후회하다	regret		
39 **share** ⓓ 공유하다	share		

들려주는 단어를 잘 듣고, 세 번씩 써 보세요.

MP3 4권 단어 **10**

40 **joy** ㊞ 기쁨	joy		
41 **fault** ㊞ 잘못	fault		
42 **fail** ㊢ 실패하다, 떨어지다	fail		
43 **subject** ㊞ 과목	subject		
44 **lonely** ㊢ 외로운	lonely		
45 **ghost** ㊞ 귀신	ghost		
46 **nightmare** ㊞ 악몽	nightmare		
47 **collect** ㊢ 모으다	collect		
48 **acorn** ㊞ 도토리	acorn		
49 **New Year's Day** ㊞ 새해	New Year's Day		
50 **soulmate** ㊞ 마음이 통하는 친구	soulmate		
51 **use** ㊢ 사용하다	use		
52 **for** ㊥ ~동안	for		

단어 쓰기 연습 11

초3800_4_w11

들려주는 단어를 잘 듣고, 세 번씩 써 보세요.

MP3 4권 단어 11

01 **bite** ⓜ 한 입	bite		
02 **leave** ⓥ 남겨두다	leave		
03 **back** ⓐ 다시, 돌아와서	back		
04 **moment** ⓜ 잠깐, 잠시, 순간	moment		
05 **step** ⓥ 밟다	step		
06 **happen** ⓥ 일어나다, 발생하다	happen		
07 **again** ⓐ 다시, 또	again		
08 **cost** ⓥ (값이)~이다[들다]	cost		
09 **finish** ⓥ 끝내다	finish		
10 **pool** ⓜ 수영장	pool		
11 **hard** ⓐ 열심히	hard		
12 **fail** ⓥ 실패하다, 떨어지다	fail		
13 **math** ⓜ 수학	math		

들려주는 단어를 잘 듣고, 세 번씩 써 보세요.

MP3 4권 단어 11

14 **test** ㉯ 시험	test		
15 **worry** ㉯ 걱정하다	worry		
16 **fine** ㉯ 괜찮은, 좋은	fine		
17 **lie** ㉯ 거짓말하다	lie		
18 **tonight** ㉯ 오늘 밤에	tonight		
19 **move** ㉯ 옮기다	move		
20 **another** ㉯ 다른	another		
21 **deliver** ㉯ 배달하다	deliver		
22 **mail** ㉯ 우편	mail		
23 **around** ㉯ 약, ~쯤	around		
24 **hold** ㉯ 개최하다	hold		
25 **next** ㉯ 다음의	next		
26 **magic** ㉯ 마술	magic		

단어 쓰기 연습 12

초3800_4_w12

들려주는 단어를 잘 듣고, 세 번씩 써 보세요.

MP3 4권 단어 12

27 **music** ⓜ 음악	music		
28 **recorder** ⓜ 리코더	recorder		
29 **xylophone** ⓜ 실로폰	xylophone		
30 **triangle** ⓜ 트라이앵글	triangle		
31 **farewell party** ⓜ 송별회	farewell party		
32 **soon** ⓟ 곧	soon		
33 **bite** ⓓ 물다	bite		
34 **stranger** ⓜ 낯선 사람	stranger		
35 **careful** ⓗ 조심하는	careful		
36 **sure** ⓗ 확신하는	sure		
37 **pass** ⓓ 통과하다	pass		
38 **exam** ⓜ 시험	exam		
39 **picnic** ⓜ 소풍	picnic		

들려주는 단어를 잘 듣고, 세 번씩 써 보세요.

MP3 4권 단어 12

40 **wash** 동 씻다	wash		
41 **dish** 명 접시	dish		
42 **forgive** 동 용서하다	forgive		
43 **listen to** 동 ~을 듣다	listen to		
44 **ready** 형 준비된	ready		
45 **fight** 명 싸움	fight		
46 **better** 형 더 나은	better		
47 **commercial** 명 광고	commercial		
48 **afternoon** 명 오후	afternoon		
49 **join** 동 함께 하다	join		
50 **return** 동 반납하다	return		
51 **baseball** 명 야구	baseball		
52 **library** 명 도서관	library		

단어 쓰기 연습 13

초3800_4_w13

들려주는 단어를 잘 듣고, 세 번씩 써 보세요.

MP3 4권 단어 13

01	**clean** ㊐ 청소하다	clean		
02	**block** ㊐ 가리다, 막다	block		
03	**wallet** ㊒ 지갑	wallet		
04	**lie** ㊐ 눕다	lie		
05	**bother** ㊐ 귀찮게 하다	bother		
06	**outside** ㊑ 밖에	outside		
07	**try** ㊐ 시도하다	try		
08	**work** ㊐ 작동하다	work		
09	**bring** ㊐ 가져오다	bring		
10	**toilet paper** ㊒ 휴지	toilet paper		
11	**ask** ㊐ 부탁하다	ask		
12	**pour** ㊐ (비가) 마구 쏟아지다	pour		
13	**bake** ㊐ 굽다	bake		

들려주는 단어를 잘 듣고, 세 번씩 써 보세요.

MP3 4권 단어 13

14 **check** ⓢ 확인하다	check		
15 **contact** ⓜ 연락, 접촉	contact		
16 **list** ⓜ 목록	list		
17 **wait** ⓢ 기다리다	wait		
18 **quiz** ⓜ 퀴즈, 시험	quiz		
19 **win** ⓢ 이기다	win		
20 **snack** ⓜ 간식	snack		
21 **chocolate** ⓜ 초콜릿	chocolate		
22 **open** ⓢ 펴다	open		
23 **wear** ⓢ 입다	wear		
24 **raincoat** ⓜ 비옷	raincoat		
25 **sneakers** ⓜ 스니커즈 운동화	sneakers		
26 **get** ⓢ ~되어지다	get		

단어 쓰기 연습 14

초3800_4_w14

들려주는 단어를 잘 듣고, 세 번씩 써 보세요.

MP3 4권 단어 14

27 **wet** ㉠ 젖은	wet		
28 **shake** ㉢ 떨다, 떨리다	shake		
29 **think** ㉢ 생각하다	think		
30 **concert** ㉣ 콘서트, 연주회	concert		
31 **waste** ㉢ 낭비하다	waste		
32 **follow** ㉢ 따라가다	follow		
33 **drive** ㉢ ~하도록 만들다	drive		
34 **care** ㉢ 신경쓰다	care		
35 **apologize** ㉢ 사과하다	apologize		
36 **mistake** ㉣ 실수	mistake		
37 **stupid** ㉠ 멍청한	stupid		
38 **daydream** ㉢ 공상하다	daydream		
39 **exercise** ㉢ 운동하다	exercise		

들려주는 단어를 잘 듣고, 세 번씩 써 보세요.

MP3 4권 단어 14

40 **kid** ⓢ 농담하다, 놀리다	kid		
41 **send** ⓢ 보내다	send		
42 **e-mail** ⓜ 이메일	e-mail		
43 **plant** ⓢ 심다	plant		
44 **charge** ⓢ 충전하다	charge		
45 **battery** ⓜ 배터리	battery		
46 **rose** ⓜ 장미	rose		
47 **wind** ⓜ 바람	wind		
48 **blow** ⓢ 불다	blow		
49 **download** ⓢ 내려받다	download		
50 **file** ⓜ 파일	file		
51 **lose** ⓢ 지다	lose		
52 **ring** ⓢ 울리다	ring		

단어 쓰기 연습 15

초3800_4_w15

들려주는 단어를 잘 듣고, 세 번씩 써 보세요.

MP3 4권 단어 15

01	**play** ⑧ (악기를) 연주하다	play		
02	**guitar** ⑲ 기타	guitar		
03	**ground** ⑲ 땅	ground		
04	**hug** ⑧ 안다	hug		
05	**camera** ⑲ 카메라	camera		
06	**secret** ⑲ 비밀	secret		
07	**late** ⑱ 늦은	late		
08	**shop** ⑧ 쇼핑하다	shop		
09	**mall** ⑲ 쇼핑몰	mall		
10	**smile** ⑧ 웃다	smile		
11	**cousin** ⑲ 사촌	cousin		
12	**work** ⑧ 일하다	work		
13	**slide** ⑲ 미끄럼틀	slide		

들려주는 단어를 잘 듣고, 세 번씩 써 보세요.

MP3 4권 단어 15

14 **cross** ⓢ 건너다	cross		
15 **monkey bars** ⓜ 구름사다리	monkey bars		
16 **seesaw** ⓜ 시소	seesaw		
17 **walk** ⓢ 걷다	walk		
18 **drive** ⓢ 운전하다	drive		
19 **front** ⓗ 앞의	front		
20 **seat** ⓜ 좌석	seat		
21 **song** ⓜ 노래	song		
22 **hair** ⓜ 머리카락	hair		
23 **answer** ⓢ 대답하다, (전화를) 받다	answer		
24 **drink** ⓢ 마시다	drink		
25 **juice** ⓜ 주스	juice		
26 **lion** ⓜ 사자	lion		

단어 쓰기 연습 16

초3800_4_w16

들려주는 단어를 잘 듣고, 세 번씩 써 보세요.

MP3 4권 단어 16

27 **kids** ⑱ 아이들	kids		
28 **swing** ⑱ 그네	swing		
29 **climb** ⑧ 오르다	climb		
30 **jungle gym** ⑱ 정글짐	jungle gym		
31 **hang** ⑧ 매달리다	hang		
32 **upside down** ⑨ 거꾸로	upside down		
33 **merry-go-round** ⑱ 회전목마	merry-go-round		
34 **spin** ⑧ 돌아가다, 회전하다	spin		
35 **green** ⑱ 초록의	green		
36 **light** ⑱ 불, 등	light		
37 **crosswalk** ⑱ 횡단보도	crosswalk		
38 **loudly** ⑨ 크게	loudly		
39 **brush** ⑧ 닦다	brush		

들려주는 단어를 잘 듣고, 세 번씩 써 보세요.

MP3 4권 단어 **16**

40 **moon** ⓜ 달	moon		
41 **rise** ⓢ 떠오르다	rise		
42 **hand** ⓜ 손	hand		
43 **forest** ⓜ 숲	forest		
44 **dizzy** ⓗ 어지러운	dizzy		
45 **host** ⓜ 진행자	host		
46 **roll** ⓢ 돌리다	roll		
47 **between** ⓙ ~사이에	between		
48 **vegetable** ⓜ 채소	vegetable		
49 **grandparents** ⓜ 할머니, 할아버지	grandparents		
50 **laugh** ⓢ 웃다	laugh		
51 **radio** ⓜ 라디오	radio		
52 **back seat** ⓜ 뒷좌석	back seat		

초3800_4_d1

Dictation Test 1

MP3 4권 받아쓰기 **01**

Name : Date : Score : /10

[01~10] 들려주는 문장을 잘 듣고 빈칸에 알맞은 단어를 채워 보세요.

01. ______ ______ at school.
그는 학교에 있었다.

02. ______ ______ happy.
너는 행복했다.

03. My dog ______ ______.
나의 개는 아팠다.

04. It ______ ______ yesterday.
어제 비가 왔다.

05. ______ ______ in the classroom.
그들은 교실 안에 있었다.

06. ______ ______ tired.
나는 피곤했다.

07. My parents ______ ______ yesterday.
나의 부모님은 어제 바쁘셨다.

08. ______ ______ a hard day.
오늘은 힘든 날이었다.

09. I ______ ______ for my age.
나는 나이에 비해 컸다.

10. My ______ ______ at the bank.
나의 엄마는 은행에 계셨다.

정답 p.270

초3800_4_d2

Dictation Test 2

MP3 4권 받아쓰기 **02**

Name : Date : Score : /10

[01~10] 들려주는 문장을 잘 듣고 빈칸에 알맞은 단어를 채워 보세요.

01. ______________ ______________ at my grandparents' house.

나는 나의 조부모님 댁에 있었다.

02. My older brother ______________ 10 years ______________.

나의 오빠는 10살이었다.

03. The final exam ______________ ______________.

기말고사는 쉬웠다.

04. ______________ ______________ my best friends.

그들은 나의 가장 친한 친구들이었다.

05. ______________ ______________ a brave person.

그는 용감한 사람이었다.

06. Yesterday ______________ my 9th birthday.

어제는 나의 9번째 생일이었다.

07. The apple ______________ ______________ in the garden.

그 사과나무는 정원에 있었다.

08. ______________ ______________ worried about you.

우리는 너를 걱정했었다.

09. ______________ ______________ cheap.

그것은 가격이 쌌다.

10. My father ______________ near my ______________.

나의 아버지는 나의 학교 주변에 계셨다.

정답 p.270

초3800_4_d3

Dictation Test 3

MP3 4권 받아쓰기 03

Name : Date : Score : /10

[01~10] 들려주는 문장을 잘 듣고 빈칸에 알맞은 단어를 채워 보세요.

01. She ____________ ____________ healthy.
그녀는 건강하지 않았다.

02. It ____________ ____________ snowy yesterday.
어제는 눈이 오지 않았다.

03. ____________ ____________ in the classroom?
넌 교실에 있었니?

04. My dogs ____________ ____________ at home.
나의 개들은 집에 있지 않았다.

05. ____________ the English ____________ difficult?
그 영어 시험은 어려웠니?

06. ____________ your ____________ in the living room?
너의 아빠는 거실에 계셨니?

07. We ____________ ____________ close at first.
우리는 처음에 친하지 않았다.

08. ____________ ____________ good at English?
그들은 영어를 잘 했니?

09. I ____________ ____________ big last year.
나는 작년에는 (덩치가) 크지 않았다.

10. ____________ ____________ busy?
그는 바빴니?

정답 p.270

초3800_4_d4

Dictation Test 4

MP3 4권 받아쓰기 04

Name : Date : Score : /10

[01~10] 들려주는 문장을 잘 듣고 빈칸에 알맞은 단어를 채워 보세요.

01. ________ ________ best friends last year?
너희들은 작년에 단짝이었니?

02. ________ Mina ________?
미나는 아팠니?

03. They ________ not ________.
그들은 행복하지 않았다.

04. The book ________ ________ interesting.
그 책은 재미있지 않았다.

05. You ________ not ________.
너는 늦지 않았었다.

06. ________ ________ with your dog?
너는 너의 개와 함께 있었니?

07. ________ the salad ________?
그 샐러드는 신선했니?

08. He ________ ________ a fool.
그는 바보가 아니었다.

09. ________ ________ hungry?
그들은 배고팠니?

10. They ________ ________ twins.
그들은 쌍둥이가 아니었다.

정답 p.270

초3800_4_d5

Dictation Test 5

MP3 4권 받아쓰기 **05**

Name : Date : Score : /10

[01~10] 들려주는 문장을 잘 듣고 빈칸에 알맞은 단어를 채워 보세요.

01. He ________________ to her house.

그는 그녀의 집에 갔다.

02. We ________________ soccer yesterday.

우리는 어제 축구를 했다.

03. The teacher ________________ my name.

그 선생님은 내 이름을 부르셨다.

04. I ________________ a book last weekend.

나는 지난 주말에 책 한 권을 읽었다.

05. You ________________ very hard.

너는 아주 열심히 공부했다.

06. My mom ________________ my test paper.

나의 엄마는 내 시험지를 보셨다.

07. She ________________ a glass of water.

그녀는 물 한 잔을 마셨다.

08. Charlie ________________ at home.

Charlie는 집에 있었다.

09. I ________________ a letter.

나는 편지를 썼다.

10. Mina ________________ loudly.

미나는 크게 웃었다.

정답 p.270

초3800_4_d6

Dictation Test 6

MP3 4권 받아쓰기 06

Name : Date : Score : /10

[01~10] 들려주는 문장을 잘 듣고 빈칸에 알맞은 단어를 채워 보세요.

01. We ________________ a comedy film.
우리는 코미디 영화를 봤다.

02. She ________________ a time capsule with a shoe box.
그녀는 신발상자로 타임캡슐을 만들었다.

03. I ________________ my ring in the box.
나는 그 상자에 나의 반지를 놓았다.

04. He ________________ a car last year.
그는 작년에 차 한 대를 샀다.

05. They ________________ at me.
그들은 나를 보았다.

06. We ________________ our homework last night.
우리는 어젯밤에 숙제를 했다.

07. She ________________ her friends.
그녀는 그녀의 친구들을 만났다.

08. My mother ________________ some cookies.
나의 엄마는 쿠키를 구우셨다.

09. They ________________ to Sihu's house.
그들은 시후의 집까지 달려갔다.

10. I ________________ my uncle on Sunday.
나는 내 삼촌을 일요일에 방문했다.

정답 p.270

초3800_4_d7

Dictation Test 7

MP3 4권 받아쓰기 **07**

Name : Date : Score : /10

[01~10] 들려주는 문장을 잘 듣고 빈칸에 알맞은 단어를 채워 보세요.

01. I ________ ________ well last night.
나는 어젯밤에 잘 자지 못했다.

02. ________ you ________ basketball yesterday?
넌 어제 농구를 했니?

03. ________ they ________ the window?
그들이 그 창문을 깼니?

04. I ________ ________ bring my notebook.
나는 내 공책을 가지고 오지 않았다.

05. The store ________ ________ fruit.
그 가게는 과일을 팔지 않았다.

06. ________ she ________ that pizza?
그녀가 저 피자를 만들었니?

07. ________ you ________ my pencil case?
넌 내 필통을 봤니?

08. We ________ ________ her name.
우리는 그녀의 이름을 알지 못했다.

09. I ________ ________ clean the classroom.
나는 그 교실을 청소하지 않았다.

10. ________ Mina ________ to see a doctor?
미나는 병원에 갔었니?

정답 p.270

초3800_4_d8

Dictation Test 8

MP3 4권 받아쓰기 08

Name : Date : Score : /10

[01~10] 들려주는 문장을 잘 듣고 빈칸에 알맞은 단어를 채워 보세요.

01. ________ you ________ to bed late yesterday?
넌 어제 늦게 잠자리에 들었니?

02. I ________ ________ that movie.
나는 저 영화를 보지 않았다.

03. ________ he ________ the secret?
그는 비밀을 지켰니?

04. He ________ ________ his umbrella.
그는 그의 우산을 가져오지 않았다.

05. Mom ________ ________ see my report card.
엄마는 내 성적표를 보지 않으셨다.

06. ________ you ________ a nightmare?
너는 악몽을 꾸었니?

07. She ________ ________ milk.
그녀는 우유를 마시지 않았다.

08. ________ I ________ you up?
내가 너를 깨웠니?

09. ________ they ________ hard?
그들은 공부를 열심히 했니?

10. The soup ________ ________ taste good.
그 수프는 맛이 좋지 않았다.

정답 p.270

초3800_4_d9

Dictation Test 9

MP3 4권 받아쓰기 09

Name : Date : Score : /10

[01~10] 들려주는 문장을 잘 듣고 빈칸에 알맞은 단어를 채워 보세요.

01. I ________________ to Mina on the ________________.
나는 전화로 미나와 이야기했다.

02. ________________ up right ________________!
지금 당장 일어나!

03. She ________________ vidco games every day.
그녀는 매일 비디오 게임을 한다.

04. We ________________ ________________ friends now.
지금은 우린 친구가 아니다.

05. She ________________ the news.
그녀는 그 소식을 들었다.

06. He ________________ lonely yesterday.
그는 어제 외롭다고 느꼈다.

07. I ________________ a great time.
나는 좋은 시간을 가졌다.

08. She usually ________________ the bus.
그녀는 보통 버스를 탄다.

09. I ________________ many coins.
나는 많은 동전들을 모았다.

10. He ________________ in his parents' room.
그는 그의 부모님 방에서 잔다.

정답 p.270

초3800_4_d10

Dictation Test 10

MP3 4권 받아쓰기 10

Name : Date : Score : /10

[01~10] 들려주는 문장을 잘 듣고 빈칸에 알맞은 단어를 채워 보세요.

01. It ________ ________ today.
오늘은 일요일이다.

02. I always ________ lunch with my friends.
나는 항상 내 친구들과 점심을 먹는다.

03. She ________ her ________.
그녀는 팔이 부러졌다.

04. He ________ a ghost.
그는 귀신을 봤다.

05. I ________ a fever.
나는 열이 있다.

06. Sihu ________ his finger.
시후는 그의 손가락을 베었다.

07. He ________ to ________ early yesterday.
그는 어제 일찍 잠자리에 들었다.

08. I ________ sleepy ________.
나는 지금 졸리다.

09. Time ________ ________.
시간은 금이다.

10. I ________ a bicycle for my birthday.
나는 내 생일 선물로 자전거를 원했다.

정답 p.270

초3800_4_d11

Dictation Test 11

MP3 4권 받아쓰기 **11**

Name : Date : Score : /10

[01~10] 들려주는 문장을 잘 듣고 빈칸에 알맞은 단어를 채워 보세요.

01. She's ______________ ______________ to go to the party.
그녀는 그 파티에 가지 않을 것이다.

02. ______________ it ______________ tomorrow?
내일 눈이 올까?

03. I'll ______________ right ______________.
나는 곧 돌아올 것이다.

04. I'm ______________ ______________ learn English.
나는 영어를 배울 것이다.

05. ______________ you ______________ to play the piano?
너는 피아노를 연주할 거니?

06. You ______________ ______________ the exam.
너는 그 시험을 통과할 것이다.

07. He is ______________ ______________ do a magic show.
그는 마술쇼를 할 것이다.

08. We ______________ ______________ play computer games.
우리는 컴퓨터 게임을 하지 않을 것이다.

09. The class ______________ ______________ at 9 o'clock.
그 수업은 9시에 시작할 것이다.

10. We are ______________ ______________ to go on a picnic.
우리는 소풍을 가지 않을 것이다.

정답 p.270

초3800_4_d12

Dictation Test 12

MP3 4권 받아쓰기 12

Name : Date : Score : /10

[01~10] 들려주는 문장을 잘 듣고 빈칸에 알맞은 단어를 채워 보세요.

01. They ______ ______ music.
그들은 음악을 연주할 것이다.

02. I ______ ______ ______ read a book this weekend.
나는 이번 주말에 책 한 권을 읽을 것이다.

03. ______ you ______ us?
우리랑 함께 할래?

04. My mom ______ ______ let me.
나의 엄마는 허락하지 않으실 것이다.

05. I'm ______ ______ to lie to you.
나는 너에게 거짓말을 하지 않을 것이다.

06. She ______ ______ forgive me.
그녀는 나를 용서하지 않을 것이다.

07. ______ you ______ to eat that?
너는 그것을 먹을 거니?

08. I ______ ______ to another school.
나는 다른 학교로 전학갈 것이다.

09. They ______ ______ ______ have lunch together.
그들은 함께 점심을 먹을 것이다.

10. ______ you study hard?
너는 공부를 열심히 할 거니?

정답 p.270

초3800_4_d13

Dictation Test 13

MP3 4권 받아쓰기 13

Name : Date : Score : /10

[01~10] 들려주는 문장을 잘 듣고 빈칸에 알맞은 단어를 채워 보세요.

01. I ________ ________ a book.
나는 책을 읽고 있다.

02. My mother ________ ________ watching TV.
나의 엄마는 TV를 보고 계시지 않아.

03. ________ it ________ outside?
밖에 눈이 오고 있어?

04. She is ________ ________.
그녀는 놀고 있지 않는다.

05. The computer ________ ________ working.
그 컴퓨터는 작동하지 않고 있다.

06. He ________ ________ with his friends.
그는 그의 친구들과 수다를 떨고 있다.

07. Suho ________ ________ for his cell phone.
수호는 그의 핸드폰을 찾고 있다.

08. ________ they ________ their homework?
그들은 숙제를 하고 있니?

09. We ________ not ________ hard.
우리는 열심히 공부하지 않고 있다.

10. The cat ________ ________.
그 고양이는 자고 있다.

정답 p.270

초3800_4_d14

Dictation Test 14

MP3 4권 받아쓰기 14

Name : Date : Score : /10

[01~10] 들려주는 문장을 잘 듣고 빈칸에 알맞은 단어를 채워 보세요.

01. ______________ she ______________ a good time?
그녀는 좋은 시간을 보내고 있는 중이니?

02. ______________ we ______________?
우리는 이기고 있는 중이니?

03. We ______________ ______________ to a concert.
우리는 콘서트에 가고 있다.

04. I ______________ ______________ following you.
나는 네 말을 이해하지 못하고 있다.

05. My mom ______________ ______________ in the kitchen.
나의 엄마는 부엌에서 요리를 하고 계신다.

06. Mina ______________ ______________ trees.
미나는 나무를 심고 있다.

07. She ______________ not ______________.
그녀는 울고 있지 않다.

08. People ______________ ______________ their umbrellas.
사람들은 그들의 우산을 펴고 있다.

09. ______________ he ______________ the dishes?
그는 설거지를 하고 있는 중이니?

10. I ______________ ______________ kidding.
나는 농담하고 있지 않다.

정답 p.270

초3800_4_d15

Dictation Test 15

MP3 4권 받아쓰기 15

Name : Date : Score : /10

[01~10] 들려주는 문장을 잘 듣고 빈칸에 알맞은 단어를 채워 보세요.

01. I ________ ________ to my cousin.
나는 내 사촌과 이야기하고 있었다.

02. Your friends ________ ________ in the playground.
너의 친구들은 놀이터에서 놀고 있었다.

03. ________ he ________ a shower?
그는 샤워를 하고 있었니?

04. I ________ not ________ TV.
나는 TV를 보고 있지 않았다.

05. She was ________ ________.
그녀는 자고 있지 않았다.

06. My father ________ ________ the car.
나의 아버지는 운전하고 계셨다.

07. ________ they ________ in the forest?
그들은 숲속에서 걷고 있었니?

08. ________ ________ playing with your friends?
너는 너의 친구들과 놀고 있었니?

09. I ________ ________ about it.
나는 그것에 대해 생각하고 있었다.

10. His mother ________ not ________ to the radio.
그의 엄마는 라디오를 듣고 있지 않았다.

정답 p.270

초3800_4_d16

Dictation Test 16

MP3 4권 받아쓰기 16

Name : Date : Score : /10

[01~10] 들려주는 문장을 잘 듣고 빈칸에 알맞은 단어를 채워 보세요.

01. The wind ________ ________.
바람이 불고 있었다.

02. She ________ ________ along with the songs.
그녀는 그 노래들을 따라 부르고 있었다.

03. ________ they ________?
그들은 쇼핑하고 있었니?

04. The baby was ________ ________.
그 아기는 자고 있지 않았다.

05. I ________ ________ for the green light at the crosswalk.
나는 횡단보도에서 녹색불을 기다리고 있었다.

06. I ________ not ________ on my cell phone.
나는 핸드폰으로 통화하고 있지 않았다.

07. He ________ ________ for me.
그는 날 기다리고 있었다.

08. We ________ ________ soccer.
우리는 축구를 하고 있었다.

09. ________ she ________ vegetables?
그녀는 야채를 자르고 있었니?

10. My friends ________ ________ in the pool.
내 친구들은 수영장에서 수영하고 있었다.

정답 p.270

단어테스트 1

다음 한글 뜻을 보고 영어 표현을 적으세요. Name : Date : Score : /26

01		형 게으른	14		형 수줍은
02		형 놀란	15		명 울보
03		명 교실	16		명 유치원
04		부 전에	17		명 아이
05		명 저녁	18		명 형, 오빠
06		명 시간	19		형 바쁜
07		부 그때	20		형 다정한
08		명 유치원생	21		명 간호사
09		형 초급의	22		명 가정주부
10		부 지금	23		명 팀, 단체
11		명 운동장	24		명 미국
12		명 나이	25		전 ~출신의
13		형 작은	26		명 은행

정답 p.270

단어테스트 2

다음 한글 뜻을 보고 영어 표현을 적으세요. Name : Date : Score : /26

01		명 소파	14		명 병원
02		전 ~에서 가까이	15		형 (가격이) 싼
03		명 도서관	16		형 조용한
04		명 중국	17		명 정원
05		형 지난	18		형 힘든, 지친
06		명 방학	19		명 생일
07		형 환상적인	20		형 멋진
08		형 걱정하는	21		명 금요일
09		부 정말	22		명 이웃
10		형 이상한	23		명 접시
11		명 배낭	24		동 깨뜨리다
12		형 마지막의	25		명 경찰관
13		명 이모	26		명 사람

정답 p.270

단어테스트 3

다음 한글 뜻을 보고 영어 표현을 적으세요.　Name :　Date :　Score :　/26

01		형 행복한	14		형 건강한
02		부 어제	15		동 울다
03		명 친구	16		형 아픈
04		명 학생	17		형 배고픈
05		형 지루해 하는	18		명 문제
06		명 교실	19		형 비슷한
07		명 선수	20		형 다른
08		명 분	21		형 같은
09		부 전에	22		명 요리사
10		명 여배우	23		명 음식
11		형 비가 오는	24		형 맛있는
12		형 기쁜	25		명 피시방
13		형 키가 큰	26		동 알다

정답 p.270

단어테스트 4

다음 한글 뜻을 보고 영어 표현을 적으세요. Name : Date : Score : /26

01		형 늦은	
02		형 귀여운	
03		부 어디에	
04		명 교무실	
05		명 잘못	
06		부 어떻게, 어떠하여	
07		형 맛있는	
08		형 재미있는	
09		명 쌍둥이	
10		형 지루한	
11		형 더 작은	
12		형 큰	
13		전 ~와 함께	
14		형 맑은	
15		형 눈이 오는	
16		형 친한	
17		명 수학	
18		형 어려운	
19		형 결석한	
20		명 복통	
21		명 샐러드	
22		형 신선한	
23		형 쉬운	
24		형 잘하는	
25		명 자전거	
26		형 낡은	

정답 p.271

단어테스트 5

다음 한글 뜻을 보고 영어 표현을 적으세요. Name : Date : Score : /26

01 ___ 명 스케이트보드
02 ___ 동 돕다
03 ___ 동 좋아하다
04 ___ 동 죽다
05 ___ 동 공부하다
06 ___ 동 즐기다
07 ___ 동 머무르다
08 ___ 부 열심히
09 ___ 동 데리고 가다
10 ___ 동 먹다
11 ___ 동 마시다
12 ___ 동 얻다
13 ___ 동 듣다
14 ___ 동 떨어지다
15 ___ 동 느끼다
16 ___ 동 자르다
17 ___ 동 놓다
18 ___ 동 치다
19 ___ 동 상처 입히다, 아프다
20 ___ 동 ~하게 하다
21 ___ 형 많은
22 ___ 명 쥐
23 ___ 명 케이크
24 ___ 명 골
25 ___ 동 웃다
26 ___ 부 크게

정답 p.271

단어테스트 6

다음 한글 뜻을 보고 영어 표현을 적으세요. Name : Date : Score : /26

01		접 왜냐하면 ~때문에	14		명 가위
02		형 웃긴	15		명 시험지
03		동 부르다	16		명 얼굴
04		동 혼내다	17		동 보다
05		명 편지	18		명 코미디 영화
06		명 사과	19		명 신발
07		명 팔	20		명 상자
08		부 많이	21		명 체스
09		동 괴롭히다	22		형 가장 좋아하는
10		명 토요일	23		명 일요일
11		부 나중에, 후에	24		동 방문하다
12		동 걱정하다	25		명 과일
13		전 ~로	26		명 시청

정답 p.271

단어테스트 7

다음 한글 뜻을 보고 영어 표현을 적으세요. Name : Date : Score : /26

01		ⓢ 자다	14		ⓢ 기억하다
02		ⓟ 잘	15		ⓜ 점심식사
03		ⓗ 이(것)들의	16		ⓢ 받다
04		ⓜ 숙제	17		ⓜ 전화
05		ⓜ 불	18		ⓜ 악몽
06		ⓢ 사다	19		ⓜ 농구
07		ⓜ 팝콘	20		ⓟ 아직
08		ⓢ 녹다	21		ⓗ 아픈
09		ⓢ 말하다	22		ⓢ 빛나다
10		ⓟ 다시	23		ⓢ 마르다
11		ⓢ (전화를) 받다	24		ⓜ 창문
12		ⓢ 이해하다	25		ⓢ 청소하다
13		ⓢ 이기다	26		ⓢ 운동하다

정답 p.271

단어테스트 8

다음 한글 뜻을 보고 영어 표현을 적으세요. Name : Date : Score : /26

번호	답	뜻	번호	답	뜻
01		동 누르다	14		동 깨우다
02		명 버튼	15		명 교과서
03		명 길	16		명 가게
04		동 가져오다	17		동 팔다
05		명 우산	18		동 존경하다
06		명 수프	19		명 공책
07		동 ~한 맛이 나다	20		동 도착하다
08		동 올리다	21		부 일찍
09		명 손	22		동 쓰다
10		명 가족	23		명 비밀
11		명 필통	24		명 성적표
12		명 알람(시계)	25		동 일어나다
13		명 침대	26		동 지키다

정답 p.271

단어테스트 9

다음 한글 뜻을 보고 영어 표현을 적으세요. Name : Date : Score : /26

번호	답	뜻	번호	답	뜻
01		명 열	14		명 모양
02		전 ~까지	15		동 (사진을) 찍다
03		명 성질	16		형 웃긴
04		동 뜨다	17		형 졸린
05		명 동쪽	18		명 교회
06		동 떨어지다	19		형 그것들의
07		명 가을	20		동 발견하다
08		명 (바느질) 땀	21		명 10월
09		동 아끼다	22		동 신경쓰다
10		동 하품하다	23		동 칠하다
11		명 백조	24		부 함께
12		동 만들다, 형성하다	25		형 화난
13		명 심장, 가슴, 하트모양	26		형 재밌는

정답 p.271

단어테스트 10

다음 한글 뜻을 보고 영어 표현을 적으세요. Name : Date : Score : /26

01	㊄ 늦게	14	㊊ 기쁨
02	㊊ 검색	15	㊊ 잘못
03	㊍ 잡다	16	㊍ 실패하다, 떨어지다
04	㊄ 또한	17	㊊ 과목
05	㊏ 가능한	18	㊏ 외로운
06	㊏ 친한	19	㊊ 귀신
07	㊍ 자르다	20	㊊ 악몽
08	㊊ 손가락	21	㊍ 모으다
09	㊍ 부러뜨리다	22	㊊ 도토리
10	㊊ 진실	23	㊊ 새해
11	㊊ 생각	24	㊊ 마음이 통하는 친구
12	㊍ 후회하다	25	㊍ 사용하다
13	㊍ 공유하다	26	㊈ ~동안

정답 p.271

단어테스트 11

다음 한글 뜻을 보고 영어 표현을 적으세요. Name : Date : Score : /26

01		명 한 입	14		명 시험
02		동 남겨두다	15		동 걱정하다
03		부 다시, 돌아와서	16		형 괜찮은, 좋은
04		명 잠깐, 잠시, 순간	17		동 거짓말하다
05		동 밟다	18		부 오늘 밤에
06		동 일어나다, 발생하다	19		동 옮기다
07		부 다시, 또	20		형 다른
08		동 (값이)~이다[들다]	21		동 배달하다
09		동 끝내다	22		명 우편
10		명 수영장	23		부 약, ~쯤
11		부 열심히	24		동 개최하다
12		동 실패하다, 떨어지다	25		형 다음의
13		명 수학	26		명 마술

정답 p.271

단어테스트 12

다음 한글 뜻을 보고 영어 표현을 적으세요. Name : Date : Score : /26

01		명 음악	14		동 씻다
02		명 리코더	15		명 접시
03		명 실로폰	16		동 용서하다
04		명 트라이앵글	17		동 ~을 듣다
05		명 송별회	18		형 준비된
06		부 곧	19		명 싸움
07		동 물다	20		형 더 나은
08		명 낯선 사람	21		명 광고
09		형 조심하는	22		명 오후
10		형 확신하는	23		동 함께 하다
11		동 통과하다	24		동 반납하다
12		명 시험	25		명 야구
13		명 소풍	26		명 도서관

정답 p.271

단어테스트 13

다음 한글 뜻을 보고 영어 표현을 적으세요. Name : Date : Score : /26

01		동 청소하다
02		동 가리다, 막다
03		명 지갑
04		동 눕다
05		동 귀찮게 하다
06		부 밖에
07		동 시도하다
08		동 작동하다
09		동 가져오다
10		명 휴지
11		동 부탁하다
12		동 (비가) 마구 쏟아지다
13		동 굽다
14		동 확인하다
15		명 연락, 접촉
16		명 목록
17		동 기다리다
18		명 퀴즈, 시험
19		동 이기다
20		명 간식
21		명 초콜릿
22		동 펴다
23		동 입다
24		명 비옷
25		명 스니커즈 운동화
26		동 ~되어지다

정답 p.271

단어테스트 14

다음 한글 뜻을 보고 영어 표현을 적으세요. Name : Date : Score : /26

01		형 젊은	14		동 농담하다, 놀리다
02		동 떨다, 떨리다	15		동 보내다
03		동 생각하다	16		명 이메일
04		명 콘서트, 연주회	17		동 심다
05		동 낭비하다	18		동 충전하다
06		동 따라가다	19		명 배터리
07		동 ~하도록 만들다	20		명 장미
08		동 신경쓰다	21		명 바람
09		동 사과하다	22		동 불다
10		명 실수	23		동 내려받다
11		형 멍청한	24		명 파일
12		동 공상하다	25		동 지다
13		동 운동하다	26		동 울리다

정답 p.272

단어테스트 15

다음 한글 뜻을 보고 영어 표현을 적으세요. Name : Date : Score : /26

번호	답	뜻	번호	답	뜻
01		동 (악기를) 연주하다	14		동 건너다
02		명 기타	15		명 구름사다리
03		명 땅	16		명 시소
04		동 안다	17		동 걷다
05		명 카메라	18		동 운전하다
06		명 비밀	19		형 앞의
07		형 늦은	20		명 좌석
08		동 쇼핑하다	21		명 노래
09		명 쇼핑몰	22		명 머리카락
10		동 웃다	23		동 대답하다, (전화를) 받다
11		명 사촌	24		동 마시다
12		동 일하다	25		명 주스
13		명 미끄럼틀	26		명 사자

정답 p.272

단어테스트 16

다음 한글 뜻을 보고 영어 표현을 적으세요. Name : Date : Score : /26

번호	답	뜻	번호	답	뜻
01		명 아이들	14		명 달
02		명 그네	15		동 떠오르다
03		동 오르다	16		명 손
04		명 정글짐	17		명 숲
05		동 매달리다	18		형 어지러운
06		부 거꾸로	19		명 진행자
07		명 회전목마	20		동 돌리다
08		동 돌아가다, 회전하다	21		전 ~사이에
09		형 초록의	22		명 채소
10		명 불, 등	23		명 할머니, 할아버지
11		명 횡단보도	24		동 웃다
12		부 크게	25		명 라디오
13		동 닦다	26		명 뒷자석

정답 p.272

워크북 정답

Dictation Test **1**

01. He, was
02. You, were
03. was, sick
04. was, rainy
05. They, were
06. I, was
07. were, busy
08. Today, was
09. was, big
10. mother, was

Dictation Test **2**

01. I, was
02. was, old
03. was, easy
04. They, were
05. He, was
06. was
07. tree, was
08. We, were
09. It, was
10. was, school

Dictation Test **3**

01. was, not
02. was, not
03. Were, you
04. were, not
05. Was, test
06. Was, dad
07. were, not
08. Were, they
09. was, not
10. Was, he

Dictation Test **4**

01. Were, you
02. Was, sick
03. were, happy
04. was, not
05. were, late
06. Were, you
07. Was, fresh
08. was, not
09. Were, they
10. were, not

Dictation Test **5**

01. went
02. played
03. called
04. read
05. studied
06. saw
07. drank
08. stayed
09. wrote
10. laughed

Dictation Test **6**

01. watched
02. made
03. put
04. bought
05. looked
06. did
07. met
08. baked
09. ran
10. visited

Dictation Test **7**

01. didn't, sleep
02. Did, play
03. Did, break
04. did, not
05. didn't, sell
06. Did, make
07. Did, see
08. didn't, know
09. did, not
10. Did, go

Dictation Test **8**

01. Did, go
02. didn't, watch
03. Did, keep
04. didn't, bring
05. did, not
06. Did, have
07. didn't, drink
08. Did, wake
09. Did, study
10. did, not

Dictation Test **9**

01. talked, phone
02. Get, now
03. plays
04. are, not
05. heard
06. felt
07. had
08. takes
09. collected
10. sleeps

Dictation Test **10**

01. is, Sunday
02. have
03. broke, arm
04. saw
05. have
06. cut
07. went, bed
08. am, now
09. is, gold
10. wanted

Dictation Test **11**

01. not, going
02. Will, snow
03. be, back
04. going, to
05. Are, going
06. will, pass
07. going, to
08. will, not
09. will, start
10. not, going

Dictation Test **12**

01. will, play
02. am, going, to
03. Will, join
04. will, not
05. not, going
06. will, not
07. Are, going
08. will, move
09. are, going, to
10. Will

Dictation Test **13**

01. am, reading
02. is, not
03. Is, snowing
04. not, playing
05. is, not
06. is, chatting
07. is, looking
08. Are, doing
09. are, studying
10. is, sleeping

Dictation Test **14**

01. Is, having
02. Are, winning
03. are, going
04. am, not
05. is, cooking
06. is, planting
07. is, crying
08. are, opening
09. Is, doing
10. am, not

Dictation Test **15**

01. was, talking
02. were, playing
03. Was, taking
04. was, watching
05. not, sleeping
06. was, driving
07. Were, walking
08. Were, you
09. was, thinking
10. was, listening

Dictation Test **16**

01. was, blowing
02. was, singing
03. Were, shopping
04. not, sleeping
05. was, waiting
06. was, talking
07. was, waiting
08. were, playing
09. Was, cutting
10. were, swimming

단어테스트 1

01. lazy
02. surprised
03. classroom
04. ago
05. evening
06. hour
07. then
08. preschool student
09. elementary
10. now
11. playground
12. age
13. small
14. shy
15. crybaby
16. preschool
17. kid
18. older brother
19. busy
20. kind
21. nurse
22. housewife
23. team
24. America
25. from
26. bank

단어테스트 2

01. couch
02. near
03. library
04. China
05. last
06. vacation
07. fantastic
08. worried
09. really
10. strange
11. backpack
12. final
13. aunt
14. hospital
15. cheap
16. quiet
17. garden
18. tired
19. birthday
20. great
21. Friday
22. neighbor
23. dish
24. break
25. police officer
26. person

단어테스트 3

01. happy
02. yesterday
03. friend
04. student
05. bored
06. classroom
07. player
08. minute
09. ago
10. actress
11. rainy

12. glad
13. tall
14. healthy
15. cry
16. sick
17. hungry
18. problem
19. alike
20. different
21. same
22. cook
23. food
24. tasty
25. Internet cafe
26. know

단어테스트 4

01. late
02. cute
03. where
04. teachers' room
05. fault
06. how
07. delicious
08. interesting
09. twins
10. boring
11. smaller
12. big
13. with
14. clear
15. snowy
16. close
17. math
18. difficult
19. absent
20. stomachache
21. salad
22. fresh
23. easy
24. good
25. bike
26. old

단어테스트 5

01. skateboard
02. help
03. like
04. die
05. study
06. enjoy
07. stay
08. hard
09. take
10. eat
11. drink

12. get
13. hear
14. fall
15. feel
16. cut
17. put
18. hit
19. hurt
20. let
21. many
22. mouse
23. cake
24. goal
25. laugh
26. loudly

단어테스트 6

01. because
02. funny
03. call
04. scold
05. letter
06. apology
07. arm
08. much
09. tease
10. Saturday
11. later
12. worry
13. with
14. scissors
15. test paper
16. face
17. watch
18. comedy film
19. shoe
20. box
21. chess
22. favorite
23. Sunday
24. visit
25. fruit
26. city hall

단어테스트 7

01. sleep
02. well
03. these
04. homework
05. light
06. buy
07. popcorn
08. melt
09. talk
10. again
11. answer

12. understand
13. win
14. remember
15. lunch
16. get
17. call
18. nightmare
19. basketball
20. yet
21. ill
22. shine
23. dry
24. window
25. clean
26. exercise

단어테스트 8

01. push
02. button
03. street
04. bring
05. umbrella
06. soup
07. taste
08. raise
09. hand
10. family
11. pencil case
12. alarm
13. bed
14. wake up
15. textbook
16. store
17. sell
18. respect
19. notebook
20. arrive
21. early
22. write
23. secret
24. report card
25. happen
26. keep

단어테스트 9

01. fever
02. until
03. temper
04. rise
05. east
06. fall
07. autumn
08. stitch
09. save
10. yawn
11. swan

12. form
13. heart
14. shape
15. take
16. funny
17. sleepy
18. church
19. those
20. discover
21. October
22. mind
23. paint
24. together
25. upset
26. fun

단어테스트 10

01. late
02. search
03. catch
04. also
05. possible
06. close
07. cut
08. finger
09. break
10. truth
11. idea
12. regret
13. share
14. joy
15. fault
16. fail
17. subject
18. lonely
19. ghost
20. nightmare
21. collect
22. acorn
23. New Year's Day
24. soulmate
25. use
26. for

단어테스트 11

01. bite
02. leave
03. back
04. moment
05. step
06. happen
07. again
08. cost
09. finish
10. pool
11. hard

12. fail
13. math
14. test
15. worry
16. fine
17. lie
18. tonight
19. move
20. another
21. deliver
22. mail
23. around
24. hold
25. next
26. magic

단어테스트 12

01. music
02. recorder
03. xylophone
04. triangle
05. farewell party
06. soon
07. bite
08. stranger
09. careful
10. sure
11. pass
12. exam
13. picnic
14. wash
15. dish
16. forgive
17. listen to
18. ready
19. fight
20. better
21. commercial
22. afternoon
23. join
24. return
25. baseball
26. library

단어테스트 13

01. clean
02. block
03. wallet
04. lie
05. bother
06. outside
07. try
08. work
09. bring
10. toilet paper
11. ask

12. pour
13. bake
14. check
15. contact
16. list
17. wait
18. quiz
19. win
20. snack
21. chocolate
22. open
23. wear
24. raincoat
25. sneakers
26. get

단어테스트 14

01. wet
02. shake
03. think
04. concert
05. waste
06. follow
07. drive
08. care
09. apologize
10. mistake
11. stupid
12. daydream
13. exercise
14. kid
15. send
16. e-mail
17. plant
18. charge
19. battery
20. rose
21. wind
22. blow
23. download
24. file
25. lose
26. ring

단어테스트 15

01. play
02. guitar
03. ground
04. hug
05. camera
06. secret
07. late
08. shop
09. mall
10. smile
11. cousin
12. work
13. slide
14. cross
15. monkey bars
16. seesaw
17. walk
18. drive
19. front
20. seat
21. song
22. hair
23. answer
24. drink
25. juice
26. lion

단어테스트 16

01. kids
02. swing
03. climb
04. jungle gym
05. hang
06. upside down
07. merry-go-round
08. spin
09. green
10. light
11. crosswalk
12. loudly
13. brush
14. moon
15. rise
16. hand
17. forest
18. dizzy
19. host
20. roll
21. between
22. vegetable
23. grandparents
24. laugh
25. radio
26. back seat

정답은 뒷면에서 확인하세요.

Match and write.

알맞은 그림과 연결하고 단어를 쓰세요.

1. bike
2. kite
3. mice
4. knife

bike

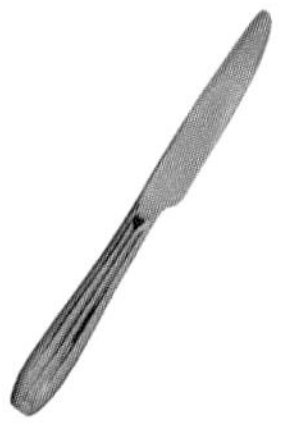

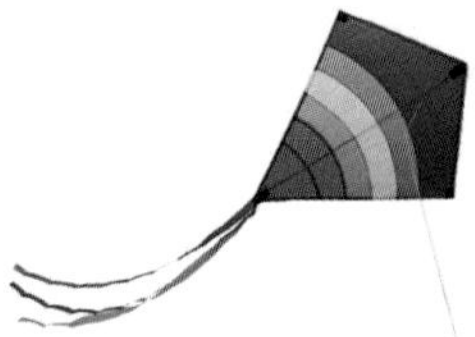

5. five
6. wipe
7. cake
8. bite

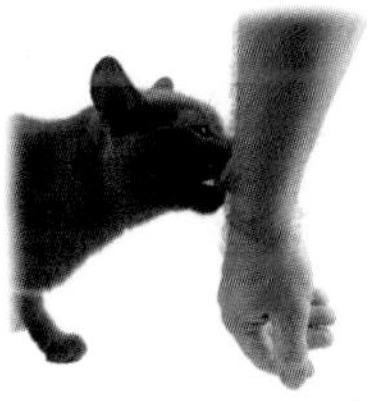

Match and write.

알맞은 그림과 연결하고 단어를 쓰세요.

1. bike 2. kite 3. mice 4. knife

mice

bike

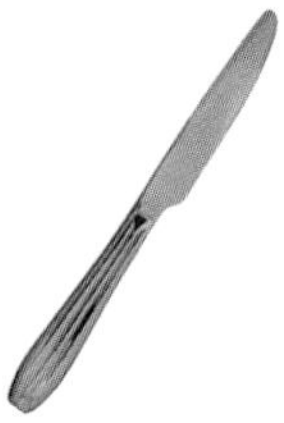

knife

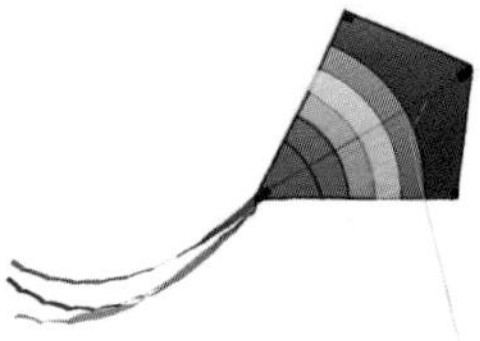

kite

5. five 6. wipe 7. cake 8. bite

cake

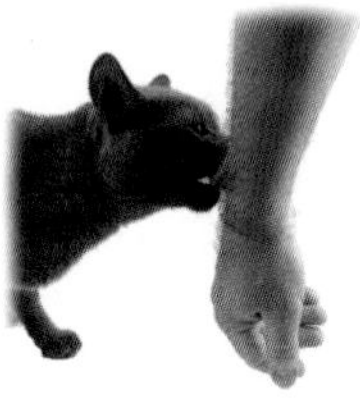

bite

five

wipe

초등영문법 3800제

정답과 해설

MOTHERTONGUE
마더텅출판사
since1999.4.1.

4
LEVEL

기초 2단계 과거시제 / 현재시제 / 미래시제 / 진행시제

영문법 판매 1위,
초등 시리즈 초등영문법 3800제 동영상 강의

초등영문법에 필요한 것만 모았습니다.
영어에 대한 고민이 있으시면 저희 마더텅과 함께 하면 달라집니다.

마더텅과 함께하는 단계별 레벨업 강의
1단계부터 8단계까지 단계별 체계적인 영문법 학습

친절한 Q&A 게시판
친절하고 자세한 Q&A 게시판에서 강의를 수강하다 생긴 모든 궁금증을 해결

오현진 선생님
초등영문법 3800제 level 1~4

어려운 영어를 쉬운 설명으로 쉽게 가보자!

- (현) 마더텅 고등영어 강사
- (현) 대치동 새움학원 대표고등강사
- (현) 강남구청 인터넷 수능 방송 강사
- (현) 수박씨닷컴 중등영어 대표강사 [수강생 강의만족도 100%]

최주영 선생님
초등영문법 3800제 level 5~8

영어, 고민하지 마시고 꽃길만 걷게 해드립니다!

- (현) 마더텅 고등영어 강사
- (현) 대치동 위자듀 재수종합 독해 강사
- (현) 전국 중고등학교 입시진로 강사
- (전) 글로벌 1st 고등 영어 전임 강사

강의 구성

※ 강의 수, 가격 등은 당사 사정에 따라 변경될 수 있습니다.

교재명	가격	강의 수	수강 기간
초등영문법 3800제 LEVEL 1	5,900원	30강	150일(무료 수강연장 1회)
초등영문법 3800제 LEVEL 2	5,900원	26강	150일(무료 수강연장 1회)
초등영문법 3800제 LEVEL 3	5,900원	30강	150일(무료 수강연장 1회)
초등영문법 3800제 LEVEL 4	5,900원	34강	150일(무료 수강연장 1회)
초등영문법 3800제 LEVEL 5	5,900원	22강	150일(무료 수강연장 1회)
초등영문법 3800제 LEVEL 6	5,900원	23강	150일(무료 수강연장 1회)
초등영문법 3800제 LEVEL 7	5,900원	22강	150일(무료 수강연장 1회)
초등영문법 3800제 LEVEL 8	5,900원	20강	150일(무료 수강연장 1회)
초등영문법 3800제 LEVEL 1~8	39,900원	207강	365일(무료 수강연장 1회)

초등영문법 3800제

정답과 해설

4

LEVEL

기초2단계

Chapter 01 be동사의 과거형

Unit 01 be동사의 과거형 (1)

Check and Write
▶ 본문 p.9

2. were 3. was 4. was 5. were

Unit 02 be동사의 과거형 (2)

Check and Write
▶ 본문 p.11

2. are 3. was 4. am 5. was

Practice 1
▶ 본문 p.12

A 2. was 3. was 4. were
5. were

B 1. was 2. was 3. were
4. were 5. was

C 1. were 2. were 3. were
4. was 5. was

D 1. was 2. was 3. was
4. were 5. were

Practice 2
▶ 본문 p.14

2. My T-shirt was clean
내 티셔츠는 깨끗했어.
3. My last vacation was fantastic
나의 지난 방학은 환상적이었어!
4. It was rainy
5. It was sunny
6. I was so shy
7. I was worried
8. That was really strange
그건 정말 이상했어.
9. My cat was in my backpack
나의 고양이는 내 배낭 안에 있었어.
10. He was a crybaby
그는 울보였다.
11. You were so cute
12. The final exam was easy
기말시험은 쉬웠어요.
13. It was an interesting day
그날은 재밌는 날이었어요.
14. I was so unhappy
난 정말 기분이 좋지 않았어!
15. My aunt was in the hospital
16. She was a nurse
그녀는 간호사였어.
17. It was really cheap
(값이) 정말 저렴했어.
18. You were a lovely baby
너는 사랑스러운 아기였어.
19. He was very quiet
그는 매우 조용했어.
20. The apple tree was in the garden
그 사과나무는 정원에 있었어.

Practice 3
▶ 본문 p.17

2. I was really tired
나는 정말 피곤했어.
3. Yesterday was my 9th birthday
어제는 나의 9번째 생일이었다.
4. Yesterday was a great day
어제는 멋진 날이었어!
5. My birthday was last Friday
내 생일은 지난 금요일이었어.
6. Sihu was my neighbor
7. They were my best friends
그들은 나의 가장 친한 친구들이었어.
8. Mina was the new girl at school
미나는 학교에 새로 온(전학 온) 여자애였다.
9. We were in the library
우리는 도서관에 있었어.
10. The dishes were broken
접시들이 깨져 있었어.
11. She was very shy
그녀는 매우 수줍어했다.
12. I was in the E-mart
나는 이마트에 있었어.
13. He was a police officer
그는 경찰관이었어.
14. You were cute
15. He was a brave person
그는 용감한 사람이었어.
17. My little brother was a preschool student last year
나의 남동생은 작년에 유치원생이었다.
18. Today was a hard day
오늘은 힘든 날이었다.
19. My cats were in my backpack
나의 고양이들은 내 배낭 안에 있었다.
20. They were at the amusement park
그들은 놀이공원에 있었다.

Let's Practice More!

SET 01
▶ 본문 p.20

02. was 03. were 04. was 05. were
06. was 07. were 08. were 09. was
10. were 11. were 12. was

SET 02
▶ 본문 p.21

02. was 03. was 04. were 05. was
06. were 07. was 08. were 09. was
10. was 11. were 12. were 13. was
14. were

SET 03
▶ 본문 p.22

02. was 03. ○ 04. were 05. were
06. ○ 07. were 08. were 09. was
10. ○ 11. was 12. ○ 13. was
14. ○

SET 04

▶ 본문 p.23

02. ~이었다　03. ~에 있었다　04. ~이었다　05. ~에 있었다
06. ~이었다　07. ~이었다　08. ~이었다　09. ~에 있었다
10. ~이었다　11. ~이었다　12. ~에 있었다　13. ~이었다
14. ~이었다

SET 05

▶ 본문 p.24

02. was　03. was　04. am　05. was
06. were　07. was　08. were　09. was
10. was　11. was　12. were

SET 06

▶ 본문 p.25

02. ○　03. ○　04. was　05. was
06. ○　07. is　08. was　09. was
10. were　11. ○　12. ○　13. was
14. was

SET 07

▶ 본문 p.26

02. They were best friends two years ago
그들은 2년 전에 단짝이었다.

03. My father was near my school two hours ago
나의 아버지는 2시간 전에 나의 학교 근처에 계셨다.

04. We were in an airport yesterday
우리는 어제 공항에 있었다.

05. My family and I were in China last year
나의 가족과 나는 작년에 중국에 있었다.

06. It was rainy yesterday evening
어제 저녁에 비가 왔어.

07. I was so shy yesterday
나 어제 너무 부끄러웠어.

08. I was so angry then
나는 그때 너무 화가 났었어!

09. My aunt was in the hospital last month
나의 이모는 지난달에 병원에 계셨어.

10. He was very quiet yesterday
그는 어제 매우 조용했어.

11. The apple tree was in the garden last year
그 사과나무는 작년에 정원에 있었어.

12. I was really tired yesterday
나는 어제 정말 피곤했어.

13. Jane was my neighbor four years ago
Jane은 4년 전에 나의 이웃이었어.

14. The dishes were broken two days ago
접시들이 이틀 전에 깨졌어.

15. They were at the amusement park an hour ago
그들은 한 시간 전에 놀이공원에 있었다.

16. He was a police officer three years ago
그는 3년 전에 경찰관이었어.

17. My little brother was a preschool student last year
나의 남동생은 작년에 유치원생이었다.

18. My cats were in my backpack yesterday morning
어제 아침 나의 고양이들은 내 배낭 안에 있었다.

19. She was very hungry two hours ago
그녀는 2시간 전에 매우 배가 고팠다.

20. We were at my grandparents' house the day before yesterday
우리는 그저께 조부모님 댁에 있었다.

SET 08

▶ 본문 p.28

02. was clean　03. were 10 years old
04. was kind　05. was from America
06. was a new kid in their class
07. were in the E-mart　08. were nurses
09. were really cheap　10. were in Jeju Island
11. was in the library　12. was in my backpack
13. was at the amusement park
14. was big for his age　15. was shy
16. was a crybaby　17. was very busy
18. were on the same soccer team
19. were best friends　20. were at the market

Unit 03 be동사 과거형의 부정문

Check and Write

▶ 본문 p.31

2. were not[weren't]
3. was not[wasn't]
4. were not[weren't]

Unit 04 be동사 과거형의 의문문

Check and Write

▶ 본문 p.33

2. Were they friends?
그들은 친구였니?

3. Was she glad?
그녀는 기뻐했니?

4. Were you bored?
너는 지루했니?

Practice 1

▶ 본문 p.34

A 2. Was　3. was, was　4. was, not
5. Is

B 1. Was　2. was, not[wasn't, sick]
3. was, not　4. was　5. was, not

C 1. Were　2. was　3. were, not
4. was　5. was　6. was, not

D 1. were　2. were, not　3. Were

Practice 2

▶ 본문 p.36

2. Was Junwoo in the classroom
준우는 교실에 있었니?

3. Where were you
너 어디에 있었어?

4. I was not late

5. Was Mr. Lee in the teachers' room
이 선생님이 교무실에 계셨니?

6. He was not in the teachers' room
그는 교무실에 계시지 않았어.

7. It was not my fault
그건 내 잘못이 아니었어!

8. How was your day
오늘 하루 어땠어?

9. Was it delicious
그것은 맛있었니?

10. The book was not interesting
그 책은 재미있지 않았어.

11. Was I cute
12. Were they twins
그들이 쌍둥이였니?
13. It was not boring
그건 지루하지 않았어.
14. Was he smaller
15. He was not big
16. I wasn't with you
나는 너와 함께 있지 않았어.
17. The sky was clear
18. It was not snowy
19. We were not in the same class
20. we were not close

Practice 3 ▶ 본문 p.39

2. They were not[weren't] close at first
그들은 처음엔 친하지 않았어.
3. Was your cat in your house
너의 고양이는 너의 집에 있었니?
4. My cat was not[wasn't] in my house
내 고양이는 우리 집에 없었어.
5. It was with your dog
그것은 너의 개와 함께 있었어.
6. My dog was not[wasn't] at home
나의 개는 집에 없었어.
7. Were you in the same class
8. I was not[wasn't] in the same class
9. I was not[wasn't] good at math
나는 수학을 잘하지 못했어.
10. Was the English test difficult
영어 시험이 어려웠니?
11. Were you best friends
12. We were not[weren't] best friends, we are[we're] (best friends)
13. Were you absent from school
14. The salad was not[wasn't] fresh
샐러드가 신선하지 않았어.
15. Was it my fault 그게 내 잘못이었니?
16. The math test was not[wasn't] easy
수학 시험은 쉽지 않았어.
17. Were they good at English
그들은 영어를 잘했니?
18. Was he a crybaby
그는 울보였어?
19. Was your bike old
너의 자전거는 낡았었니?
20. My bike was not[wasn't] too small

Let's Practice More!

SET 01 ▶ 본문 p.41

02. ×	03. ×	04. ×	05. ○
06. ×	07. ×	08. ○	09. ○
10. ○	11. ×	12. ×	

SET 02 ▶ 본문 p.42

02. was not	03. was not	04. was not
05. were not	06. was not	07. were not
08. was not	09. was not	10. were not
11. were not	12. was not	13. were not
14. was not		

SET 03 ▶ 본문 p.43

02. ○	03. wasn't	04. wasn't
05. wasn't	06. weren't	07. wasn't
08. wasn't	09. ○	10. ○
11. ○	12. ○	13. weren't
14. ○		

SET 04 ▶ 본문 p.44

02. weren't	03. wasn't	04. weren't	05. wasn't
06. weren't	07. wasn't	08. wasn't	09. weren't
10. weren't	11. wasn't	12. wasn't	

SET 05 ▶ 본문 p.45

02. Was	03. Was	04. Were	05. Were
06. Was	07. Were	08. Was	09. Was
10. Was	11. Were	12. Was	13. Was
14. Were			

SET 06 ▶ 본문 p.46

02. she was, she wasn't	03. they were, they weren't
04. I was, I wasn't	05. you were, you weren't
06. he was, he wasn't	07. she was, she wasn't
08. it was, it wasn't	09. it was, it wasn't
10. he was, he wasn't	11. it was, it wasn't
12. she was, she wasn't	13. she was, she wasn't
14. we were, we weren't	

SET 07 ▶ 본문 p.48

02. He was not[wasn't] hungry
그는 배고프지 않았어.
03. My mom was not[wasn't] a housewife
우리 엄마는 전업주부가 아니셨어.
04. Were they healthy
그들은 건강했니?
05. He was not[wasn't] sick
그는 아프지 않았어.
06. Mom was not[wasn't] at home
엄마가 집에 안 계셨어.
07. Were your dreams the same, too
너희들의 꿈도 똑같았니?
08. Was she a cook
그녀는 요리사였니?
09. You were not[weren't] in an Internet cafe
너는 피시방에 없었어.
10. Was I cute when I was young
내가 어렸을 때 나는 귀여웠어요?
11. Was the sky clear last year
작년에 하늘은 맑았니?
12. Was Junwoo in the classroom
준우는 교실에 있었니?
13. Was Mr. Lee in the teachers' room
이 선생님이 교무실에 계셨니?
14. Was it delicious
그것은 맛있었니?
15. He was not[wasn't] big last year
그는 작년에는 (덩치가) 크지 않았다.

16. I was not[wasn't] with you
나는 너와 함께 있지 않았어.

17. It was not[wasn't] snowy yesterday
어제는 눈이 오지 않았어.

18. He was not[wasn't] lazy
그는 게으르지 않았어.

19. Were my cats in my house
내 고양이들은 우리 집에 있었니?

20. Were you with your dog
너는 너의 강아지와 함께 있었니?

SET 08 ▶ 본문 p.50

02. What, was	03. Were	04. was, not
05. Where, were	06. Was	07. Was
08. How, was	09. was, not	10. Were
11. was, not	12. Was	13. was, not
14. was, not	15. was, not	16. was, not
17. Was	18. was, not	19. Was
20. were, not		

Chapter 02 일반동사의 과거형

Unit 01 일반동사의 과거형(규칙변화)

Check and Write
▶ 본문 p.55

2. looked 3. studied 4. liked

Unit 02 일반동사의 과거형(불규칙변화)

Check and Write
▶ 본문 p.57

2. wrote 3. put 4. made

Practice 1
▶ 본문 p.58

A	2. got	3. won	4. gave
B	1. read	2. laughed	3. called
	4. scolded	5. wrote	6. hurt
C	1. knew	2. heard	3. felt
	4. went	5. had	
D	1. told	2. ran	3. played
	4. got	5. wanted	

Practice 2
▶ 본문 p.60

2. I got up late
난 늦게 일어났어.
3. I arrived home early
4. I cut the paper
5. My mom saw my test paper
우리 엄마는 내 시험지를 보셨다.
6. I saw her angry face
나는 그녀의 화난 얼굴을 보았다.
7. we went to a movie
8. We watched a comedy film
우리는 코미디 영화를 보았다.
9. I had a lot of dreams
10. I made a time capsule
11. We played chess
우린 체스를 했어.
12. She drank a glass of water
그녀는 물 한 잔을 마셨다.
13. I read a book
14. I believed them
나는 그들을 믿었어.
15. Charlie stayed at home
16. I put my favorite toy

Practice 3
▶ 본문 p.62

2. I felt good
나는 기분이 좋았다.
3. I visited my uncle
4. I got up at 9 o'clock
나는 9시에 일어났어.
5. The class started early
수업은 일찍 시작했다.
6. I met him on Friday
나는 금요일에 그를 만났다.
7. She ate fruit
그녀는 과일을 먹었다.
8. She took care of her little brother
그녀는 그녀의 남동생을 돌봤다.
9. We went to city hall
10. He saw "Pororo"
11. They took a picture
그들은 사진을 찍었다.
12. Leaves fell from the tree
나뭇잎들이 나무에서 떨어졌다.
13. He fell asleep
그는 잠이 들었다.
14. She told a lie
그녀는 거짓말을 했다.
15. She met her friends
그녀는 그녀의 친구들을 만났다.
16. Her father wrote a letter
그녀의 아버지는 편지를 썼다.
17. He hit a home run
그는 홈런을 쳤다.
18. She answered my question
그녀는 나의 질문에 대답했다.
19. He bought a car
20. He cried all day long
그는 하루 종일 울었다.

Let's Practice More!

SET 01 ▶ 본문 p.64

02. ○	03. ×	04. ○	05. ×
06. ○	07. ○	08. ○	09. ○
10. ×	11. ○	12. ×	

SET 02

▶ 본문 p.65

02. played	03. helped	04. stayed
05. visited	06. lived	07. called
08. scolded	09. wanted	10. arrived
11. watched	12. believed	13. started
14. cried		

SET 03

▶ 본문 p.66

02. cried	03. baked	04. lived
05. laughed	06. played	07. helped
08. stayed	09. visited	10. watched
11. called	12. scolded	13. wanted
14. arrived		

SET 04

▶ 본문 p.67

02. ○	03. gave	04. ○	05. wrote
06. hurt	07. ○	08. ○	09. met
10. drank	11. took	12. ○	

SET 05

▶ 본문 p.68

02. got	03. won	04. felt	05. went
06. told	07. ran	08. did	09. cut
10. saw	11. drank	12. had	13. made
14. read			

SET 06

▶ 본문 p.69

02. went	03. watched	04. fell	05. bought
06. played	07. hurt	08. told	09. got
10. got	11. wrote	12. heard	13. went
14. did			

SET 07

▶ 본문 p.70

02. We played chess
우린 체스를 했어.

03. We win the game
우리는 그 경기를 이긴다.

04. Nayeon knew Mina's secret
나연이는 미나의 비밀을 알았다.

05. Junwoo felt sorry
준우는 미안함을 느꼈다.

06. I run to Sihu's house
나는 시후의 집으로 달려간다.

07. She gets a phone call
그녀는 전화를 받는다.

08. I got up late
난 늦게 일어났어.

09. I cut the paper with scissors
나는 가위로 종이를 잘랐다.

10. My mom saw my test paper
우리 엄마는 내 시험지를 보셨다.

11. He watches a comedy film
그는 코미디 영화를 본다.

12. They put their favorite toys in the box
그들은 그들이 가장 좋아하는 장난감들을 그 상자에 넣는다.

13. Jane went to school
Jane은 학교에 갔다.

14. My younger brother felt good
내 남동생은 기분이 좋았다.

15. Janet and I get up at 9 o'clock
Janet과 나는 9시에 일어나.

16. They took a picture
그들은 사진을 찍었다.

17. She told a lie
그녀는 거짓말을 했다.

18. Her father wrote a letter
그녀의 아버지는 편지를 썼다.

19. He hits a home run
그는 홈런을 친다.

20. She drank a glass of water
그녀는 물 한 잔을 마셨다.

SET 08

▶ 본문 p.72

02. saw	03. went	04. played	05. had
06. made	07. read	08. put	09. felt
10. got	11. met	12. ate	13. lived
14. fell	15. told	16. wrote	17. hit
18. bought	19. drank	20. took	

Unit 03 일반동사 과거형의 부정문

Check and Write

▶ 본문 p.75

2. didn't buy　3. didn't melt　4. didn't talk

Unit 04 일반동사 과거형의 의문문

Check and Write

▶ 본문 p.77

2. Did they remember you
그들은 너를 기억했니?

3. Did she have lunch
그녀는 점심을 먹었니?

4. Did you get the call
너는 전화를 받았니?

Practice 1

▶ 본문 p.78

A	2. didn't, sleep	3. didn't, stop	4. Did, have
	5. didn't, have	6. didn't, get	
B	1. Did, play	2. didn't	3. played
	4. Did, win	5. did	6. got
	7. Did	8. didn't	
C	1. Did, answer	2. didn't	3. Did, come
	4. didn't	5. Did, go	6. did

Practice 2

▶ 본문 p.80

2. The playground didn't dry
운동장이 마르지 않았어.

3. we didn't play soccer

4. Did you break the window
네가 창문을 깼니?

5. didn't clean the classroom

6. I didn't talk to him
나는 그에게 말을 건네지 않았어.

7. We didn't exercise
우리는 운동을 하지 않았어.

8. Did you make that pizza
네가 그 피자를 만들었니?

9. Did you push the button

너가 버튼을 눌렀니?

10. Did you see Sihu
11. I didn't see him
12. Did you watch that movie
너 그 영화 봤니?
13. I didn't watch that movie
나는 그 영화를 보지 않았어.
14. Did you have lunch
너 점심 먹었니?
15. He didn't bring his umbrella
그는 그의 우산을 갖고 오지 않았어.
16. The soup didn't taste good
그 수프는 맛이 좋지 않았어.
17. Did he raise his hand
그는 손을 들었니?
18. We didn't know her name
우리는 그녀의 이름을 몰랐어.
19. She didn't have a family
그녀는 가족이 없었어.
20. Did you see my pencil case
너 내 필통 봤니?

Practice 3

▶ 본문 p.82

2. Did I wake you up
내가 너희들을 깨웠니?
3. Did you go to bed late last night
너 어젯밤에 늦게 잤니?
4. Mom did not[didn't] wake me up
엄마는 나를 깨우지 않으셨어.
5. The school bus did not[didn't] come in time
학교 버스는 제 시간에 오지 않았어.
6. I did not[didn't] bring my textbook
나는 내 교과서를 가져오지 않았어.
7. Did you do your homework
너 숙제 했어?
8. I did not[didn't] want to study
나는 공부하고 싶지 않았어.
9. The store did not[didn't] sell fruit
그 가게는 과일을 팔지 않았어.
10. I did not[didn't] bring my notebook
나는 내 노트를 가져오지 않았어.
11. Did he arrive early
그는 일찍 도착했니?
12. Did you write a letter of apology
너 반성문 썼니?
13. Did they study hard
그들은 공부를 열심히 했니?
14. Mom did not[didn't] see my report card
엄마는 내 성적표를 보지 않으셨어.
15. Did it happen at night
그것은 밤에 일어났니?
16. Did he keep the secret
그는 비밀을 지켰니?
17. They did not[didn't] fight
그들은 싸우지 않았어.
18. Did you respect him
너는 그를 존경했니?
19. Did you get your report card
너 네 성적표 받았니?
20. He did not[didn't] drink milk
그는 우유를 마시지 않았어.

Let's Practice More!

SET 01

▶ 본문 p.85

02. ○	03. have	04. ○	05. win
06. ○	07. get	08. come	09. shine
10. ○	11. clean	12. ○	

SET 02

▶ 본문 p.86

02. watch	03. taste	04. know	05. have
06. ring	07. wake	08. come	09. sell
10. bring	11. see	12. fight	13. drink
14. stop			

SET 03

▶ 본문 p.87

02. didn't	03. ○	04. didn't	05. ○
06. didn't	07. ○	08. didn't	09. didn't
10. ○	11. ○	12. ○	13. ○
14. didn't			

SET 04

▶ 본문 p.88

02. like	03. Did	04. do	05. Did
06. Did	07. go	08. break	09. make
10. Did	11. see	12. watch	13. Did
14. Did			

SET 05

▶ 본문 p.89

02. Did	03. do	04. Did
05. write	06. Did	07. Did
08. Did	09. see	10. Did
11. have	12. watch[see]	13. Did
14. do[wash]		

SET 06

▶ 본문 p.90

02. he did, he didn't	03. she did, she didn't
04. I did, I didn't	05. they did, they didn't
06. I did, I didn't	07. we did, we didn't
08. they did, they didn't	09. he did, he didn't
10. we did, we didn't	11. you did, you didn't
12. I did, I didn't	

SET 07

▶ 본문 p.92

02. Did the store sell fruit
그 가게는 과일을 팔았니?
03. He did not[didn't] have a nightmare
그는 악몽을 꾸지 않았어.
04. We did not[didn't] play basketball
우리는 농구를 하지 않았어요.
05. We did not[didn't] play soccer
우린 축구를 하지 않았어요.
06. Did Sihu get a goal
시후가 골을 넣었니?
07. I did not[didn't] get the call
나는 전화를 못 받았어.
08. Did she come to school
그녀가 학교에 왔니?

09. Did Junwoo clean the classroom
준우는 교실 청소를 했니?

10. I did not[didn't] talk to him
나는 그에게 말을 건네지 않았어.

11. We did not[didn't] exercise
우리는 운동을 하지 않았어.

12. Did they see him
그들은 그를 봤니?

13. Did he bring his umbrella
그는 그의 우산을 갖고 왔니?

14. I did not[didn't] watch that movie
나는 그 영화를 보지 않았어.

15. Did the soup taste good
그 수프는 맛이 좋았니?

16. We did not[didn't] know her name
우리는 그녀의 이름을 몰랐어.

17. Did the alarm ring
알람이 울렸니?

18. Mom did not[didn't] wake me up
엄마는 나를 깨우지 않으셨어.

19. I did not[didn't] bring my textbook
나는 내 교과서를 가져오지 않았어.

20. I did not[didn't] want to study
나는 공부하고 싶지 않았어.

SET 08 ▶ 본문 p.94

02. Did, you	03. Did, do	04. did, not
05. Did, write	06. Did, study	07. didn't
08. Did, you	09. did, not	10. Did, keep
11. didn't	12. didn't	13. Did, get
14. didn't	15. Did, him	16. Did, drink
17. didn't	18. didn't	19. Did
20. didn't		

Chapter 01~02 실전테스트 ▶ 본문 p.96

01. (1) was (2) weren't[were not]
(3) wasn't[was not]

02. ③	03. ①	04. ④
05. ④	06. ②	07. ②
08. ①	09. ④	10. ①
11. ②	12. ②	13. ③

14. We didn't[did not] eat pizza.
우리는 피자를 먹지 않았다.

15. She didn't[did not] wake up early this morning.
그녀는 오늘 아침에 일찍 일어나지 않았다.

16. I didn't[did not] do my homework.
나는 내 숙제를 하지 않았다.

17. They aren't kind to my kids.
그들은 내 아이들에게 친절하지 않다.

18. I didn't wash the dishes.
나는 설거지를 하지 않았다.

19. He wasn't a scientist.
그는 과학자가 아니었다.

20. You weren't his friend.
너는 그의 친구가 아니었다.

21. was	22. are
23. were	24. is
25. she, wasn't	26. it[he/she], didn't
27. Did, he, did	28. they, weren't

29. We watched a movie yesterday.
우리는 어제 영화를 보았다.

30. She went to Japan last week.
그녀는 지난 주에 일본에 갔다.

Chapter 03 현재시제 / 과거시제

Unit 01 현재시제

Check and Write ▶ 본문 p.103

2. form 3. take 4. is

Unit 02 과거시제

Check and Write ▶ 본문 p.105

2. played 3. was 4. had

Practice 1 ▶ 본문 p.106

A	2. went	3. did	4. played
	5. was	6. had	
B	1. Get	2. am	3. is
	4. want	5. did	6. went
	7. did	8. talked	
C	1. did	2. is	3. is
	4. play	5. is	

Practice 2 ▶ 본문 p.108

2. The sun rises in the east
태양은 동쪽에서 떠오른다.

3. He laughed at me
그가 나를 비웃었어.

4. They were close
그들은 친했었잖아.

5. My mother is not inside the house
6. He went to bed early
7. It is quiet
8. Sihu cut his finger
시후는 그의 손가락을 베였어.

9. He heard the news
10. She broke her foot
그녀는 발이 부러졌어.

11. They didn't know the truth
그들은 진실을 몰랐어.

12. It is not a good idea
그건 좋은 생각이 아니야.
13. I may regret it
나는 그것을 후회할지도 몰라.
14. I can understand you
15. I always share joy
16. I fell down on the playground
난 운동장에서 넘어졌어.
17. It was not your fault
그건 너의 잘못이 아니었어.
18. I was not with you
난 너와 함께 있지 않았어.
19. I failed some subjects
난 몇몇 과목에서 낙제했어.
20. He felt lonely

Practice 3

▶ 본문 p.111

2. It was a big doll
그것은 커다란 인형이었어.
3. We go to school
우리는 학교에 가.
4. had a nightmare
5. he sleeps in his parents' room
6. It was not[wasn't] a ghost
그건 귀신이 아니었어.
7. I collected many acorns
나 도토리 많이 모았어!
8. Today is Dana's birthday
오늘은 다나의 생일이야.
9. Yesterday was New Year's Day
어제는 새해 첫날이었어.
10. I felt lonely
11. We were best friends once
12. We are soulmates
13. I used my smartphone
14. Mom was upset
15. I play video games
16. He lived on the farm
17. He knocked on the door
그는 문을 두드렸어.
18. They ate some pizza
19. We arrived early
20. She usually takes the bus
그녀는 보통 버스를 타.

Let's Practice More!

SET 01

▶ 본문 p.114

02. met	03. went	04. aren't[are not]
05. ate	06. cut	07. plays
08. heard	09. broke	10. fell
11. sleeps	12. did	

SET 02

▶ 본문 p.115

02. 현재의 상태	03. 불변의 진리	04. 현재의 습관
05. 현재의 상태	06. 격언	07. 현재의 상태
08. 현재의 습관	09. 불변의 진리	10. 현재의 상태
11. 현재의 습관	12. 현재의 상태	13. 속담
14. 현재의 상태		

SET 03

▶ 본문 p.116

02. 과거의 사실	03. 과거의 사실	04. 과거의 사실
05. 현재의 습관	06. 역사적 사실	07. 과거의 사실
08. 과거의 사실	09. 과거의 사실	10. 현재의 습관
11. 역사적 사실	12. 과거의 사실	13. 과거의 사실
14. 역사적 사실		

SET 04

▶ 본문 p.117

02. ○	03. went	04. ○
05. had	06. was	07. broke
08. ○	09. is	10. ○
11. arrived	12. are	

SET 05

▶ 본문 p.118

02. laughed	03. is	04. used
05. cut	06. takes	07. heard
08. collected	09. am	10. ate
11. failed	12. rises	13. was
14. knocked		

SET 06

▶ 본문 p.119

02. is	03. ○	04. ate
05. felt	06. takes	07. ○
08. share	09. ○	10. am
11. were	12. ○	13. lived
14. is		

SET 07

▶ 본문 p.120

02. She broke her arm
그녀는 팔이 부러졌어.
03. She wants a bicycle for her birthday
그녀는 그녀의 생일 선물로 자전거를 원해.
04. He saw a ghost
그는 귀신을 봤어.
05. It is a big doll
그것은 커다란 인형이야.
06. I collected many coins
나는 동전을 많이 모았어!
07. It is not a ghost
그건 귀신이 아니야.
08. He slept in his parents' room
그는 그의 부모님 방에서 잤어.
09. He lived on the farm
그는 농장에 살았어.
10. We are best friends
우리는 가장 친한 친구야.
11. I used your headphones
나는 너의 헤드폰을 사용했어.
12. Mom was upset about it
엄마는 그것 때문에 속상해 하셨어.
13. They eat some pizza
그들은 피자를 먹어.
14. I felt sad
나는 슬펐다.
15. What did you do there
거기서 뭘 했는데?
16. I go to bed at 1:00 a.m
저는 새벽 한 시에 자요.

17. Why did you stay up late
너 왜 늦게까지 깨어있었니?

18. He knocked on the door
그는 문을 두드렸어.

19. My mother is not inside the house
나의 엄마는 집 안에 없어요.

20. They don't know the truth
그들은 진실을 몰라.

SET 08 ▶ 본문 p.122

02. sleeps 03. did 04. went
05. played 06. Was 07. had
08. broke 09. was 10. felt
11. are 12. painted 13. fell
14. play 15. did 16. arrived
17. saves 18. were 19. got
20. wants

Chapter 04 미래시제

Unit 01 미래시제 will

Check and Write ▶ 본문 p.127

2. will snow 3. will go 4. will study

Unit 02 미래시제 be going to

Check and Write ▶ 본문 p.129

2. is going to sleep
3. are going to watch
4. am going to study

Practice 1 ▶ 본문 p.130

A 2. are, going, to
B 1. am, going, to, deliver 2. will, arrive
3. will, arrive 4. will, be
5. Will, be 6. will, deliver
C 1. will, hold 2. are, going, to, dance
3. is, going, to, do 4. will, play
5. will, play 6. will, play
7. is, going, to, play
D 1. will, move 2. will, hold
3. will, not, go

Practice 2 ▶ 본문 p.133

2. When will we meet
우리 언제 만날 거야?
3. We will watch a movie
4. Will you come
5. My mom won't let me
우리 엄마는 허락하지 않으실 거야.
6. It will be interesting
재미있을 텐데.
7. The dog is not going to bite
그 개는 물지 않을 거야.
8. I'll be careful
조심할게요.
9. It will snow
10. I won't tell you
나는 너에게 말해주지 않을 거야.
11. you will pass the exam
12. She is going to watch TV
13. We will go on a picnic
14. I am going to read a book
15. They are going to have lunch
16. He will wash the dishes
17. She will forgive me
그녀는 나를 용서해 줄 거야.
18. Will you listen to some music
너는 음악을 좀 들을 거니?
19. it will rain
20. The class will start

Practice 3 ▶ 본문 p.136

2. I will[I'll] be right back
전 금방 돌아올 거예요.
3. We will[We'll] hold a party for her
우리는 그녀를 위해 파티를 열 것이다.
4. Will you come
너 올 거니?
5. I will not[I'll not/I won't] go to the party
나는 파티에 가지 않을 거야.
6. Tomorrow will be better
내일은 더 나을 것이다.
7. We will[We'll] be right back
8. We will[We'll] play "League of Legends"
9. Will you join us
너도 우리와 함께 할래?
10. I will[I'll] return this book
12. I am[I'm] going to go to the library
나는 도서관에 갈 거야.
13. You are[You're] going to enjoy the game
14. I am[I'm] going to deliver your parcel
15. Are you going to stay at home
당신은 집에 계실 건가요?
16. I am[I'm] going to be at school
17. We are[We're] going to go to a concert
18. I am[I'm] going to learn English
나는 영어를 배울 거야.
19. The final exam is going to be held
20. is going to ride a bicycle

Let's Practice More!

SET 01
▶ 본문 p.138

02. arrive 03. be 04. be 05. play
06. play 07. move 08. meet 09. watch
10. be 11. be 12. snow

SET 02
▶ 본문 p.139

02. are 03. are 04. is 05. play
06. is 07. is 08. bite 09. is
10. going 11. are 12. be 13. am
14. deliver

SET 03
▶ 본문 p.140

02. study 03. deliver 04. ○ 05. ○
06. ○ 07. ○ 08. going 09. going
10. be 11. join 12. ○ 13. is
14. is

SET 04
▶ 본문 p.141

02. Will it snow tomorrow
내일은 눈이 올까?
03. You will not[won't] pass the exam
너는 시험에 통과하지 못할 거야.
04. We will not[won't] go on a picnic this Saturday
우리는 이번 토요일에 소풍을 가지 않을 거야.
05. Will he wash the dishes
그가 설거지를 할까?
06. Will she forgive me
그녀가 나를 용서해줄까?
07. Will you listen to some music
너는 음악을 좀 들을거니?
08. Will anyone be there tomorrow
내일은 그곳에 누군가 계신가요?
09. Will you join us
너도 우리와 함께 할래?
10. Dinner will not[won't] be ready
저녁식사는 준비되지 않을 거야.
11. Will you come
너 올거니?
12. We will not[won't] play games this afternoon
우리는 오늘 오후에 게임을 하지 않을거야.

SET 05
▶ 본문 p.142

02. She is not[She's not/She isn't] going to watch TV after dinner
그녀는 저녁식사 후에 TV를 보지 않을 거야.
03. I am[I'm] not going to go to the library
나는 도서관에 가지 않을 거야.
04. Are they going to have lunch together
그들이 함께 점심을 먹을까?
05. I am[I'm] not going to deliver your parcel today
저는 오늘 당신의 택배를 배달하지 않을 것입니다.
06. Are they going to stay at home
그들이 집에 있을까?
07. He is not[He's not/He isn't] going to be at school
그는 학교에 있지 않을 거예요.
08. I am[I'm] not going to learn English
나는 영어를 배우지 않을 거야.
09. Is the final exam going to be held tomorrow
기말고사가 내일 실시될까?
10. Is Sihu going to ride a bicycle
시후가 자전거를 탈까?
11. She is not[She's not/She isn't] going to learn Japanese
그녀는 일본어를 배우지 않을 거야.
12. I am[I'm] not going to read a book this weekend
나는 이번 주말에 책을 읽지 않을 거야.
13. Are you going to enjoy the game
너는 게임을 즐길거니?
14. Is the baseball game going to be fun
그 야구 경기가 재미있을까?

SET 06
▶ 본문 p.144

02. Dinner will[is going to] be ready
저녁식사는 준비될 거야.
03. Sihu will[is going to] ride a bicycle
시후는 자전거를 탈 거야.
04. I will[am going to] study at home
나는 집에서 공부할 거야.
05. We will[are going to] hold a school talent show
우리는 학예회를 개최할 것이다.
06. I will[am going to] deliver a piece of registered mail soon
제가 곧 등기우편 한 통을 배달할 거예요.
07. Jinwoo will[is going to] do a magic show
진우는 마술쇼를 할 것이다.
08. Suho and his friends will[are going to] play music
수호와 그의 친구들은 음악을 연주할 것이다.
09. You will[are going to] pass the exam
너는 시험에 통과할 거야.
10. My mom will not[is not going to] let me
우리 엄마는 허락하지 않으실 거야.
11. It will[is going to] be interesting
재미있을 텐데.
12. The dog will not[is not going to] bite
그 개는 물지 않을 거야.
13. We will[are going to] watch a movie
우리는 영화 볼 거야.
14. He will[is going to] wash the dishes
그는 설거지를 할 거야.

SET 07
▶ 본문 p.146

02. Is he going to sleep
그가 잠을 잘 거니?
03. The baseball game is not[isn't] going to be fun
그 야구 경기는 재미있지 않을 거야.
04. I am[I'm] not going to go to the library
나는 도서관에 가지 않을 거야.
05. You are not[You're not/You aren't] going to enjoy the game
너는 게임을 즐기지 않을 거야.
06. I am[I'm] not going to learn English
나는 영어를 배우지 않을 거야.
07. They are not[They're not/They aren't] going to be right back
그들은 금방 돌아오지 않을 거야.
08. Is tomorrow going to be better

내일은 더 나을까?

09. She is not[She's not/She isn't] going to go to the party
그녀는 파티에 가지 않을 거야.

10. Is the class going to start at nine o'clock
수업이 9시에 시작할까?

11. We are not[We're not/We aren't] going to go on a picnic this Saturday
우리는 이번 토요일에 소풍을 가지 않을 거야.

12. Are you going to come with us
너도 우리랑 같이 갈래?

13. It is not[It's not/It isn't] going to snow tomorrow
내일은 눈이 오지 않을 거야.

14. Is Jane going to tell you
Jane이 너에게 말해줄까?

15. Is Taeyeon going to move to another school
태연이가 다른 학교로 전학을 갈 거니?

16. It is not[It's not/It isn't] going to rain
비가 오지 않을 거야.

17. Is Jinwoo going to do a magic show
진우가 마술쇼를 할까?

18. I am[I'm] not going to deliver a piece of registered mail
저는 등기우편 한 통을 배달하지 않을 것입니다.

19. Is anyone going to be there tomorrow
내일은 거기 누군가 계신가요?

20. We are not[We're not/We aren't] going to hold a school talent show
우리는 학예회를 개최하지 않을 것입니다.

SET 08 ▶ 본문 p.148

02. They will[They'll] stay at home
그들은 집에 있을 것입니다.

03. Mina and Sihu will play the recorder
미나와 시후는 리코더를 연주할 것이다.

04. Some of the students will not[won't] have a farewell party
몇몇 학생들은 송별회를 하지 않을 것이다.

05. I am[I'm] not going to go to the party
나는 파티에 가지 않을 것이다.

06. We will[We'll] watch a movie
우리 영화 볼 거야.

07. I will[I'll] be careful
조심할게요.

08. She will[She'll] forgive me
그녀는 나를 용서해 줄 거야.

09. I am[I'm] going to be at school
저는 학교에 있을 거예요.

10. I think it will[it'll] rain
내 생각엔 비가 올 것 같아.

11. The class is going to start at nine o'clock
수업은 9시에 시작할 거야.

12. Dinner is going to be ready
저녁 식사가 준비될 거야.

13. We will[We'll] hold a party for her
우리는 그녀를 위해 파티를 열 것이다.

14. We will[We'll] be right back
저희는 곧 돌아오겠습니다.

15. We will not[won't] play games
우리는 게임을 하지 않을 것이다.

16. I am[I'm] going to return this book
난 이 책을 반납할 거야.

17. I will[I'll] deliver it
제가 그것을 배달할게요.

18. I think I will[I'll] arrive
도착할 거 같아요.

19. Sihu is going to ride a bicycle
시후는 자전거를 탈 거야.

20. Dana and I are going to play the xylophone
다나와 나는 실로폰을 연주할 것이다.

Chapter 05 현재진행시제

Unit 01 현재진행시제

Check and Write ▶ 본문 p.153

2. They are lying on the beach
그들은 해변에 누워 있어.

3. You are taking a shower
너는 샤워를 하고 있어.

4. I am listening to music
나는 음악을 듣고 있어.

Unit 02 현재진행시제의 부정문과 의문문

Check and Write ▶ 본문 p.155

2. I am not[I'm not] playing
나는 놀고 있지 않아.

3. The dog is not[isn't] playing with a ball
그 개는 공을 가지고 놀고 있지 않아.

4. Are you swimming
너 수영하고 있니?

Practice 1 ▶ 본문 p.156

A 2. am, trying 3. is, not, working

B 1. am, watching 2. am, asking 3. am, coming

C 1. Is, raining 2. is, pouring 3. is, doing 4. is, watching 5. are, making 6. am, baking

D 1. am, checking 2. am, waiting

E 1. am, not, studying 2. am, playing 3. am, playing 4. are, winning

Practice 2
▶ 본문 p.159

2. We are having chocolate ice cream
우리는 초콜릿 아이스크림을 먹고 있어.
3. I am coming
4. It is raining
5. People are opening their umbrellas
사람들은 우산을 펼치고 있다.
6. I am wearing my raincoat
나는 비옷을 입고 있다.
7. My sneakers are getting wet
내 운동화가 젖고 있다.
8. I am shaking
9. I am thinking
난 생각하는 중이야.
10. We are going to a concert
우리는 콘서트에 가는 중이야.
11. I am not following
12. You are driving me crazy
네가 나를 미치게 하고 있어(너 때문에 미치겠다)!
13. I am crying
14. I am calling
15. Are you saying
16. I am daydreaming
나는 공상 중이야.
17. Are they exercising
그들은 운동하고 있니?
18. I am not kidding
나 농담하고 있는 거 아니야.
19. They are having a good time
그들은 좋은 시간을 보내고 있어.
20. He is not exercising
그는 운동하고 있지 않아.

Practice 3
▶ 본문 p.162

2. The rain is pouring down
비가 쏟아지고 있어.
3. It is not[It's not/It isn't] snowing
눈이 오고 있지 않아.
4. We are planting trees
우리는 나무를 심고 있어.
5. I am studying
6. He is charging a battery
그는 배터리를 충전하는 중이야.
7. My roses are dying
내 장미들이 죽어가고 있어.
8. The wind is blowing
9. He is downloading a file
그는 파일을 다운로드하고 있어.
10. She is cooking in the kitchen
그녀는 부엌에서 요리하는 중이야.
11. We are playing soccer
우리는 축구를 하고 있어.
12. Our team is losing
우리 팀이 지고 있어.
13. Your phone is ringing
네 전화가 울리고 있어.
14. You are wasting your time
너는 네 시간을 낭비하고 있는 거야.
15. He is chatting
16. is looking for his cell phone
17. his mother is using his phone
18. Are they sitting
그들은 앉아있니?
19. Are they doing their homework
그들은 숙제를 하고 있니?
20. Are you teasing me
너 나를 놀리고 있는 거야?

Let's Practice More!

SET 01
▶ 본문 p.165

02. cleaning	03. stopping	04. talking
05. raining	06. swimming	07. lying
08. singing	09. reading	10. looking
11. coming	12. dying	

SET 02
▶ 본문 p.166

02. am	03. making	04. is
05. shopping	06. winning	07. opening
08. are	09. kidding	10. taking
11. wasting	12. sitting	13. Are
14. using		

SET 03
▶ 본문 p.167

02. having	03. ○	04. swimming
05. ○	06. coming	07. ○
08. dying	09. cutting	10. ○
11. losing	12. raining	13. ○
14. running		

SET 04
▶ 본문 p.168

02. making	03. ○	04. ○
05. getting	06. are	07. ○
08. going	09. am	10. taking
11. ○	12. daydreaming	

SET 05
▶ 본문 p.169

02. Is she doing the dishes
그녀는 설거지를 하고 있니?
03. The computer is not[isn't] working
그 컴퓨터는 작동하지 않고 있어.
04. Is it snowing a lot outside
밖에 눈이 많이 오고 있니?
05. It is[It's] raining outside
밖에 비가 오고 있어.
06. I am not[I'm not] asking you
나는 너에게 물어보고 있지 않아.
07. Are you baking cookies
너는 쿠키를 굽고 있니?
08. He is not[He's not/He isn't] studying now
그는 지금 공부하고 있지 않아.
09. Are they lying on the beach
그들은 해변 위에 누워 있니?
10. Sihu is not[isn't] sending an e-mail
시후는 이메일을 보내고 있지 않아.
11. I am not[I'm not] shaking now

나는 지금 떨고 있지 않아.

12. Are they having a good time
그들은 좋은 시간을 보내고 있니?

13. Is he wearing his raincoat
그는 그의 우비를 입고 있니?

14. He is planting trees
그는 나무를 심고 있어.

SET 06 ▶ 본문 p.171

02. 씻고 있다	03. 보았다	04. 오고 있다
05. 확인할 것이다	06. 기다리고 있다	07. 비가 오고 있니?
08. 구웠다	09. 보내고 있다	10. 운동한다
11. 쏟아지는 중이다	12. 심을 것이다	13. 이기고 있다
14. 누워 있다		

SET 07 ▶ 본문 p.172

02. He is[He's] chatting with his friends
그는 그의 친구들과 잡담을 하고 있어.

03. She is[She's] looking for her wallet
그녀는 그녀의 지갑을 찾고 있어.

04. We are[We're] playing soccer
우리는 축구를 하고 있어.

05. Our team is losing
우리 팀은 지고 있어.

06. Your phone is ringing
너의 전화기가 울리고 있어.

07. You are[You're] wasting your time
너는 너의 시간을 낭비하고 있어.

08. His mother is using his phone
그의 엄마는 그의 전화를 사용하고 계셔.

09. Are they sitting
그들이 앉아 있니?

10. Are you teasing me
너는 나를 놀리고 있는 거니?

11. I am[I'm] washing my hair
나는 머리를 감고 있어.

12. The wind is blowing hard
바람이 세게 불고 있어.

13. He is[He's] downloading a file
그는 파일을 다운 받고 있어.

14. My roses are dying
내 장미들은 죽어가고 있어.

15. He is[He's] charging a battery
그는 배터리를 충전하고 있어.

16. I am[I'm] checking my contact list
나는 내 연락망을 확인하고 있어.

17. We are[We're] having chocolate ice cream
우리는 초콜릿 아이스크림을 먹고 있어.

18. People are opening their umbrellas
사람들은 그들의 우산을 펴고 있어.

19. My sneakers are getting wet
내 운동화는 젖고 있어.

20. We are[We're] going to a concert
우리는 콘서트에 가고 있어.

SET 08 ▶ 본문 p.174

02. is, snowing	03. am, checking	04. am, waiting
05. is, pouring	06. are, playing	07. Are, exercising
08. am, following	09. are, driving	10. is, crying
11. am, calling	12. Are, saying	13. are, planting
14. is, studying	15. am, kidding	16. are, winning
17. am, working	18. is, wearing	19. am, trying
20. are, watching		

Chapter 06 과거진행시제

Unit 01 과거진행시제

Check and Write ▶ 본문 p.179

2. She was hugging her dog
그녀는 그녀의 개를 안고 있었어.

3. We were looking at the camera
우리는 카메라를 보고 있었어.

4. I was telling my secret
나는 내 비밀을 말하고 있었어.

Unit 02 과거진행시제의 부정문과 의문문

Check and Write ▶ 본문 p.181

2. Was the cow looking at us
그 소가 우리를 쳐다보고 있었니?
The cow was not looking at us
The cow wasn't looking at us
그 소는 우리를 쳐다보고 있지 않았어.

3. Were they smiling
그들은 웃고 있었니?
They were not smiling
They weren't smiling
그들은 웃고 있지 않았어.

Practice 1 ▶ 본문 p.182

A 2. was, talking 3. was, meeting

B 1. were, playing 2. was, playing
3. was, crossing 4. were, playing
5. were, playing 6. was, walking

C 1. going 2. driving
3. sleeping 4. listening
5. singing 6. feeling
7. blowing

D 1. Were, sleeping 2. was, sleeping
3. was, taking

Practice 2 ▶ 본문 p.184

2. The lion was sleeping
3. The kids were playing

4. Sihu was going down the slide
시후는 미끄럼틀을 타고 내려오고 있었다.

5. Taeyeon was playing on the swing
태연이는 그네를 타고 있었다.

6. Suho was climbing the jungle gym
수호는 정글짐을 오르고 있었다.

7. Mina and Yuri were playing on the seesaw
미나와 유리는 시소를 타고 있었다.

8. Mike was hanging

9. The merry-go-round was spinning
회전목마가 돌아가고 있었다.

10. What were you doing

11. I was doing my homework
나는 숙제하고 있었어.

12. She was waiting for the green light

13. He was not feeling well
그는 몸이 좋지 않았다.

14. He was singing

15. She was brushing her teeth
그녀는 양치하고 있었다.

16. The evening moon was rising
저녁달이 떠오르고 있었다.

17. My parents were looking for

18. Mom was waiting for me
엄마가 나를 기다리고 계셨다.

19. I was thinking about it
나는 그것에 대해 생각하고 있었다.

20. He was washing his hands
그는 손을 씻고 있었다.

Practice 3

▶ 본문 p.186

2. They were walking in the forest
그들은 숲 속을 걷고 있었다.

3. Were you playing with your friends
너는 친구들과 놀고 있었니?

4. I was not[wasn't] watching TV
나는 TV를 보고 있지 않았어.

5. I was walking my dog
나는 내 개를 산책시키고 있었어.

6. What were you doing
너는 무엇을 하고 있었니?

7. I was sleeping
나는 자고 있었어.

8. Suho was going to his grandparents' house

9. I was feeling dizzy
나는 어지러웠다.

10. They were eating popcorn
그들은 팝콘을 먹고 있었다.

11. His father was looking at

12. I was not[wasn't] feeling well

13. The host was talking about

14. He was rolling a pencil

15. She was cutting vegetables
그녀는 야채를 자르고 있었다.

16. They were taking a break
그들은 휴식을 취하고 있었다.

17. His grandparents were waiting for him
그의 할아버지, 할머니가 그를 기다리고 계셨다.

18. He was laughing
그는 웃고 있었다.

19. His mother was listening to the radio
그의 어머니는 라디오를 듣고 있었다.

20. Suho was sleeping

Let's Practice More!

SET 01

▶ 본문 p.189

02. waiting	03. sleeping	04. cutting
05. playing	06. driving	07. snowing
08. fighting	09. visiting	10. running
11. watching	12. listening	

SET 02

▶ 본문 p.190

02. were	03. were	04. were
05. was	06. was	07. were
08. were	09. driving	10. listening
11. was	12. was	13. sleeping
14. were		

SET 03

▶ 본문 p.191

02. ○	03. was waiting
04. were walking	05. was feeling
06. ○	07. were looking
08. was singing	09. was brushing
10. Were	11. ○
12. was thinking	13. were eating
14. was washing	

SET 04

▶ 본문 p.192

02. Was the lion sleeping in a tree
사자가 나무에서 자고 있었니?

03. Mina and Yuri were not[weren't] playing board games
미나와 유리는 보드게임을 하고 있지 않았다.

04. Was the merry-go-round spinning
회전목마가 돌아가고 있었니?

05. My mother was not[wasn't] meeting her friends
어머니는 그녀의 친구들을 만나고 계시지 않았어.

06. The kids were not[weren't] playing in the playground
아이들이 놀이터에서 놀고 있지 않았어.

07. Was he going down the slide
그는 미끄럼틀을 타고 내려오고 있었니?

08. Taeyeon was not[wasn't] playing on the swing
태연이는 그네를 타고 있지 않았어.

09. Was he climbing the jungle gym
그는 정글짐을 오르고 있었니?

10. Were they taking a break
그들은 쉬고 있었니?

11. Was she cutting vegetables
그녀는 야채를 자르고 있었니?

12. She was not[wasn't] hanging upside down from the monkey bars
그녀는 구름사다리에 거꾸로 매달려 있지 않았어.

13. His grandparents were not[weren't] waiting for him
그의 할아버지, 할머니는 그를 기다리고 계시지 않았어.

14. He was not[wasn't] laughing loudly
그는 크게 웃고 있지 않았어.

SET 05

▶ 본문 p.194

02. I was[we were]
03. they weren't[were not]
04. I was[we were]
05. they were
06. she wasn't[was not]
07. he wasn't[was not]
08. they weren't[were not]
09. she wasn't[was not]
10. I was[we were]
11. it wasn't[was not]
12. she was

SET 06

▶ 본문 p.195

02. was, walking
03. are, going
04. was, listening
05. is, singing
06. was, feeling
07. is, blowing
08. was, sleeping
09. am, taking
10. is, drinking
11. was, sleeping
12. were, swimming
13. is, driving
14. was, cooking

SET 07

▶ 본문 p.196

02. was spinning
03. climbed
04. played
05. were playing
06. went
07. talked
08. was washing
09. were walking
10. was playing
11. walked
12. was having
13. ate
14. was going
15. was looking
16. met
17. were playing
18. was hanging
19. was doing
20. watched

SET 08

▶ 본문 p.198

02. was, cutting
03. was, waiting
04. was, not, feeling
05. was, rising
06. were, singing
07. was, running
08. were, looking
09. were, eating
10. was, thinking
11. was, washing
12. was, looking
13. was, listening
14. was, talking
15. were, sleeping
16. were, doing
17. were, taking
18. was, laughing
19. was, not, watching
20. was, rolling

Chapter 03~06 실전테스트

▶ 본문 p.200

01. ②
02. 불규칙 동사(과거형): took, went, felt
규칙 동사(과거형): liked, studied, watched
03. is snowing
04. Is, playing
05. ①-ⓒ, ②-ⓐ, ③-ⓑ
06. ③
07. ④
08. ①, ③
09. singing
10. went
11. 현재시제, 미래시제, 과거시제, 과거진행시제
12. (1) (g)oing, to (2) (w)ill
13. bought, buy
14. arrived, arrive
15. drinking
16. wearing
17. am reading
18. was taking
19. ②
20. ③
21. 과
22. 현
23. 과
24. 현
25. 현
26. (1) did (2) looking
27. I went to an English lesson last week.
나는 지난주에 영어 수업에 갔다.
28. I was sitting on the bench.
나는 벤치에 앉아 있었다.
29. I will play baseball next weekend.
나는 다음 주말에 야구를 할 것이다.
30. What did you do yesterday?
너는 어제 무엇을 했니?

Game 정답

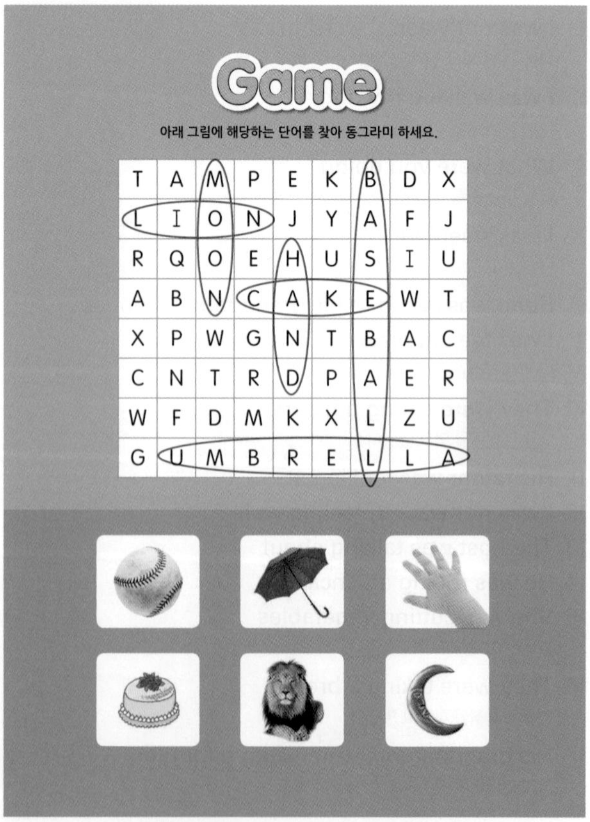

초등영문법 3800제 서평

초등3학년 아이.. 원서는 어느 정도 잘 읽는데.. 글씨 쓰는 걸 많이 어려워해요. 그래서 문법을 알면 도움이 되지 않을까 싶어서 찾다가 3800제를 만났네요. 초등 저학년 아이가 혼자서 하는데 있어서 어려움이 없어요. 쉬운 단어로 설명을 해주니 쉽게 이해하고 공책에 배운 걸 써보기도 하면서 혼자서 열심히 공부하고 있어요. 2번, 3번 쭈욱~~ 3800제로 나갈까 합니다. *YES24* / 은**주

형이 중학교 진학 전부터 중학생용 3800제를 풀고 있었고 3800제 구성이 만족스러워서 초등 동생도 풀기 시작했어요. 개념도 구체적이고 다양한 내용이 있어서 좋았어요. 지루하지 않게 그림이 자주 삽입되어 있으니까 덜 삭막해요^^ 무엇보다 다각도로 연습문제가 진짜진짜 많아요. 어설프게 알고 진도 나가면 나중에 다시 봤을 때 까먹게 되고 제대로 이해 못하게 되거든요. 다양한 방식의 문제를 풀면서 영어실력이 확장되는 게 느껴져요. 게임, 마크만 성실, 꼼꼼하게 하지 공부는 대충 해치우고 마는 아이인데 이 교재를 통해서 언젠가는 영어 실력이 차곡차곡 쌓이길 기대해봅니다. 뒷편에는 단어 공부, 받아쓰기 연습을 할 수 있는 것도 있어요. 아이 핸드폰에 mp3파일을 넣어주면 스스로 할 수 있겠더라구요. 아직은 진도를 빨리 빼느라 숙제주진 않았는데 방학 시작하면 이 한권으로 영어공부는 충분할 것 같습니다. 핸드폰이 게임, 유튜브 보는 것만이 아닌 공부할 적에도 사용하는 것이라는 것을 알게 되길~^^; *YES24* / 희*

잠수네로 별칭되는 엄마표 영어를 한 지 몇 년 되었는데 엄마가 너무 띄엄띄엄 지도하다 보니 아이 단어와 문법이 많이 약한 것 같아 문법 교재로 구매했습니다. Unit 시작할 때 단어가 스물 몇 개 있고 의미를 인지하고 있는지 셀프 테스팅 하도록 구성되어 있고 개념 문제 뒤 연습문제가 쭉 있어서 아이가 스스로 정리하며 공부할 수 있어요. 난이도는 쉬운 편이라 차라리 부담 없이 스르륵 풀 수 있어서 좋아요. *YES24* / d**rh0424

문법은 실제로 문장 속에서 활용해봐야 이해가 쉽기 때문에 예제 중심의 반복학습이 가능한 책을 찾다가 선택한 교재입니다. 여러 형식으로 문제 풀이가 다양하게 제시되어 있어 문제를 풀다보면 그 원리가 절로 체득되어 정말 좋습니다. 아직 문법이라는 추상적인 개념을 이해하기 어려워하는 초등학생들에게 좋은 교재예요. 기존에 기초 문법의 틀이 조금 잡혀 있는 학생들은 자습용으로도 좋고 처음 문법을 접하는 학생들에게는 단계적으로 심화되는 문제 구성을 차근차근 밟아가며 공부하기에 좋습니다. *YES24* / a**owa

---

아이 문법 학습을 위해서 구입을 하게 되었습니다. 큰아이 중학영문법 3800제를 가지고 학습을 한 경험이 있어 믿고 구입하게 되었는데 역시나 초등문법도 많은 연습문제로 아이들이 같은 내용을 꾸준히 반복 연습하게 구성이 되어있어서 마음에 듭니다. 초등학생용이라 글씨도 큳 직큼직하고 페이지마다 빈공간도 많이 있어 답답하지도 않아서 좋아요. 초등학 생 아이들은 일단 글씨가 작고 빽빽하면 보면서 질려하는 경향이 있는데 이 교재는 그런 점에서는 후한 점수를 주고 싶네요. 단순 객관식 문제 풀이로 학습시키고 싶은 분들에게는 추천하지 않구요. 객관식 문제풀이가 단원 끝에 단원테스트에 조금 밖에 없어서요. 객관식 문제풀이가 아닌 아이가 문장을 만들면서 학습하기를 원하시는 분들에게는 강추합니다. 타 학습서들이 보통 초등문법을 2권 내지 3권에 끝내는 것을 이 초등영문법 3800제는 1권부터 8권까지에 연습할 부분을 나누어 놓았으니 얼마나 많은 반복을 시킬 수 있는지 권수만 봐도 알 수 있지요. 어쨌든, 초등학교 4학년 아이 8권까지 열심히 공부할 예정입니다. *YES24* / j**onim

book.toptutor.co.kr

구하기 어려운 교재는
마더텅 모바일(인터넷)을 이용하세요.
즉시 배송해 드립니다.

마더텅 학습 교재 이벤트에 참여해 주세요. 참여해 주신 모든 분께 선물을 드립니다.

이벤트 1 1분 간단 교재 사용 후기 이벤트

마더텅은 고객님의 소중한 의견을 반영하여 보다 좋은 책을 만들고자 합니다.
교재 구매 후, <교재 사용 후기 이벤트>에 **참여해 주신 모든 분**께는 감사의 마음을 담아 **모바일 문화상품권 1천 원권**을
보내 드립니다. 지금 바로 QR 코드를 스캔해 소중한 의견을 보내 주세요!

이벤트 2 학습계획표 이벤트

STEP 1 책을 다 풀고 SNS 또는 수험생 커뮤니티에 작성한 학습계획표 사진을 업로드

필수 태그 #마더텅 #초등영어 #초등영문법3800 #학습계획표 #공스타그램
SNS/수험생 커뮤니티 페이스북, 인스타그램, 블로그, 네이버/다음 카페 등

STEP 2 왼쪽 QR 코드를 스캔하여 작성한 게시물의 URL 인증

참여해 주신 모든 분께는 감사의 마음을 담아 **CU 모바일 편의점 상품권 1천 원권** 및 **B 북포인트 2천 점**을 드립니다.

이벤트 3 블로그/SNS 이벤트

STEP 1 자신의 블로그/SNS 중 하나에 마더텅 교재에 대한 사용 후기를 작성

필수 태그 #마더텅 #초등영어 #초등영문법3800 #교재리뷰 #공스타그램
필수 내용 마더텅 교재 장점, 교재 사진

STEP 2 왼쪽 QR 코드를 스캔하여 작성한 게시물의 URL 인증

참여해 주신 모든 분께는 감사의 마음을 담아 **CU 모바일 편의점 상품권 2천 원권** 및 **B 북포인트 3천 점**을 드립니다.
매달 우수 후기자를 선정하여 **모바일 문화상품권 2만 원권**과 **B 북포인트 1만 점**을 드립니다.

B 북포인트란? 마더텅 인터넷 서점 http://book.toptutor.co.kr에서 교재 구매 시 현금처럼 사용할 수 있는 포인트입니다.

※자세한 사항은 해당 QR 코드를 스캔하거나 홈페이지 이벤트 공지글을 참고해 주세요.
※당사 사정에 따라 이벤트의 내용이나 상품이 변경될 수 있으며 변경 시 홈페이지에 공지합니다. ※만 14세 미만은 부모님께서 신청해 주셔야 합니다.
※상품은 이벤트 참여일로부터 2~3일(영업일 기준) 내에 발송됩니다. ※동일 교재로 세 가지 이벤트 모두 참여 가능합니다. (단, 같은 이벤트 중복 참여는 불가합니다.)
※이벤트 기간: 2024년 12월 31일까지 (*해당 이벤트는 당사 사정에 따라 조기 종료될 수 있습니다.)

정답은 뒷면에서 확인하세요.

Circle and write.

알맞은 것에 동그라미 하고 쓰세요.

1.

ike

ine

pineapple

2.

ike

ime

l___

3.

ime

ine

l___

4.

ine

ike

str___

5.

ike

ine

w___

6.

ime

ine

t___

Circle and write.

알맞은 것에 동그라미 하고 쓰세요.

1.

ike

ine

pineapple

2.

ike

ime

like

3.

ime

ine

lime

4.

ine

ike

strike

5.

ike

ine

wine

6.

ime

ine

time